OLD VIC DRAMA

From the etching by Gwen May, A.R.E.

I.—*Hamlet* in Modern Dress (1938). The Death of Hamlet.

OLD VIC DRAMA

A Twelve Years' Study
of Plays and Players

by

AUDREY WILLIAMSON

FOREWORD BY
DAME SYBIL THORNDIKE
D.B.E., LL.D.

ROCKLIFF

SALISBURY SQUARE
LONDON

MADE AND PRINTED IN ENGLAND
BY
LOXLEY BROS. LTD., LONDON AND SHEFFIELD

THIS BOOK IS DEDICATED
TO
THOSE OLD VIC ACTORS,
ACTRESSES AND PRODUCERS
WHOSE WORK MADE THESE
PRODUCTIONS POSSIBLE
AND TO
THOSE WHO PRECEDED AND
WILL SUCCEED
THEM

FOREWORD

BY DAME SYBIL THORNDIKE, D.B.E., LL.D.

T H I S book about the Old Vic and its achievements starts its recording and criticism from the year 1934. By this time, however, the Old Vic had been in existence for twenty years and it is of its beginning that I am to write a few words, as I was in nearly at the start.

In the spring of 1914 Lilian Baylis decided she wanted to start a Shakespeare Company. Already an Opera Company was in existence and much appreciated, but this wasn't enough for Lilian—not enough, she felt, for the people for whom the Old Vic was intended, the hard-working-class people round about the Waterloo Road. So, after discussion with various members of the theatrical profession, a season was started by Rosina Filippi, that grand actress and teacher, and the play was *Romeo and Juliet.* Rosina's daughter, Rosemary—sixteen years old—was the Juliet. This met with the usual response that pioneers in the theatre expect and generally get, so another short season was given by Mr. and Mrs. Matheson Lang, who appeared in *The Taming of the Shrew.* The Langs were really the two people who fired Lilian Baylis with determination to go on and struggle through, and indeed they were strong friends of the Old Vic throughout the rather discouraging start. They all seized on Ben Greet to do the productions, knowing he was the sort of person who was never discouraged if only one man and a baby were in the audience : and with Estelle Stead to help him, both as organiser and player, the real beginning of the Home of Shakespeare was launched.

It was in the early autumn of 1914, when the war had already started, that the Old Vic adventure began. A very good company was formed, with William Stack as leading man, Andrew Leigh and others. I joined them in October and we had years of exciting work. The beginning was tough going ; it takes time in England for a theatrical venture to take root, and they were troublous times. Some nights it seemed as if it were hardly worth while ringing up the curtain, so small was the audience, but Lilian Baylis

would never give in. She'd say to us " Only a handful in front, dears.
Would you like me to give them their money back and all go home—
safer with all these raids?"; but a look in her eyes made us realise
that she'd kill us outright unless we said " Let's ring up!", and we
always did ! Many times, if a raid was in progress (and Waterloo
Road often had it good and hot), our audiences had to stay a long
while after the end of the play ; but we all kept cheerful, with
impromptu performances and songs to make us forget the bombs.

We played alternately with the opera, and so had some free
nights. The opera always had the Saturdays, for it was more
popular than the drama, and we Shakespearites used to be sent
off to Bethnal Green to give performances at the swimming baths,
which were converted into a very good theatre on Saturdays. We
had very big Jewish audiences there, and how appreciative they
were ! We played real repertory, doing as many plays as we could
cram in : always three different ones in a week and three operas.
Children's matinées were a great feature. Ben Greet enjoyed them
more than we did—and the company grew into a very good team.

Robert Atkins joined in 1915 (he afterwards, as Producer, set
the traditional standard of good solid Shakespearean playing), and
my brother, Russell Thorndike, joined in 1916, after being invalided
back from the Dardenelles. Fisher White and Henry Kendall were
early members ; and Beatrice Wilson and Mary Sumner were two
strong actresses. It was a hand-to-mouth affair : no minimum
salaries—*all* minimum salaries we were ! And gradually the
audiences grew, and for men home from the front it was the one
theatre where they could get something more meaty than the usual
froth provided for fighting men. In the last year of the war packed
houses and an eager public had been achieved. Each Christmas
we gave them a topical revue, guying all the work we had done in
the season. We played an enormous repertory. The Four Great
Tragedies were a regular occurrence, and all the well-known Comedies besides the lesser-known ones and the best-known Histories.
We had few men during the war, though any actor home from
France was welcomed as a player. My husband and my young
brother Frank played often during their leave time. We women
had to fill the male gaps, however, and we weren't so bad ! In
fact I think many of us were glad to play men's parts in order to
get away from the hampered feeling women always have in a

Shakespeare Company, for it is the men who get the fat parts. There are a few good ones, however, for the women!

We did the Sheridan Three, Goldsmith, *Everyman* and other plays of the same class. It was a hard-working theatre with lots of spirit and keenness, and in the audience, too, there was this spirit—this good, co-operative spirit. We did seasons at Stratford-on-Avon, and in the summer vacation we occasionally kept the theatre open with Dickens.

When 1918 came, and peace, some of us moved off to the West End, anxious for careers; but the Home of Shakespeare went on with various producers—Atkins, Thorndike, Leigh. Atkins produced the first performances of *Peer Gynt* in the early twenties, with Russell as Peer Gynt. None of us who had been in at the start ever felt the same about any other theatre, and we'd go back from time to time again, for Lilian Baylis had a real hold on us all.

When in 1927 considerable alteration had to be done to the theatre, Lewis Casson and I did a season at the Lyric Theatre, Hammersmith, with Andrew Leigh producing. Eric Portman, Hay Petrie and many other now well-known film and theatre players were in the company, and the faithful Old Vic audience followed us there. It was a People's Theatre in the truest sense. It started a tradition. The Old Vic Company is a much grander company now and at a grander theatre, but still the same spirit, of which Lilian Baylis was the inspirer, persists—the play was the thing that mattered and individual success came second. If some of us older actors miss the metaphorical smell of sawdust and the non-metaphorical chops being cooked in the wings—well, it's a different age and the tremendous influence of the cinema has produced more luxurious ideas. But the Theatre is there, and we all hope that some time in the future the not-so-highly-incomed workers will be provided with a branch of the Old Vic with good seats to suit not-too-well-furnished pockets.

This twenty years chapter (Edith Evans's first season, so interesting and exciting, came into this period) finished with the distinguished productions of Harcourt Williams, and those who saw the Hamlet of John Gielgud have a memory of something hauntingly beautiful for which to be grateful all their lives.

A great tradition was started in this twenty years by one woman's tremendous idea and faith. This idea and this faith will live.

S Y B I L   T H O R N D I K E

April, 1947

CONTENTS

LIST OF PLATES

xiii

PAGES 158-9

INTRODUCTION

THIS book was planned as dramatic criticism, but for the sake of continuity and historic interest I have referred briefly to Old Vic events and changes of policy during the period covered. Though the judgments are purely personal, the book will, I hope, have some value as a complete record and analysis of the productions presented by the Old Vic Theatre Company in London since the autumn of 1934. This represents less than half of the Company's active history, but the twelve years' period dealt with has been one of important development and achievement.

A bibliography of books to which reference is made, directly or indirectly, in the text appears at the end of the book. To this I would add prefaces or introductions by Edmund Gosse (*The Country Wife*), Ernest Rhys (*The Witch of Edmonton*) and J. Dover Wilson (*King John* and *Henry IV*). "The Old Vic and Sadler's Wells Magazine", which was issued monthly until 1939, provided some useful information.

I wish to acknowledge with special gratitude the assistance of of Mr. John Burrell, Mr. Glen Byam Shaw and the Old Vic staff in providing certain data and lending me plays I found otherwise unobtainable. I should like also to thank Dame Sybil Thorndike for her valuable Foreword, Mr. Robert Helpmann for the loan of several photographs, Miss Margaret Rankin, Secretary of the Vic-Wells Association, for providing me with an almost complete set of programmes and Miss Gwen May, A.R.E., for permission to reproduce her fine etching as a frontispiece. My thanks are also due to those friends who lent me further books and programmes and to the photographers whose work has provided so valuable a pictorial record of many Old Vic productions. I should like specially to mention Mr. John Vickers, who kindly provided me with photographs in spite of the fact that he was, at the time, planning a book of his own on the same subject.

London,   AUDREY WILLIAMSON
April, 1947.

CHAPTER I

MAURICE EVANS AT THE OLD VIC

RICHARD II

M Y first memory of the Old Vic is of the clash of voices : the silver trumpet of Richard II pitched above the angry throbbing bass of Bolingbroke and Norfolk.

It was the second production of a new era. Harcourt Williams had left the Old Vic in 1933 after four years of production—years made notable by a new and at the time controversial insistence on speed of speech and production, and by the bright rising star of the young John Gielgud. Tyrone Guthrie had succeeded him for the following year, bringing with him Charles Laughton and Flora Robson to break the Old Vic tradition of discovering its own stars instead of importing them from the West End or the cinema ; and in the early autumn of 1934 Henry Cass followed Guthrie as producer with a production of *Antony and Cleopatra* in which Mary Newcombe played Cleopatra, Wilfred Lawson Antony and Maurice Evans' Octavius Caesar.

It was Lawson's only appearance at the Vic ; but the American actress Mary Newcombe stayed for several more productions, and it was obvious from the critical comments on Maurice Evans' Octavius, a far from foolproof part, that the Old Vic had gained from the West End a young actor of shining promise, inexperienced in Shakespeare yet capable of bringing to the plays voice, presence and freshness and intelligence of approach. I did not see this production ; but in it Cass doubtless followed his own preliminary statement that the keynote of his productions would be simplicity. " A use of modern simplified production seems to me the best method of expressing the full richness of Shakespeare's plays. Good verse-speaking, combined with sincerity and understanding, will be our aim."

1

It was an aim precipitated, no doubt, by pecuniary necessity as well as genuine belief. The Old Vic was still, under Lilian Baylis's valiant direction, essentially a suburban theatre, with a loyal and regular audience drawn from the ranks of serious playgoers and its local environs, but hardly touching the fringe of West End theatregoers and the great general public. Some of these had seeped into the audience during the Laughton season, attracted by the glitter of famous names and the current notoriety of the film *The Private Life of Henry V I I I :* but their Shakespearean interest proved ephemeral and the Old Vic found itself once again fighting a constant battle in the face of limited resources and often pitifully small audiences.

That the first of Cass's aims—simplicity of production—did not necessarily involve drabness and lack of invention was, however, apparent in his *Richard I I*, and throughout the season his team, led by Maurice Evans, were to make good his theory of the value of clear verse-speaking, sincerity and understanding. A young artist, David Ffolkes, gave to the play a bare sweep of stage and sky in which a single mast, as in the Barkloughly Castle scene, would achieve a spare but vivid suggestion. His costumes had a pastel elegance, and those of Richard—the peach-gold fantastic short tunic of the early scenes, the long pale green gown with lemon sleeves on his return from Ireland, the sombre purple of his robe of imprisonment—unobtrusively echoed the changes of the play's mood and the King's character. Three years later, at the Queen's Theatre, John Gielgud was to stage a far richer and more elaborate production of the play, but in comparison the pictorial design distracted from the action. Only Motley's exquisite pallid tourney scene, with its white-robed King and Queen and single pennon etched against a pale blue sky, offset the drama with the lucidity and directness of Henry Cass's more subdued and less ambitious production.

What of Cass's other aims ? I have already said my first memory of the Old Vic is centred in the actors' voices in the opening scene, and this clarity and fire of speech and sincere understanding of the text were to prove predominant factors in this production. Maurice Evans's voice as Richard II, rather light in texture but flexible, attuned to the emotion and music of the verse, capable of sudden touching quietudes or ringing head-tones, kept a melodic line in brilliant contrast to the deep harmony of the voices of

Abraham Sofaer as Bolingbroke and Leo Genn as Norfolk. That opening clash of wills had vocal as well as dramatic excitement, and Richard's " I was not born to sue, but to command !" cut across the quarrel, " the bitter clamour of two eager tongues ", with the ringing sharpness of a steel blade.

This sudden cry of angered authority was a key to Evans's interpretation. It recognised in Richard that same fatal and insane trust in royalty, the Divine Right of Kings, which a couple of centuries later was to cost another King of England, as it cost Richard himself, his crown and his life. Again and again, during the course of the play, Richard's defiance blazes out in a precarious glory of omnipotence, and the justification of the actor in stressing it is in the royal death at the last, when the imaginative, capricious, unstable King makes his last bid for life with a fierce flare of courage that fells two of his attackers before Exton can strike his fatal blow. And even then the reaction is majestic :

> That hand shall burn in never-quenching fire
> That staggers thus my person—

" As full of valour as of royal blood" is Exton's epitaph.

Another side of Richard, not often stressed, Evans brought out with particular skill. This was a natural streak of irony through which the King subtly, at times cruelly, lashed Bolingbroke with his scorn. " We will descend and fold him in our arms ": the mockery with which this was said drove home the inference in the duel as bitingly as the sardonic " *King* Bolingbroke " and gibe at Northumberland—" You make a leg, and Bolingbroke says ' Ay ' "—later.

> Fair cousin, you debase your princely knee
> To make the base earth proud with kissing it . . .
> Up, cousin, up ;—your heart is up, I know,
> Thus high at least (*touching his crown*) although your
> knee be low.

Though quietly spoken the taunt burnt to the bone.

The advantage of this irony—and I think it is an advantage and an absolutely legitimate reading of the text—is that it emphasises that intellectual detachment from the brawl and swagger of the war-mongers that Gordon Daviot made a key-note of the character in her *Richard of Bordeaux*, and which even in Shakespeare separates the indolent and art-loving King from the materialistic Bolingbroke. Richard's caprice in stopping the duel becomes in this reading

something more than a weak assertion of power ; it is a challenge to
the followers of a different code of living, as well as a stroke of
policy that removes from the kingdom at one blow two potentially
dangerous rebels. For Richard's foppery and raillery mask a
quick enough brain, and Evans made one aware of this through all
the impudent glitter of his early scenes.

C. E. Montague in his famous essay on Benson in this part solves
the riddle of Richard in the phrase, " The capable and faithful
artist in the same skin as the incapable and unfaithful King ".
It was the special grace of Maurice Evans's performance that he
never lost sight of Richard's passion for turning his grief into
words—that artistic impulse that Montague describes as " his
own quick and glowing apprehension of what is about him "—
while giving due emphasis to the irony and that " rash, fierce blaze
of riot " in which Gaunt foresees Richard's doom.

" Say that again. The shadow of my sorrow ? " Here indeed
was that sense of fondling a phrase that links Richard, in Montague's
mind, with the writer in creation, and throughout the play Evans
gave the rich imagery and music of the words a lovely pliancy
and lyric expression. In sheer sound the performance approached
virtuosity, and the delivery ranged from pure rhetoric to genuine
force of suffering.

> Oh that I were as great as is my grief
> Or lesser than my name . . .

The heart of Richard was packed into that bitter cry, and the
King's uneasy fluctuations from hope to despair were played with
emotional variety and an imaginative feeling for gesture. I am
still moved by the memory of the way this Richard flung wide his
arms to his friends at the words " I live with bread like you, feel
want, taste grief—need friends ": in that one moment of distrust
in the Divinity of Kings, the sudden pang of loneliness, Richard
touched true pathos. But the " Death of Kings " and " little
grave " speeches, and the whole of the Renunciation scene, with
its final exit shaken by quiet weeping, were equally moving, and
the great Pomfret soliloquy was delivered with masterly lucidity.
One felt poignantly here the battle to retain sanity within prison
walls : " Yet I'll hammer it out . . . . " The parting from the Queen,
and from the aged Groom in the prison, had in contrast natural
tenderness. Evans, in fact, turned over and exposed every facet of the
part with the loving care of a connoisseur examining a prized jewel.

Abraham Sofaer was in this production a forthright Bolingbroke, admirably realising the watchful unruffled calm of the man who knows his power and can afford to let his enemy rail.

> Be he the fire, I'll be the yielding water.
> The rage be his—

This is the essence of Bolingbroke, and in his monosyllabic comments in the Renunciation scene there lies the unspoken contempt of the man of action for the artist, the natural poet who " unpacks his heart with words " and can do nothing.   Frank Napier got a good deal of fun and bustle out of the Duke of York, and Morland Graham, one of the finest of Old Vic character actors, played the Gardener and the Groom with a moving simplicity.   Nancy Hornsby as the Queen struck me as over-plaintive, but when the play was revived for two weeks towards the end of the season Vivienne Bennett gave to the character a wistful grace that touched the heart. Alfred Sangster, author of *The Brontës*, was the John of Gaunt, a well-played characterisation which, as in so many cases, failed to lift the famous " Royal throne of kings " speech above the hackneyed.   Only Leon Quartermaine, in my experience, has struck a new fire out of the words and given the whole death scene the unearthly majesty of the " prophet new inspir'd".

MUCH ADO ABOUT NOTHING: THE TAMING OF THE SHREW

T H E advantage of the three-week run to which each Old Vic play was limited at this period was that it enabled the leading players to be seen in a greater variety of parts than became possible some two years later, when the six or eight-week run began to be introduced.   Since at this time it was customary for the same company to remain throughout the season, the demands made on the actors' versatility were considerable.   With an average of nine productions a season the repertoire of necessity was a varied one, and although miscasting inevitably occurred something in the actor seemed genuinely to respond to the artistic pressure and variety of the work.

It is doubtful if any Old Vic leading actor has surpassed Maurice Evans's range of character and achievement in his single nine-month season at this theatre.   While many actors before and since have taken both tragedy and comedy in their stride, his was that rarer type of versatility which encompassed both with a natural ease that made it difficult to affix a label to him at all.　To qualities of pity and drama he added a dash and humour that made it possible for him to step from Richard II to Benedick, from Petruchio to the Dauphin in *Saint Joan*, without ever seeming to have left his natural medium ; and still his range was not exhausted, leaving a Iago, Hippolytus, Adolphus Cusins and Hamlet still to be accounted for.　In America he has since added a Falstaff and Romeo with equal success.

In England his Benedick immediately followed his Richard II, and a Petruchio early the same season consolidated his success in that particular type of Shakespearean comedy in which the qualities of the romantic actor must be allied to great wit, spirit and invention. It is the heritage of the Lewis Wallers, Fred Terrys and Martin Harveys, and Evans indeed had something of the litheness and sparkle of Harvey, although he lacked his romantic beauty.

Much Ado About Nothing is the wittier play, and where gusto will suffice in *The Taming of the Shrew* the actor of Benedick is lost unless he can catch the quick wit as well as the rattle of the repartee.　He must suggest too that essential honesty, courage and good nature that his friends never cease to admit in him even when their badinage is at its height.　The soldier, also, is very near the surface in the earlier scenes, and if the actor captures the fun and drollery of the famous scene in which Benedick is baited with Beatrice's supposed love, and the beautifully phrased and timed soliloquy that closes it, he has still to carry the hurdle of that sudden real tenderness for Beatrice that trembles beneath the surface in the Church Scene and later love passages.　Evans presented as nearly complete a Benedick as is possible and only Donald Wolfit, in an equally dashing performance, has matched him in recent years in either this character or Petruchio.

The comedy of *Much Ado About Nothing*, however, depends not upon one fine performance but on two.　At a pinch Petruchio may carry his play without a Katharine, but a Benedick without a Beatrice is like a bird with a broken wing.　The " merry war " between the two must have wit and resource on both sides and indeed Beatrice is in some ways the better part, lifting the mechanics of the comedy plot into a new world that touches both enchantment and feeling.　Who has not responded to the picture that has been handed down to us of Ellen Terry picking up her skirts and, " like a lapwing ", skimming across the ground, of that quality in her that a critic described as "chequered sunshine", and which must have made it seem that not one but a myriad stars had danced when she was born ? Mary Newcombe's star glowed rather than sparkled, and the clouds of tragedy still tended to trail about her ; but everything that brain and spirit could do was there. The husky voice added its own charm to the wit of the words, and in the Church Scene her warmth of feeling and fine blaze of anger at her cousin's wrong gave the character its true basis of feminine sympathy and generosity. No actress has more sincerely caught the spirit of the words " taming my wild heart to thy loving hand".

A programme note by the producer explained that the choice of costumes of different periods for the male and female characters was intended to " remove the Play from any definite time or place and make it what it really is—a Masque ". Since the two periods chosen were quite recognisable and definite I do not think the device succeeded: but, though the production was generally plain, the use of colours, masks and gay dance figurations in the ball scene did achieve a quality of masquerade that was the most charming note in the production.

The sub-plot of the defamed Hero and her peculiarly unlikeable lover Claudio always takes some swallowing, and the actor of Claudio in this production was not helped by an unhappy idea of the designer to give point to Beatrice's " civil as an orange " quip through the colour of his costume. In his sympathetic playing of the scene at Hero's tomb Alan Webb did his best to make amends : but Claudio by then is beyond all hope. Nancy Hornsby was a charming and delicate Hero, and Leo Genn played that melancholy bore, Don John, with a suitable air of sombre villainy and a voice that seemed wrapped, like his person, in black velvet. How much Mrs. Malaprop owes to Dogberry it is difficult to say ; probably a good deal, though to compare the two parts is like comparing plain homespun and priceless satin. Jay Laurier, a magnificent natural droll and mime, is the only modern actor I have seen to raise the character into the realms of pure Munden comedy. Morland Graham's Dogberry in this Old Vic production has left no impression on me.

There were no attempts at " fancy " production in *The Taming of the Shrew*, which was given its first performance at Sadler's Wells on New Year's Day, 1935. The fun was allowed to sweep the play along on its own velocity, buoyed up by Maurice Evans's irrepressible Petruchio, which had the flash and spirit of an Italian desperado as well as that " lyrical touch of romance " that Montague discerned in Benson's performance.   It is, of course, possible to present Petruchio as pure bully ; but half the gaiety is lost if the minds of feminists in the audience are allowed to wander in the direction of handcuffs and iron railings.   There is, moreover, a good humour in some of Petruchio's raillery, a lurking pride in Kate's spirit, that fully justifies the actor in taking the action in the spirit of a joke or charade.   And under her flame of temper isn't Katharine herself a little enamoured of this disarming termagant, won against her will by his glib and unblushing recital of her charms and " mildness ", and the note of real admiration she perhaps senses, with a woman's acuteness, beneath it ?   The best Katharines have certainly suggested this.   Cathleen Nesbitt, who appeared as guest in this production, seemed to me to play Katharine on too sour and spiteful a note ; she was shrewish in the petty, rather than the larger, way, though she allowed this Petruchio to toss her about the stage with an intrepidity that won one's ungrudging admiration.

Andrew Leigh, always a delightful Shakespearean clown, returned to play Christopher Sly, Raymond Johnson as the page Biondello rattled off his description of Petruchio's arrival with the machine-gun speed of a Gilbert and Sullivan patter song, and Morland Graham as Grumio represented the cheeky and indulged servant, with a sneaking pride in his master, to the life.   A great deal of fun was got out of the wedding scene, with Petruchio in a many-coloured patchwork cloak which raised clouds of dust and a hat that made him look like a battered D'Artagnan.   The general riot was accentuated by a small white terrier which clung to Grumio's neck with inexorable patience, and which was identified as the wistful West Highland to be seen frequently at this time in Maurice Evans's car in the Waterloo Road.   The play, wrote Montague, is "a roaring extravaganza only to be carried off at all upon the stage by a sustained rush of high spirits that leaves no time to think ".   This production and performance caught the idea admirably.

Since the re-opening of Sadler's Wells Theatre in 1931 the various Old Vic companies had constantly interchanged between the two theatres.   Except for a revival of *Peer Gynt* the following season, *The Taming of the Shrew* was the last play to be given at Sadler's

Wells, the acoustics of which had never been good for drama. Thereafter the dramatic company remained permanently at the Old Vic and the opera and ballet companies at the Wells, and there was no recurrence of that unfortunate mistake by which a famous dramatic critic, setting out as he thought to see this play, found himself listening to a suspicious amount of incidental music and as a result produced a notice, the following Sunday, headed " *The Taming of Eugene Onegin* "!

SAINT JOAN

S H A W ' S *Saint Joan* succeeded *Much Ado about Nothing* at the Vic on 26 November, 1934, and, transferring to Sadler's Wells for two additional weeks on 18 December, preceded the production of *The Taming of the Shrew* at that theatre. Between the two Shakespearean comedies this greatest of modern historical plays drove like a mighty engine : a bigger play, both in theme and mental faculty, than either of the others, it more than justified its appearance in the repertoire and the policy, encouraged by Harcourt Williams several years before, of making the Old Vic a national centre for the production of classics other than the plays of Shakespeare.

The outstanding characteristic of Shaw's *Saint Joan* is not only that it gives humanity and dramatic fire to a character which might so easily become, on the stage, a popular saint drawn " in the flat," but also that it takes as its basis historical truth and makes that truth live without the traditional stage impositions of black and white on the leading characters. The time-honoured belief in the theatre that history can only appear dramatic on the stage if it is falsified and cheapened into a melodramatic formula was finally swept away by this play. Joan's accusers are painted as men inspired not by personal malice but a mistaken, fanatic but absolutely sincere faith in the political or religious system they represent. The ruin Joan's new idea of individual responsibility might bring to that system, be it feudal or Catholic, is the determining factor in their persecution ; and though the system to our eyes may be pernicious it is not so to theirs. Joan suffers not for herself but for her quite unconscious personal representation of the dangerous new forces of protestantism and nationalism. That is the true tragedy of the play and the darkest evidence of the perniciousness, not of her accusers and judges, but of the systems they represent.   The individual is crushed in the machine ; a great wrong perpetrated for an issue which dwindles, in historical perspective, into insignificance.

Historical truth has been observed in this play in the sense that documentary facts and even something of the dialogue are authentic as far as the time limits and shape of a theatrical representation will allow. It is a period picture painted without distortion, although inevitably as seen from the outside.   Shaw has given to his noblemen and priests the heightened political and ecclesiastical vision of his own twentieth-century detachment ; to their conscious motives and half-nebulous sense of larger issues at stake he has added a prophetic insight they could hardly, in their own period, have possessed.   Generalisations such as " protestantism " and " nationalism " give verbal expression to forces of which they must have been dimly aware, but could not at the time have so clearly discussed.   The truth, then, of Shaw's picture is relative, not absolute, but within the limits of this relativity it is complete.

The important thing from the dramatic point of view is the amazing potency of this form of representation in the theatre. I have seen four separate productions of *Saint Joan* in London and the provinces and on every occasion the tent scene, in which action is reduced to the purely stylised formula of three men arguing round a table, has been followed by the audience with an almost fanatical absorption.   The reason is, I think, that with Shaw argument is never negative but positive : with him words and ideas have the living force of dramatic action, his mental conflicts are more vital than the physical clashes of ninety per cent. of contemporary dramatists.

Yet his plays, and particularly *Saint Joan*, do not lack character interest, though the people generally live through the expression of their ideas and points of view rather than through their actions. Our knowledge of them is, perhaps, the deeper for this reason ; it is a knowledge of their minds, not simply of their superficial bodily actions and desires.   In how many plays produced each year the characters, for all their emotional activity, seem essentially enigmatic and sterile, mere pawns in the action of the " well-made play !"   How much do we sense of the inmost recesses of their thought and beliefs, their active life outside the enclosing box of the stage ?   In most cases we never even learn how they earn their living.   The distinguishing factor, perhaps, of Shaw's characters is that they have minds to express, whereas the puppets of too many modern dramatists have only the limbs and outward flourishes.

With what brisk, acute strokes, too, Shaw indicates the characters in his stage directions.   The pen sketches give the actor all he needs from which to develop a full-scale portrait.   Take, for instance, those at the very beginning of this play :

> *Captain Robert de Baudricourt, a military squire, handsome and physically energetic, but with no will of his own, is disguising that defect in his usual fashion by storming terribly at his steward, a trodden worm, scanty of flesh, scanty of hair, who might be any age from 18 to 55, being the sort of man whom age cannot wither because he has never bloomed.*

Two characters leap not merely to the eye but to the understanding in one sentence.   De Baudricourt's psychological weakness under the bluster is the key to the character, though it is surprising the number of actors who have missed it.   Note too that vivid little pointer to the actor of Gilles de Rais, which, if followed, can give this tiny part a sinister twist his subsequent history (not mentioned in the dialogue) fully justifies :   " *He is determined to make himself agreeable, but lacks natural joyousness, and is not really pleasant.*" Yet actors still say Shaw does not provide opportunities for acting ! The tradition that " acting " is a matter only of emotional display and not subtle characterisation dies hard : it is a legacy, perhaps, of the actor-manager tradition.

Some key to the playing of Joan is indicated before she makes her appearance, when her voice, " *bright, strong and rough,*" is heard off-stage.   Later we are to see how well the epithets fit not only Joan's voice but her " bright, strong, rough " peasant cheerfulness, that positive certainty and daring instinct that extract from Dunois the shrewd comment that she is in love with War.   But if Joan is not the plaster saint of the stained-glass window neither is she all warrior and peasant ; behind the scorching logic is a flame of genuine inspiration and imagination, that imagination through which she says she hears her voices and which presents to her so vividly the picture of a life of perpetual imprisonment that she chooses death—and a particularly horrible death—rather than face it.   The poet in Joan is here, and significantly Shaw's spare, rhythmic prose quickens in her great speech of recantation to a new and urgent music.

No actress I have seen in the part has combined as well as Sybil Thorndike, its creator, the common sense of the peasant, the reckless vision of the fighter and the rapt apprehension of beauty of this moment ; nor has any other actress seen so clearly that the imagination that reveals to her the full horror of captivity will also present to her no less clearly the terror and pain of the fire that must replace it. This Joan went into the market place with her eyes wide open, and when the executioner put his heavy hand on her shoulder her momentary collapse at the knees, and the white flash of fear in her face, revealed a terrible comprehension.

Perhaps for this reason the Epilogue, in the production in which Sybil Thorndike appeared, seemed furthest from flippancy and most movingly to justify Shaw's own defence : " Without it the play would be only a sensational tale of a girl who was burnt, leaving the spectators plunged in horror, despairing of humanity. The true tale of Saint Joan is a tale with a glorious ending ; and any play that did not make this clear would be an insult to her memory." It is difficult to understand how, unless it is seriously botched in performance, that scene in which Joan's companions and former enemies kneel and praise her can fail in its effect of moving simplicity ; the final glory is concentrated in these few moments, and in Joan's last cry—" How long, O Lord, how long ? "—to which Sybil Thorndike gave an echoing poignancy.

Mary Newcombe's performance of Joan at the Old Vic caught nearly everything of the character except the naïve serenity. Most of the players in this production tended to shout ; but noise is not a substitute for drama and Joan's passion is a matter of inward conviction, not of outward show. Apart from this tendency to force the note Mary Newcombe played with a strong mental grasp of Shaw's intentions and considerable emotional fire. Morland Graham was outstandingly good as de Stogumber, a part that can easily be clowned but which loses all possible pathos and conviction in the last scene if this happens. Blind prejudice, not farce, must be the keynote of the characterisation if we are to believe in, and be moved by, that mental collapse of the unimaginative man brought face to face with a cruelty he had advocated but never truly envisaged.

The Dauphin also is a part that tends in performance to overstep the borderline into farce ; but Shaw emphasises the sharpness under the weak impudence, and Maurice Evans, playing the charac-

ter as a shrivelled monkey of a man with a lisp, brilliantly underlined the shrewd wit while preserving the ineffectual pathos. The
rest of the playing was clear and forceful if not distinguished by
any great subtlety of characterisation. The beautiful and picturesque Charles Ricketts costumes, designed for the original
production, were used, but both costumes and characters lost
something of their colour against new settings which lacked the
severe simplicity and dignity of Ricketts's own conception.

OTHELLO

T H E tragedy of *Othello*, produced by Henry Cass at the Old Vic
on 21 January, was pictorially the most beautiful production of
the season. The austerity imposed upon the producer at this time
through lack of funds tended to throw the plays and characters
into sharp relief, but the sharpness was at times monotonous and
hard on the eyes. Shakespeare's verbal richness requires in certain
plays a visual richness to give credence to the atmosphere it en-
genders. A producer of imagination may achieve this with the
barest of materials, but rarely in a long succession of plays ; and
Cass was not primarily an imaginative producer. His particular
qualities were incisiveness and lucidity, an intellectual apprehension
that often penetrated to the physical bones of the play but rarely
illuminated its spirit with outward impressions or imagery.

Othello had the advantage of settings and costumes which had
been originally designed by E. McKnight Kauffer for Ernest
Milton's production at the St. James's Theatre three years before.
Their splendour of line and colour caught the glowing opulence
of Renaissance Venice and the East, and Abraham Sofaer's Othello,
sheathed from sari to feet in cloth of gold, became a figure of
oriental royalty, his lean hawk's profile carved out of mahogany.

There is an advantage in this stressing of the exoticism of the
Moor, and Irving seems to have tested it, since although in his
earliest production of the play he suggested the fully civilised
alien aping the Venetian magnifico, in his later performances,
according to Dutton Cook, he assumed the costume of " an Eastern
king pictured by Paolo Veronese." Venetian habit may well have
suited Othello's position as a trusted general of the State, but the
harping of the Venetians on his colour suggests his assimilation
into their ways of life was far from complete. Certainly the stage

presentation of the Moor as an oriental in costume (or perhaps merely details of costume) as well as physique satisfies *l'optique du théâtre* and gives visual vividness to the emergence of the barbarian later.

There are, however, degrees in national characteristics and the first consideration of the actor is to present not only an oriental but a particular kind of oriental. If Othello has the nobility of the savage whose descent is royal, he has also his simplicity and gulli- bility, that sensitivity to a hint that springs not from the brain but from primitive emotional instinct. In his profession he has brain and to spare, but his generalship represents the mind of a calculating mathematician. Emotionally, and in all personal contacts, he is a child.

It was in this aspect of Othello's exoticism that Abraham Sofaer failed, and it was a failure not of understanding but of physical and racial disability. This actor's Jewish shrewdness would have penetrated Iago's insinuations at the start, even if it had not pierced the Ancient's deceptive armour of honesty before he even began them. He was noble, keen and phlegmatic, never " perplexed," and although the fit of epilepsy did magnificently let loose the animal and savage its effect was vitiated because one had no glimpse of the barbarian until that moment and little afterwards. The man struck one as without passion, where passion should well up in him like molten lava, shrivelling up everything in its path. Unless we see this, and the terrible degeneration of that public castigation of Desdemona in which Othello's veneer of civilisation slips and crashes into the mud, we lose the full effect of the reversion to majestic calm—" It is the cause, my soul, it is the cause "—when purged of the last torturing doubt, Othello knows his course and comes to follow it. Sofaer's performance was dignified, intelligent and sonorously spoken, but it rarely struck at the roots of Othello.

On the other hand Maurice Evans, brilliant and sinuous as quicksilver, caught the essence of Iago and gave a performance which, although lightweight, drove the play before it with a Machiavellian force. Unless we accept Hazlitt's rather far-fetched theory that the references by the other characters to " honest Iago " are ironic, and arise out of " something suspicious in his appearance," the difficulty facing the actor of this part is to make credible his reputation of bluff honesty while leaving no doubt in the audience's mind as to the character's essential malignancy, his callous relish in evil for the sake of evil. He must look the innocent flower and be the serpent under it. Evans's elastic walk, slight compact physique and boyish countenance helped him to present a credible mask of candour and good-humour ; but there was danger in the alert carriage, suggesting the egoist and opportunist, and the quick bright brown eyes darted mischief. Subtle, plausible, cynical, the performance had the menace of a hidden dagger and cleverly suggested the vanity and corroding jealousy of a man who, pitiless and baulked of authority, finds a distorted power in plotting the ruin of others. Iago's instinct for evil grows by what it feeds on. It is an obsession that takes increasing hold and eventually destroys him, and the value of Maurice Evans's portrait was that it conveyed this without melodrama but through the wit and easy grace of the Renaissance adventurer.

The enchantment of Vivienne Bennett's Desdemona in this production aroused wide critical comment. A young actress whose early stage appearances had been as a dancer as well as Chorus Leader in Greek tragedy, she had slipped unobtrusively into the company in the small part of Bianca in *The Taming of the Shrew.* Desdemona gave her her first major opportunity and her performance remains the most moving and completely satisfying of any I have seen. Its special grace was in its delicate perception of that magic that holds Othello in thrall and seems always on the brink of disarming his suspicion. Her solicitation for Cassio had the gay and winning cajolery of a child, and her pleading for her own life at the end something of a child's terror of the dark. No actress has more touchingly presented the dazed bewilderment of that " What horrible fancy's this ? " in which Desdemona's love and trust are at last fatally shaken by doubt, and the tragic feyness of the Willow Scene. There was a golden chiaroscuro about this portrait, as if the painter, like Turner in his later sunrises, had dipped his brush in sunlight.

Mary Newcombe chose to play Emilia rather than Desdemona ; she lacked something of the waiting woman's coarseness of fibre but her loyalty and devotion rang true. Leo Genn as Cassio packed a true dignity into his " Dear general, I never gave you cause "—that final unexpected nobility in the man that hints neither at blame nor forgiveness—and Alan Webb's Roderigo was a not unlikeable grotesque, as weak in the brain as in the knees.

A memorable Iago and Desdemona do not alone make a great

Othello, but if the tragedy lacked here its full passion and stature, it attained through these performances intellectual drive and poetry of a high order.

HIPPOLYTUS : THE TWO SHEPHERDS

ON 11 February Henry Cass produced the *Hippolytus* of Euripides in Professor Gilbert Murray's translation, and the Old Vic audience had an opportunity to compare the classic of Elizabethan England with the classic of ancient Greece, and at the same time to see one of the greatest lyrical tragedies in the world's dramatic history. That it did not avail itself of the opportunity—the audiences were the poorest of the whole season and on some nights could be easily counted—is one of the dark blots in the annals of this theatre ; for some fine acting was to be seen in this production, if only the public which now flocks to the performances of Laurence Olivier and Ralph Richardson at the New Theatre had made the short journey to the Waterloo Road to discover it.

The reference to Shakespearean comparisons is not a loose one, for as more than one commentator has pointed out the character of Phaedra's Nurse in the Greek tragedy had a later development in Seneca, and it was from the influence of Seneca that many Elizabethan characters, such as the Nurse in *Romeo and Juliet*, derived.

The Nurse in the *Hippolytus* is not only, like the Nurse in *Romeo and Juliet*, the devoted attendant of a heroine in the stress of a tragic passion ; she represents the coarser-grained feeling, the bludgeoning logic of the natural materialist, which acts as contrast to the more delicate senses of her noble mistress and finally revolts them. Emilia in *Othello* is of much the same company, although as a younger woman—more waiting gentlewoman than servant, as Granville-Barker has pointed out—she does not venture too far and retains her position of trust to the end. The advice of Euripides' Nurse to Phaedra—to yield to her passion and grasp her happiness without regard to conscience or ethics : " A straight and perfect life is not for man "—is of a piece in cynicism with the Nurse's advice to Juliet to " marry with the County." In the end it wins her the same fierce repudiation ; a rending the more cruel and bitter in Phaedra's case since, in spite of her first perception of the " fair, false words ", she had half-willed the Nurse's fatal action on her

behalf and only turned on her in wrath when it had brought disaster.
If the Nurse's confession of her mistress's secret love had won
Phaedra her Hippolytus, instead of alienating and nauseating him,
would her reaction have been the same ? The temptation, certainly, was there, for Phaedra's was a nature consumed and weakened
by guilty passion and not, like Juliet's, matured and given a new
spiritual freedom by a radiant first love.

In what subtle strokes, too, Euripides brings out the unimaginative,
dog-like devotion of the Nurse, attending her mistress with a hungry
and jealous affection yet blind to the real nature of her spiritual
crisis. To Phaedra's wild and fevered longing for escape—that
nostalgia for the free country freshness of mountain and spring,
away from the fetid atmosphere of the town and human malice,
that tends to assail the sensitive in moments of great unhappiness—
she can only advance the blank and prosaic :

> What wouldst thou with them—fancies all !—
> Thy hunting and thy fountain brink ?
> What wouldst thou ? By the city wall
> Canst hear our own brook plash and fall
> Downhill, if thou wouldst drink.

It is the same quick psychological intuition that lifts the Chorus,
with its cowardly hesitation to interfere at Phaedra's death, from
an abstract commentary into a band of living women whose re-
actions differ little from those of a human crowd in our own day.

> Nay, are there not men there ? 'Tis an ill road
> In life, to finger at another's load.

It happens again at the end of the Henchman's pitiful description
of Hippolytus' death in the chariot, one of the most wonderful
and exciting passages in the play, when he ends the tearing and
almost impersonal pathos of his story with that truculent, savage,
magnificently loyal :

> All women born may hang themselves for me
> And swing their dying words from every tree
> On Ida ! For I know that he was true !

And this to Theseus' face ! The conventional Greek messenger
of disaster becomes in three lines a living character, rough in
devotion, uncowed by authority and loyal to the bone.

The real tragedy of *Hippolytus* is the conflict of passion and
asceticism. The Goddesses Aphrodite and Artemis were to the
sceptic Euripides the physical embodiment of these two forces,

governing the lives of Phaedra, with her wild incontinent love, and of Hippolytus, the natural ascetic and dedicated worshipper of Artemis, or Diana, the chaste. The illicit passion of a young stepmother for her stepson has not for us the dark incestuous significance that it had for the Greeks, but if we cannot share Euripides' horror we can share his pity, which he has wrung from us by showing Phaedra as a woman caught in the toils of a love beyond her control, but which she resists with a wasting fever of grief. Phaedra's tragedy to us is not that her love was evil but that it was hopeless ; and that she herself was aware of this, and it was the real basis of her despair, is suggested by her instinctive prevision of disaster at the Nurse's revelation of it. The momentary hope which prevents her from restraining the Nurse is a chimera that evaporates with her first dulled acquiescence. Thereafter she stares straight into the bottomless pit of her own empty life, and as Hippolytus' bitter words scald and revile her the thin thread of her reason weakened, by fever, snaps, and the one course open to her throws its grim shadow across her face. The great love that so often hovers on the brink of a great hate is lashed by Hippolytus' cruelty into the savage self-defence of revenge, and with the reckless :

> He shall not stand so proud where I have lain
> Bent in the dust ! O he shall stoop to share
> The life I live in, and learn mercy there !

a cry of anguish echoing in the void, she turns like a distraught thing and rushes from our sight for ever. " Gone like a wild bird, like a blowing flame . . . ."

Every actress of the part of Phaedra must match her genius against Lewes's description of Rachel in Racine's version of the play : " You felt that she was wasting away under the fire within." The greatest actress must fail with an audience whose imagination has been heightened by such descriptions as this, and the superb " Rachel was the panther of the stage : with a panther's terrible beauty and undulating grace she moved and stood, glared and sprang." She is faced not with ordinary standards but a legend magnified by time and poetic expression. Mary Newcombe's pale honey-coloured beauty had in it nothing of Rachel's midnight malevolence and smouldering fire ; but she beautifully conveyed the wan and leaden weakness of a withering nervous disease and a mind fitfully racked by poetry and despair.

Phaedra is a short part in which the effect must be vivid and

concentrated, so much so that the character lives on in our imagination, an avenging ghost looming behind the action, throughout
the second half of the play. But where until that last mad lie of
revenge our pity is all for her, it is now switched to Hippolytus,
who begins to reap in suffering the harvest of that sin of pride on
which the Aged Huntsman comments in the first moments of the
play. For Hippolytus' youthful boast of chastity is grounded at
least partly in egoism, and that form of asceticism that mistakes
natural coldness for virtuous abstinence. He has the intolerance
and thoughtless cruelty of the very idealistic and the very young ;
nothing could more underline his lack of imagination than that
astounded " 'Tis most strange . . . Wherefore did she die ? "
when he learns of Phaedra's death. Passionless, he has no conception of the spiritual agony of unrequited love, and the suicidal
desperation to which his repudiation might have brought its victim.
To him love is purely sexual and depraved, woman a " gleaming
snare " to " dog us on the happy earth " ; that earthly love might
have anything of the selfless spirituality of his own love for the
Goddess Artemis does not occur to him. In giving to his Hypolite
a lover, Aricie, Racine in his *Phèdre* missed the real significance of
his rejection of Phèdre and distorted the psychological structure
of the original tragedy.

It was perhaps this natural purity of Hippolytus, his horror of
sex, that first aroused Phaedra's consuming devotion. There is a
streak in women, the eternally pursued, that despises the pursuer
and the unobtainable is often alluring. There was nothing of
effeminacy in Maurice Evans's performance of Hippolytus, which
had a clean-limbed and agile grace, but there was an icy brittleness
about it that perfectly conveyed the personality of a man whose
passions were the servant of his brain. Yet something in its
ringing and silvery eloquence struck pathos too, and the blind cry
at the inexplicable Fate that has struck him down gave to the death
scene the anguish of youth betrayed. The entire death scene,
played with the lacerated head flung back over the edge of the bier
and a voice drained white with pain, was a miracle of virtuosity,
and the melting sweetness of that new pity that springs from
suffering beautifully conveyed. For with his pride and bright
youth laid low Hippolytus gains a new maturity and a new self-
lessness : in his last agony he can think of another's pain before his
own, and rend Theseus with his :

> I pity thee in this coil ;
> Aye, more than me.

The entrance of Theseus at the moment of the discovery of his dead wife marks a turning point in the tragedy. With that dramatic irony of which the Greeks were masters he comes garlanded as for a festival, and his first grief is succeeded by a terrible and hasty ire. It is typical of the man that he cries out his fatal curse against Hippolytus without waiting even to see him or hear his defence, although his son's spotless character and reputation were well-known to him. Perhaps intentionally Euripides emphasises the " hot strained fury " of which Hippolytus speaks in order to turn our sympathy from Theseus to Hippolytus, the true hero now of the tragedy and the one in whom our pity must centre.   Hippolytus' unlucky reference to his own bastardy and Theseus' sin against his mother lashes his father's rage still further, and his lame defence and thwarted cry—" Ye stones, will ye not speak ? "—stress the pathos of his position, unable to tell the whole truth because of his oath.   Only at the end do we again feel the tragedy of Theseus' love for his wife and son and pity him in the coil into which his trust in the one, and too-hasty judgment of the other, have led him.   In the brief space of time between the suicide of Phaedra and Hipploytus' terrible death in the chariot he has lost wife and son twice over.   His pride, too, is in the dust.

Theseus in the Old Vic production was played by Abraham Sofaer with a judicious mixture of dignity, anger and grief.   Evelyn Hall, who appeared only in this one production, was excellent as the Nurse, and Vivienne Bennett, a striking Chorus Leader and Goddess Artemis, gave to the lyric cadences of Murray's verse a golden flood of sound and dramatic excitement.   Alan Webb also declaimed the speech of the Henchman with great beauty and feeling, even though his personality did not match the rough edge of those last surly and passionate lines.

This was a plain, homespun production, with cardboard scenery and no great imagination of detail ; but the emotional sweep of the drama never faltered in the performance and the characters became human beings suffering, as people of our own time may suffer, from their own passions and spiritual blindness as well as the tragic pressure of outside forces.   With Euripides the span of two thousand years separating his age from our own seems at times but the passing of an hour.

Martinez Sierra's *The Two Shepherds,* in the translation of Helen and Harley Granville-Barker, preceded the *Hippolytus.* It was a gentle, dim little play about life in a Spanish backwater ; a village of hard hearts and hard soil to which the local priest and doctor, after many years of wrestling with a tough native material, have become rooted by a curious affection. In the end they are swept aside for younger men of more up-to-date theoretic knowledge, and in a tender last scene, like a faint echo of *The Cherry Orchard,* the aged priest takes leave of his home and village while the doctor stays bitterly to watch his successor. The play was like a pool so calm that scarcely a ripple disturbed its surface, but it was written with insight, character and a Shavian irony. Perhaps it was this last quality that attracted the translator. Cecil Trouncer played the sceptical and Shavian old doctor with great relish, and as the Priest Morland Graham once again distinguished himself by a character study of exquisite delicacy.

MAJOR BARBARA

I T had been intended to follow the *Hippolytus* with a new adaptation of *The Lady of the Camellias,* but as Francis Toye's translation was not ready the project was abandoned and Shaw's *Major Barbara* substituted at the Old Vic on Monday, 4 March.

It was an admirable choice and not only for the purely coincidental reason that the part of Adolphus Cusins, the Professor of Greek, in the Shaw play is said to have been inspired by the distinguished translator of the *Hippolytus,* Professor Gilbert Murray. Shaw's brilliant dramatic juxtaposition of the creed of the Army of religion and that of the international arms manufacturer is timeless in its applications, and in 1935, with the Japanese Manchurian adventure much in public thoughts, the lines about a Japanese victory in Manchuria, written thirty years before, proved as startlingly topical as much of the rest of the war talk would prove to-day. For the firm of Undershaft and Lazarus is still with us, together with Bodger who destroys with whisky instead of gunpowder, and the Salvation Army which, fighting both, must still depend on wealth tainted by this or similar sources.

Major Barbara is a dramatisation of the irony of spiritual integrity defeated by this vicious circle of material power and dependence, and finding in the end that " the way of life lies through the factory of death " : in other words that that " war against war " which excited Shelley and Leigh Hunt can only be carried out through the weapons and resources of the enemy itself. Thus the pacifist Professor of Greek moves into the armament factory as heir apparent to its forces of destruction, and Major Barbara into its model workers' estate where she may save souls without the bribery of food and shelter for the starving.

The hero of this play, nevertheless, is not Major Barbara but the Armament King her father, whose " *kindly, patient manners and engaging simplicity of character* " do not blind the ironic Cusins to his essential ruthlessness and ability. Cusins's murmured " Machiavelli " has in it, nevertheless, a tincture of humorous admiration as well as disgust, and the men understand each other at sight. Barbara is too much her father's daughter to see him with the same acuteness, or to realise that her own managing temper and natural capacity to do exactly as she likes are the precise counterparts of his ; even their driving vision is the same, although his is of the domination of steel and gunpowder while hers is of the saving of men's souls. Add to this intellectual trio the earthy realism of the Army shelter denizens, Rummy Mitchens, Bill Walker, Peter Shirley and Snobby Price, the satiric Lady Brittomart, apostle of wealth and respectability, and the *Times*-reading prig Stephen who is ripe for Cabinet futility, and it is easy to see why this play retains its vitality and force. The characters, with the exception of the last two, are nearer to life and further from caricature than in most Shaw plays, yet in no play does the wit flow with more ease and point and remain less blunted by time. The success of a wartime film version proves this.

At the Old Vic the acting was first-class and for a repertory company chosen chiefly for its Shakespearean capacity the casting was quite remarkably successful. Mary Newcombe played Major Barbara with the right air of school-teacher competence and passionate sincerity, and Cecil Trouncer as Undershaft, in his most important Old Vic part to date, attracted attention as a new Shavian actor of unmistakable incisiveness and quality. If he lacked a little of that deceptive gentle absent-mindedness that Robert Morley so perfectly brought into his film characterisation, he pointed the speeches with abundant wit and presented with gusto the picture of a man who was master of himself and of others, and fully knew it.

II.—*Richard II* (1934). Pomfret Scene : Maurice Evans as
Richard II.

III.—*Richard II* (1934). "Up. cousin, up—your heart is up I know . . ." Maurice Evans as Richard and Abraham Sofaer as Bolingbroke.

IV.—*Hamlet* (1935). Maurice Evans as Hamlet.

V.—*Hippolytus* (1935). Mary Newcombe as Phaedra with Evelyn Hall (left) as the Nurse.

J. W. Debenham.

J. W. Debenham.

VI.—*The Three Sisters* (1935). Marie Ney as Olga, Vivienne Bennett as Masha and Nancy Hornsby as Irina.

J. W. Debenham.

VII.—*Richard III* (1936). Helen Haye as Margaret and William Devlin as Richard.

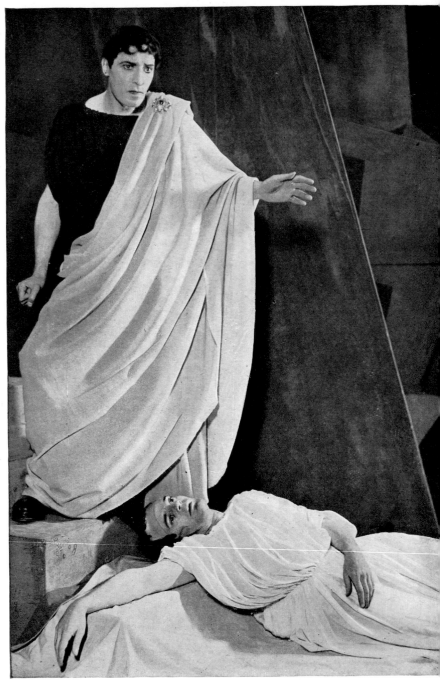

VIII.—*Julius Caesar* (1935). "I come to bury Caesar . . ." Ion Swinley as Marc Antony and Cecil Trouncer as Caesar.

IX.—*Macbeth* (1935). Leo Genn as Macduff, William Devlin as
Banquo and Vivienne Bennett as Lady Macbeth.

X.—*Peer Gynt* (1935). William Devlin as Peer and Vivienne Bennett
as Solveig.

The difficulty facing the player of Cusins, who for love of Barbara beats a Salvation Army drum with his tongue just perceptibly in his cheek, is to make credible the Professor of Greek beneath the light façade of irony and comic importunity. Maurice Evans, taking as his make-up cue, with some textual justification, not Gilbert Murray but the young red-haired, red-bearded George Bernard Shaw, brilliantly combined intellectual and clown, and shot his bolts of wit with a satiric marksmanship. As Rummy Mitchens and Peter Shirley, Buena Bent and Morland Graham seemed to have sprung straight from the soil and dust of the West Ham shelter. Leo Genn as Bill Walker put up, for so polished a Shakespearean, a portrait of truculent Cockney humour, there was a good attempt at Snobby Price by a youthful actor Richard Warner, and as the Salvationist, Mrs Baines, Ruth Hermansen waved an Army banner and screamed the Christian " Blood and Fire ! " with a cannibalistic frenzy. Alan Webb's Stephen revealed an unexpected gift for pompous satire, and as the amiable but foolish " Cholly " a young actor named Alec Clunes, hitherto seen in very minor parts, made his first noticeable success. Looking back it is possible to see in this genial and humorous sketch the first seeds of his dazzling Charles Surface and Sir Harry Wildair of later days.

HENRY IV, PART II.

T H E isolated production of *Henry I V, Part I I*, is much rarer in the English theatre than that of Part I : it stands less on its own, being a direct continuation of the rebellious movement that was shattered at Shrewsbury at the end of Part I. Dr. Dover Wilson has aptly remarked that the final scenes of Part I mark a crest in the drama more normally associated with the third Act of the other Shakespeare plays. The fact that Part II begins in the slough of that wave, with the depressing backwash of the Battle of Shrewsbury and the bringing of news confusing to an audience unacquainted with Part I, adds to the difficulties of the play. The device of the Chorus " Rumour," emphasising the falseness of the news brought to Northumberland, shows that Shakespeare himself was not unaware of these difficulties.

There is another reason for some of the slackening of interest in Part II, at least on the political side. The death of Hotspur and disappearance of Glendower leave the conspirators without any comparable characters, characters able to strike fire from the damp tinder of rebellion. The intrigue sags, and far more than in Part I the dramatic interest rests on the mighty shoulders of Falstaff. It has, though, two lively rustic character additions in Shallow and Silence, Henry IV himself takes a rather more prominent par:, and Prince Hal is still a leading figure even though his manner of rejecting Falstaff loses our sympathy at the end. Given good acting of these characters, and particularly of Falstaff, Part II may still prove a coherent narrative with some richnesses of wit, phrase and character that exceed those in Part I.

The production of *Henry I V, Part I I* at the Old Vic at the end of March, 1936, did not stand in complete isolation, since it coincided with Sydney Carroll's production of Part I at His Majesty's Theatre, featuring George Robey as Falstaff. Another George, George Merritt, came as guest artist to the Vic to play Falstaff, but his genial characterisation lacked spiritual " bigness " and never placed Falstaff within what Dover Wilson terms " the greatest rout of unseemly, and often indecent, disreputables that ever teemed from a dramatist's brain." He was too little the rapscallion, and merged without prominence into the play's team of characters where he should have bestrode the play like a Colossus.

The great successes of this production were the Justice Shallow of Morland Graham and the Doll Tearsheet of Vivienne Bennett, who also brilliantly " doubled " the part of Rumour in a costume like tongues of flame. Both performances were perfectly conceived as a part of their rural and urban surroundings, and both reflected the faint glint of melancholy that seeps through the rustic humours and ribaldry of the play. Graham's Shallow, cackling of his dead acquaintances, touched the very kernel of senile reminiscence ; he was dry and bitter as a nut from the woods of his native Gloucestershire, and his very laughter seemed to echo from the edge of the grave. It was Doll Tearsheet, not Falstaff, who caught that same prevision of death in the tavern scenes, and her talk of Falstaff's patching up his old body for heaven had a slatternly tenderness. There was a raddled glamour of fading beauty about this portrait, but it had gusto also and with the roaring young Pistol of Alec Clunes made enough noise to split the ears of the groundlings.

Abraham Sofaer as Henry IV presented a later phase of his Bolingbroke with skill, suggesting the increase of royalty and statesmanship as well as the wasting uneasiness of the head that

wears a crown.   The player of Prince Hal is faced here with a
cleavage of personality which Alan Webb failed to compass.   The
Prince of Part II, even in the tavern scenes, already shows signs
of satiety in indulgence, and it is impossible not to recognise the
growing bitterness and sense of responsibility in such dialogue
as the following, with its reference to his father's sickness :

> HAL : What wouldst thou think of me if I should weep ?
> POINS : I would think thee a most princely hypocrite.
> HAL : It would be every man's thought, and thou art
>   a blessed fellow to think as every man thinks.

Yet the lively scapegrace is still much in evidence, and was missed
in the performance of this actor, whose talents were never those
of the romantic leading player although they have proved con-
spicuous since in certain character rôles.   In the trappings of
royalty he was happier, he spoke the " golden care " speech with
eloquence and feeling and his sympathy did much to take the edge
of coldness from that cruel " I know thee not, old man."

It is the manner of Prince Hal's rejection of Falstaff that revolts
us ;   analyse the situation and it is difficult to see how the young
King, eager to recognise his political responsibility, could have
acted otherwise.   Faced with such companions at such a moment
(one must remember the cut-throat and cut-purse Pistol was of
the party), how could he publicly acknowledge and encourage them
without jeopardising the whole apparent course of his future conduct ?   As companions and advisers to a King they were impossible
and he knew it : better cut the bond at once, since it must be done,
though, as appears quickly in the text, his treatment was not otherwise ungenerous and he saw to it they were materially well provided
for.   Yet how much more tactfully the situation might have been
handled !   That stark, uncompromising " I know thee not, old
man " shows a cruelty we look for in vain in the later Henry V,
but which down the ages has thrown its grim unlikeable shadow
across the character, a dark blot on the future brightness.

Maurice Evans, preparing to don the mightier cloak of Hamlet,
took a brief holiday in this production in the small part of Silence.
Perhaps the gala spirit too obviously infected his performance,
with its sombre raising of a tall conical hat at every reference to
Shallow's acquaintances who had passed on.   As I write a critic
of my own generation has just recalled its irreverences in print with
pious horror.   It was, nevertheless, an inventive riot of tippling

senile comedy, enjoyed as much by the audience as by the actor, and there are moments in the histories when we welcome such diversions, whatever our critical faculties tell us we ought to write about them afterwards.

Rumour has it that Henry Cass produced this play for the nett sum of £10. Allowing such financial restriction to be necessary at the time, it was an achievement of some merit, making up in some attractive lighting what it lacked in substance. A warm glowing of embers transformed the bareness of the tavern, the King paced with nocturnal restlessness in the violet shaft of a stained-glass Gothic window, and the one piece of material richness, Doll Tear-sheet's tarnished tapestry gown, held the eye with a tawdry magnificence.

HAMLET

I T was customary at the Old Vic to include a number of performances of *Hamlet* in its entirety each time the play was produced. John Gielgud's first Hamlet under Harcourt Williams had been in an entirety version, with some performances of a shorter version, and the same procedure was adopted in the three weeks' season beginning on 29 April, 1935, when Maurice Evans played Hamlet in the nine " entirety " performances and several of the shorter ones. At the remaining six performances of the shorter version Marius Goring took the part of Hamlet. He was a young actor who had made a brilliant impression, two years previously, as Romeo to Peggy Ashcroft's Juliet, and a little while before this, when scarcely twenty, had played Macbeth at short notice in place of Malcolm Keen, who had met with an accident. I saw neither of these early Old Vic performances and regret very much I also missed his Hamlet, which in spite of its immaturity must, to judge by the actor's later work, have been both intelligent and interesting. At other performances he played Fortinbras and nicely hit off the eager and capable spirit of Hamlet's spiritual " opposite."

The advantage of playing Hamlet in his eternity, as the Old Vic actors were wont to put it, is that it enables the whole Prince to be revealed in his psychological contradictions and variety, and the purely sentimental reading encouraged by some " cut " versions becomes impossible. In particular the scenes most often omitted— all the vivid hue and cry after Hamlet's killing of Polonius and the morbid satire of his taunts at the King—reveal a flashing Renaissance Hamlet irreconcilable with the " sweet Prince " of Victorian tradition, and also with Goethe's celebrated half-truth of the " lovely, pure and most moral nature, without the strength of nerve which forms a hero," sinking " beneath a burden which it cannot bear and must not cast away." Modern scholarship and the introduction of entirety stage versions by the Old Vic company have stripped the sugar-coating from Hamlet, and revealed the tormented and at moments corroding savagery beneath without obscuring the essential sensibility and grace of intellect. For Hamlet's cruelty is never more than word-deep, and under the tarnish of disillusion we glimpse continually the ingenuous charm and glowing genius of the natural Prince.

There is more, of course, to Hamlet even than this ; the emotional instability which after the revelation of the Ghost brings him to the verge though never over the precipitous brink of madness, the inexplicable and frustrating weight of melancholy, the self-torturing doubts and introspection and procrastination, the rapier-like wit, the idealistic affection thrown out of balance by the discovery of human perfidy. What we see is a nature on the rack, and the actor must show this whatever his individual interpretation of other aspects of the rôle. For the actor, as Granville-Barker has so acutely pointed out, is bound to reconstruct the character in terms of his own personality. " He realises himself in Hamlet. And if he did not his performance would be lifeless."

Evans's Hamlet was quick with life, and practically everything was in it except the fatal irresolution. It lacked natural melancholy and natural antipathy to violence, and the intellect was a shade too calculating to suggest a mind torn by doubt and girded to action only by extreme emotional stress. This Hamlet would, one suspected, have dispatched the King within a few scenes and with no shriving time allowed. Given this defect, a matter of personality rather than interpretation, it was a performance of mobility, suffering and whiplash intelligence, every word lucid in meaning and with reserves of genuine pathos and tenderness. One touch of imaginative insight I have never seen repeated by any other actor : it was in the response " Well, well, well " to Ophelia's query, " How does your honour for this many a day ? ", which most actors and commentators take as an impatient and half-automatic reply without psychological significance. At the third

" well " Evans's voice broke and he turned quickly from Ophelia
and the audience, as if suddenly shaken by the irony of his own
reply. It was a revealing flash of anguish and in the contracted
shoulders and instinctive lift of the hand to the face one had the
impression of tears rising to the surface and with an effort suppressed.

Apart from Evans's performance this tended to be a " routine "
Hamlet production. An Elizabethan setting was chosen, and although intellectually it fits the play's outlook and philosophy
there was a restrictive coldness about the atmosphere, as if the
action as well as the characters were cribb'd, cabin'd and confin'd
in ruffles and farthingales. The impression of a blameless Court
was not mitigated by a King (Abraham Sofaer) of subtle treachery
but almost ascetic lack of wantonness, and Dorothy Green's beautifully played and spoken Gertrude was hardly more suggestive of
illicit passion.

Alec Clunes's Laertes, in the young and still inexperienced actor's
more explosive vein, gave too much of water to the drowned Ophelia,
but Morland Graham performed an unusual and interesting "double"
as Polonius and the Gravedigger. Leo Genn was a quiet, watchful
and devoted Horatio, although his crimson costume and raven's-
wing hair suggested more a Renaissance Roman than a Dane.
At the first performances Vivienne Bennett's Ophelia seemed
somewhat subdued by a blonde wig of quite revolting artificiality ;
when this was removed we were able to appreciate the pathos of
her mad scene and the extreme sensitivity with which, in the Play
Scene, she hinted at future mental unbalance. Her white face and
revealing hands suggested bewildered suffering and intolerable
nervous strain. This is one of the few Ophelias I have seen which
has made an unmistakable attempt to prepare one for the girl's
later madness.

Hamlet was Maurice Evans's last complete performance not only
at the Old Vic but in England. Guthrie McClintoc, the American
producer, saw the play while on a visit to this country in search
of an actor to play Romeo with his wife, Katherine Cornell, as
Juliet. The result was inevitable, and the young actor departed
within a few weeks for the United States, where after successful
appearances as Romeo and the Dauphin in *Saint Joan*, both with
Katherine Cornell, he played Richard II under his own management
and laid the foundation-stone of his future eminence as America's
leading Shakespearean actor. On the last night of the Old Vic

season, on Monday, 20 May, 1935, scenes from *Richard II*, *Hamlet* and *The Taming of the Shrew* were given, and Evans's *tour de force* in the contrasting rôles of Richard, Hamlet and Petruchio must live in the memory of all who witnessed it.

CHAPTER II

THE SECOND HENRY CASS SEASON

PEER GYNT

T H E new season, with Henry Cass again as producer and William Devlin and Ion Swinley as leading actors, opened at the Old Vic on 23 September, 1935, Ibsen's *Peer Gynt* being chosen for the occasion.

This was not the first Old Vic production of *Peer Gynt* : it had been performed in 1922 with Russell Thorndike in the part of Peer, now chosen to mark the Old Vic début of the 24-year-old actor William Devlin. Devlin had achieved some distinction as Sophocles' King Oedipus in an O.U.D.S. production performed in the original Greek, and at the age of twenty-two had again won high critical praise for his performance of King Lear at the Westminster Theatre. His interpretation of the part of Ibsen's rapscallion, which makes tremendous demands on the poetic imagination of the player, as well as his ability to encompass three distinct character phases of youth, middle age and senility, was awaited with some interest. Swinley, a more experienced actor of great beauty of voice and elocution, returned to the theatre where he had played many leading parts with success in 1923 and 1924. A noble, sensitive and frequently moving actor, he was content—like Laurence Olivier ten years later—to play the small but significant part of the Button-Moulder in the last few scenes of the play.

Henry Cass opened with a judiciously " cut " version of the play, but for the last two weeks of the season—in May, 1936—the production was revived at Sadler's Wells Theatre, where several performances of the play in its entirety were performed with a dinner interval. This entirety version was magnificently revealing and many of the audience must have found, as in the case of *Hamlet*, that no " cut " version seemed afterwards completely satisfactory. In Cass's first production at the Vic both the intensely significant " Onion " soliloquy and the Lunatic Scene were omitted : in

Tyrone Guthrie's more recent version at the New Theatre these were included, but the scene of the funeral and great oration of the Priest, which throw Peer's own psychology so strikingly into relief, disappeared entirely. Only in the full version was one able to gain a valid impression of Ibsen's complete play, with its finely correlated technical machinery in which even the smallest episodes are designed to heighten the theme, and to provide a suggestive link with later character developments and events.

In comparison with Ibsen's later compact sociological dramas *Peer Gynt* is a sprawling masterpiece, half-fantasy, half-morality, and making huge demands on the scenic resources of the producer. Yet how beautifully, even here, every cog in the technical machine works, and plays its part in driving the whole. The degrading adventures of Peer's youth become comically idealised, in his elderly memory, as glittering romance ; the forest lad who, in the horrified presence of the young Peer, mutilates himself to avoid military service is the subject of the Priest's funeral oration half a century later ; the casting ladle which Åse discovers on her death bed, the toy of the child Peer, becomes the symbol of the messenger of Death, the Button-Moulder, who appears to him in his age ; Solveig's silver-clasped Prayer Book haunts Peer from youth to age, a re-minder of his true self smothered in self-glorification and romancing ; the Boyg reappears in the riddling Spinx of the desert and the King of the Dövre in the statue of Memnon. And for all the occasional philosophic obscurity and muddle (no one that I know has yet produced a plausible explanation of the Boyg) there are beauties of scene and ironies of pattern that rank with Ibsen's best.

The scene in which Solveig comes to Peer across the snow, cutting herself off without compromise from all she holds dear, has a tranquil poetry that shines through the play until his return to her at the last. The contrast of her serene courage with his own attempts at compromise, his fatal propensity to " go roundabout " life's difficulties and always leave a gap for retreat, is ironically pointed. There is a similar irony in the placing of Solveig's song of changeless love in the forest immediately after the scene in which Peer, tricked by the strumpet Anitra in the desert, goes his way with a wry com-ment on the worthlessness of women. The death scene of Åse is moving because both she and Peer retain their true characters throughout. Peer, driving his mother in an imaginary sledge to her death, is merely plunging into that same feverish world of fancy she herself first encouraged him to create and share with her. The excitement kills her, but there is no suggestion in the text that she would have had him act otherwise. Both are blinded by the white heat of their own passion for escapism.

Peer is the mainspring of the play, the character around whom all the Norwegian folk-lore is set spinning. The political satire at the expense of Norwegian isolationism is, in comparison, unimportant. Yet he is by no means the only character drawn "in the round." Åse is finely conceived and her relationship with her son drawn with vitality and truth. There is a dogged scolding peasant devotion in her pride of him : she will revile him to his face as a liar and good-for-nothing, but defend him as fiercely if he is attacked from outside. Nor is Solveig's sweetness without moral fibre ; even in her first child-like shyness one catches a glint of steel, and at the end she is the strongest character in the play.

Peer himself is an idealist, although an utterly selfish one. Finding life, and the part he must play in it, so much beneath his ideal, he gets round the facts by covering them with the shining veil of his own poetic imagination. He is a Don Quixote who sees himself, not as Knight Errant, but as King and Tyrant. In the end he loses his true soul under the false erection of his fantasy, and only in Solveig's love finds the real, the intended Peer, untouched. By then there is piled up behind him the whole tinsel fabric of a wasted life ; the sententious ex-slave trader, the ridiculous middle-aged lover, the ancient home-comer thrusting the ship's cook from his shipwrecked spar to drown (the darkest episode in all Peer's history) have smothered the original, not unlikeable, rapscallion, and Ibsen is too little the sentimentalist to suggest that Solveig's love will wipe the slate clean. Peer must still meet the Button-Moulder at the next cross-roads. But Solveig has shown him what is, I think, the real point behind Ibsen's theme ; that true self-realisation can only come, not from egotism and self-sufficiency, but through one's relationship and contact with others.

In his youth Peer's charm saves him from despicability and his romancing, full of lyric fire, shows at moments a hint of shame or disillusion that is not without pathos. The actor who can suggest this as well as the fecklessness will catch the magic of Peer, and Devlin did so with impetuosity and the right air of tussled bravado. He was equally successful in the pompous satire of middle age and the craggy harshness of senility, and for so young an actor the achievement here was perhaps the greater. A deep musical voice helped to give weight and maturity to the portrait and richness to the words.

Max Beerbohm's wife, Florence Kahn, returned to the stage to play Åse at the Old Vic and was succeeded in the Sadler's Wells revival by Susan Richards ; both gave true and moving performances. There was a fascinating sketch of the Strange Passenger by Alec Clunes—at his fey and gentle " What I specially seek is the seat of dreams " the blood ran cold—and Vivienne Bennett conveyed Solveig's spiritual integrity with a touching candour ; but perhaps the outstanding achievement after Devlin's was that of Ion Swinley, who combined a magnificently satirical and buoyant sketch of the German, Von Eberkopf, with a Button-Moulder of quiet and persuasive humour. At the Wells he also played the Boyg and filled the theatre with a voice that seemed to acquire, without mechanical aid, a power treble life-size. Never in the theatre have I heard anything to match the splendour of this natural organ. Memorable, too, were Keneth Kent's dwarfish and sinister Troll King, and the exquisitely delivered and moving speech of the Priest by Cecil Trouncer in the first production and Christopher Casson in the full-length one.

The translation of R. Ellis Roberts, designed to retain the complicated rhyme-schemes and metres of the original, was used in preference to William Archer's more literal translation in blank verse. This meant one did get some impression of the poetic variety and impulse of the play, although it involved too an occasional awkwardness of phrasing—the kind of awkwardness one meets in operatic librettos, where the translator has been forced to follow the musical " line " at the expense of grammar and common sense. Henry Cass's production, with rather austere scenery by Eric Newton and most charming hand-painted Norwegian costumes by Betty Dyson, used lighting to heighten the fantasy, often with considerable imaginative effect. His Troll Scene, dissolving in flames with the coming of the dawn, was his finest single achievement as producer at the Old Vic. Herbert Menges, a fine and insufficiently appreciated conductor (his symphonic concerts at Brighton provided me with my own first schooling in classical music), directed an enlarged orchestra with vitality and expression, and one was able for the first time to appreciate the full variety and dramatic impetus of Grieg's incidental music. Menges has done a great deal of useful work, both in arranging and composing scores, as musical director of Old Vic plays, but it is only on rare occasions that he steps into the limelight and gets the acknow-ledgment he deserves.

JULIUS CAESAR

JULIUS CAESAR, produced by Henry Cass on 22 October, 1935, is the only production of this play to have been seen at the Old Vic during the last twelve years. This is surprising, since recent political events have given the subject a certain contemporary significance (a modern-dress production at the Embassy Theatre during the War emphasised this by turning Antony's faction into militant fascists). The play is, moreover, one of the most exciting of the histories, magnificently supple in stagecraft and with the psychological conflicts sharply outlined and developed. " There is a powerful ease in the construction of *Julius Caesar* which shows us a Shakespeare master of his means," writes Granville-Barker, and Bradley makes a similar comment on the play's " easy mastery and complete harmony," although he remarks at the same time that it does not give so strong an impression as the later tragedies of " inner power bursting into outer life." The characters are, indeed, more classically controlled, less inclined to sweep the play up into the turbulent skies of their emotion and imagination ; but they are vigorously and dramatically drawn and the clash of personality, rather than the clash of arms, remains the keynote of the play.

In no play before this does Shakespeare play so freely and so vividly with contrasts of character, and the contrasts are within the group of conspirators themselves no less than in the opposing factions. The emotional and intellectual differences between Brutus and Cassius are as striking as those between either of them and the quick-witted opportunist Antony, and they precipitate in the Quarrel Scene a dramatic climax comparable to that at the killing of Caesar. So much, indeed, is the interest concentrated in the psychological cleavage and strange mutual attraction of these two that when they finally sink their differences, and advance to their defeat at Philippi, there is an appreciable slackening in the tension of the play. We do not again see them in opposition, and the verbal scrimmage with Antony and Octavius catches a spark of the old fire only at Antony's characteristic " Old Cassius still "—a mocking response to the other's equally characteristic taunt. But with Cassius' over-hasty suicide at a piece of false news—typical of the " rash humour " of the man—the pace quickens afresh, and in the final catastrophe we see Shakespeare's theme move to its logical conclusion. The political end has not justified the means, and the victory of the unscrupulous triumvirate marks the tragic fallacy of that theory.

Brutus has been described as a first sketch for Hamlet. He is the noble idealist led fatally into action, spurred to murder only after an intense spiritual conflict and moral argument. Even more than Hamlet he is " sicklied o'er with the pale cast of thought," and he lacks entirely the emotional volatility as well as the charm of his great dramatic successor. Cassius' is the warmer temperament, and under the quick passionate envy, the corruption and dubiousness of motive, his attachment has a more genuine basis. There is something of a child's hero-worship in his persistent submission to Brutus' political decisions, though they are invariably fatal : his abnormal sensitivity to blame, his tormented jealousy, spring from the same root. In spite of his natural shrewdness his heart and temper invariably rule his head, and in the end his rash impatience kills him. Around the marble stoic Brutus he rages like an angry fire, and only the poorest actors can fail to make the contrast dramatically potent.

At the Old Vic Leo Genn was a handsome and dignified Brutus, giving full value to the man's quiet integrity but failing, I think, to mark sufficiently the early mental indecision. He was admirably supported by his Cassius, William Devlin, who gave the man a lean and hungry look of livid intensity, and a feverish and leaping intelligence that quickened the pulse of the play. As Marc Antony Ion Swinley was, to my mind, incomparable. The easy rhetoric of the funeral oration became in his declamation a torrent of music swept by dissonance, a masterly playing on the feelings of the mob with enough core of genuine grief to lash his hearers to frenzy. The sardonic " honourable men " was virulently pointed, and the inclusion of the rarely played scene with Lepidus and Octavius, in which the three " masters of the world " seal the fate of their enemies and sow the first seeds of their own dissension, enabled Swinley to reveal a further aspect of Antony : the dissolute cynic and unscrupulous politician, already shadowed by the rising sun of the calculating Octavius. This performance looked forward to the Antony of *Antony and Cleopatra*, and beneath its ringing challenge one felt already the stir of future ruin.

Shakespeare is not considered to have done well by Caesar, but Cecil Trouncer came nearer than any actor I have seen to suggesting the flash of greatness as well as the weakening assault of the falling sickness. At his " I *will* not go " the theatre quailed. Keneth Kent, in a brilliant cameo, gave an acrid sting to Casca's sardonic humour, and in the small part of Marcellus in the opening scene a young Anglo-American actor, Clement McCallin, suddenly gripped the mind with a dark flood of bitter invective. He did little work at the Vic, but in the Stratford-on-Avon festival of 1937 played a Henry V of fire and promise.

Once again Betty Dyson designed the costumes, and, working on the theory that our conception of the Roman toga as white may be influenced by surviving sculpture, she brightened her Roman fashions with a variety of colour. The scene as a result leapt to life, and Henry Cass, marshalling his crowds against skies of flame-red and cobalt blue, achieved some picturesque effects. His tattered army, straggling in silhouette against the skyline, solved the problem of Philippi with economy and ease, but although the mob at Caesar's funeral had both liveliness and verbosity their comments struck one as more natural to the Waterloo Road than the Capitol. Certainly they weren't to be found in current editions of Shakespeare.

THE THREE SISTERS

THE THREE SISTERS, produced by Henry Cass on 12 November, 1935, was not the first of Tchehov's plays to be produced at the Old Vic, but it remains at the time of writing the only Old Vic production of this particular play. The unforgettable production by Michel St. Denis, in John Gielgud's repertory season at the Queen's Theatre three years later, attained a higher degree of imagination and atmosphere, and Komisarjevsky's earlier production at Barnes was recalled by many critics for its achievement in suggesting the spasmodic glow of the fire in the third Act ; but with one exception the acting at the Old Vic compared favourably with any one has seen or can imagine in this play, and the moving qualities of Tchehov's character-symphony were realised with delicate perception.   Henry Cass's direction did not challenge the haunting guitar-playing Slav melancholy, with its rippling under-currents of mirth, of St. Denis's masterly composition ;   but it was subtle and intelligent, and the settings, designed by Bagnall Harris from photographs of the Moscow Art Theatre production, effectively suggested the oppressive, shabby-genteel atmosphere of the provincial town at the beginning of the century.

It is this confined provincial atmosphere that is the very essence of the play ; it seeps into everything on the stage, and the characters are slowly and irresistibly enmeshed by it.   Thornton Wilder in his *Our Town* has caught something of the same changeless and trivial treadmill of existence, translated into an American setting and expressionistic terms, and in his ballet *Pillar of Fire* Antony Tudor, striking deeper into psychological instincts, has presented with vividness a choreographic picture of the loneliness, gossip and social restrictions of American small-town life of the same period. Tudor's is also a tale of three sisters, although only one of them, the sex-starved Hagar, breaks momentarily and fatally through the moral conventions of her surroundings.   In neither of the American works do we get Tchehov's tragic sense of characters reduced by circumstances and environment to a littleness which is below their natural stature ;   of refinement and intelligence warped in a town in which " to know three languages is an unnecessary luxury," and the presence of a military garrison the only antidote to boredom.

In a perfect first scene of reminiscence and introduction he places before us his characters : the schoolmistress, Olga, regretfully accep-ting her spinsterhood ;   the married sister, Masha, bored and whist-ling a tune as she reads ;   the youngest, Irina, radiant with a reason-less optimism ;   the irresponsible old doctor who has lost all his illusions, but not his tenderness for the three girls whose mother he had loved ;   the feckless, violin-playing brother for whom the sisters have such high hopes ;   the chattering, philosophic Colonel Vershinin ; the rich, ugly young Baron, dreaming like an idealistic Communist of happiness through work ;   the kind, pedantic school-teacher Kuligin, blind to his wife's discontent ;   the vulgar Natasha and strange and terrifying Solyony.   And as the play proceeds the quenching of their hopes, their fleeting evasions of life through love or work, their inescapable unhappiness, are revealed in innumerable little glancing lights of dialogue and action.   Irina's glowing Spring fades into an overcast Summer, the love of Masha and Vershinni burns with a brief and ineffectual fire, the brother Andrey marries a commonplace scold and ends by sitting ignobly on the local Rural Board and pushing a perambulator about the garden, the gentle Baron dies in a duel with Solyony. At the last the regiment is called away to another district, and those left behind subside in bleak boredom to the sound of echoing good-byes.

The three sisters will never return to Moscow, the centre of their hopes and longing. Life has passed them by ; but in the continual coming and going, talking and making of tea, the restless trivialities of daily life, there emerge little flashing patterns of poetry and pathos. Tusenbach going to his death with a fey perception of the loveliness of trees he had never noticed before, and a last shy prosaic request for a cup of coffee he will not live to drink ; Andrey pouring out his unhappiness and resentment to the aged servant who cannot hear him and the mute, unresponsive screens round his sisters' beds ; Kuligin, blundering into nobility, trying to distract his wife from thoughts of her lost lover by putting on the comic beard he had taken from a schoolboy—in moments such as these life takes on a heightened intensity, like a figure marked by a spotlight on a darkened stage. At the end the three sisters, locked together in misery, radiate a queer quality of hope, and Olga's quiet voice has in it the echo of wondering eternity :

> Time will pass, and we shall go away for ever, and we shall be forgotten, our faces will be forgotten, our voices, and how many there were of us ; but our sufferings will pass into joy for those who will live after us, happiness and peace will be established upon earth, and they will remember kindly and bless those who have lived before. Oh, my dear sisters, our life is not ended yet. We shall live ! The music is so gay, so joyful, and it seems as though a little more and we shall know what we are living for, why we are suffering . . . If we only knew—if we only knew !

Lovely performances by Marie Ney, Vivienne Bennett and Nancy Hornsby brought to full flower Olga's resigned grief, Masha's bitter irritability and brief awakening passion, Irina's joyousness and disillusion ; and as the weak, introspective brother Keneth Kent gave a perfect performance that touched both pathos and ineffectuality. Unlike Gielgud several years later, Ion Swinley did not attempt a Stanislavsky make-up as Vershinin, but gave the talkative, dreaming and unhappy Colonel the backwash of his own sensitivity and elegance. I found the performance less amusing and superficial than Gielgud's, less of a "character," but considerably more moving. Vershinin's parting with Masha—the two clinging like lost souls in a last helpless and lingering embrace—is memorable still. As the ugly young Baron Tusenbach William Devlin also modestly, and I think mistakenly, played without make-up ; it was otherwise a performance of genuine feeling and intelligence. Andrew Leigh was the schoolmaster, Myrtle Richardson the scolding Natasha, and Cecil Trouncer outstanding as the fuddled, affectionate, incompetent and drunken old Doctor.

The flaw to my mind was the Solyony of George Woodbridge, a forthright actor here completely miscast. The chilling, humourless interruptions of this sinister romantic, obsessed by a vision of himself as the poet Lermontov and terrifying Irina with his jealousy and love, throw a bleak neurotic shadow across the play which was brilliantly conveyed by Glen Byam Shaw in the St. Denis production. At the Old Vic one missed the chill and venom, and even that final eerie revelation that the man scents his hands because they smell like a corpse failed to curdle one's blood.

MACBETH

MACBETH, produced on 3 December, 1935, was a major failure. In it Ion Swinley played his greatest rôle this season, but his interpretation failed to reveal either the variety or imaginative impulse of the character, and Henry Cass's production plodded equally far behind the swift dramatic course and poetry of the play.

Macbeth is, above all things, a play of poetic imagination, and Macbeth a character whose vaulting ambition is fatally checked and precipitated by its ravagings. His imagination is his conscience, an airborn dagger driving through the layer of ruthlessness with phantoms of terror and blood, dyeing his hand until it seems to him the stain will penetrate the multitudinous seas of the earth, revealing to him in sudden blinding flashes—" Wake Duncan with thy knocking ! *Would thou couldst* ! "—the whole disintegrating futility of his crime. Yet his is not the nature to give way ; racked by the cry " Macbeth shall sleep no more ! ", able to feel the bitter regret of age unaccompanied by honour and friends, he steps joylessly, savagely, almost dementedly from crime to crime, and to the last refuses to " play the Roman fool " and die on his own sword. The Macbeth of the end of the play, hardened in tyranny and seeing life without hope—

> a tale
> Told by an idiot, full of sound and fury,
> Signifying nothing—

is not the Macbeth of the beginning of the play. He has over-ridden his imagination and scruples while his wife, blind to the horror of her act until, as Bradley has acutely pointed out, she sees its hideousness " reflected in the faces of her guests," sinks under the strain of a guilt-complex she had never for one moment foreseen.

It is a mistake, I feel sure, to look on Macbeth as a man of honour poisoned by the revelations of the Weird Sisters. *Macbeth* is not a play of Grecian destiny, but of character. Twice in the first scenes Macbeth is referred to as " rapt," and one senses a mind already familiar with the gnawing and glittering temptation that now possesses it utterly. The supernatural enflames his resolution, never creates or controls it. Yet the poet in him is not easily suppressed, and if the murderer wins in the end it is a barren victory, and he knows it. That is his tragedy, and the actor who fails to point it reduces the stature both of the play and character.

Swinley, I think, did fail, and in spite of the fact that he had, one would have thought, all the natural mental and spiritual equipment for the part. He was himself a poet, and an actor of sensibility and passion who had recently scored brilliantly in the more unscrupulous aspect of Marc Antony. Yet of Macbeth's physical ruthlessness we saw as little as of his doubts and hesi-tations. " There is no sign whatever in the play that Shakespeare meant the actions of Macbeth to be forced on him by an external power," wrote Bradley, but this Macbeth seemed actually through-out to be acting in a kind of spell, without personal volition. Poetry was lost in declamation, and imagination reduced to the prosaic.

What was the reason for this failure ? Did the actor, feeling his own natural antipathy to " bloody execution " and his poetic bent, attempt to " tone down " the metaphysical side for fear of its overwhelming the warrior ? If so, he made the same mistake as Robert Harris more recently at Stratford-on-Avon, and without bringing the murderer to life suffocated all the free flow of dark imaginings with a forced and inflexible recitation. It is an easy pit for the actor, who tends to forget that until the final fight Macbeth's warlike prowess is spoken of but never put to proof on the stage. Practically the whole business of the play is concentrated on the mind and imagination of the poet, not the feats of the man of action. It was his realisation of this fact that invested John Gielgud's Macbeth with such compelling power ; he gave just as much weight to the man of action as his personality and physique (aided by an excellent costume and make-up) would allow, and then brought the whole iridescent splendour and vigour of his imagination to bear on the spiritual revelation of the verse. As a result he created a murderer and poet too, and his " To-morrow and to-morrow and to-morrow " became, most movingly, the last spent and bitter flame of a furnace that we had seen, in the murder scene, blaze white-hot.

Swinley was admittedly not helped by his production, which gave the colour of dust to a play Bradley felt to be saturated with the colour of blood, and inflicted on him in the murder scene a pair of squeaking boots which prated of his whereabouts more than any mere stones could hope to do. Vivienne Bennett's Lady Macbeth was also condemned by some critics. Playing against her personality, she seemed to me to achieve a performance of some power : unyielding as hardened ice, conscienceless, dominating Macbeth without affection and by sheer force of will. The trouble with this was that it did not sufficiently prepare us for the sleepwalking, which the actress played beautifully. Lady Macbeth should crack sooner, and we should be aware of the rift even though she never " lets on " and rallies superbly in the Banquet Scene when her husband needs her. Leo Genn and Clement McCallin were a presentable Macduff and Malcolm but Cecil Trouncer as Duncan was fatally miscast, the wonder being not that there was so much blood in this vigorous martinet but so little.

The finest and most complete performance came from William Devlin, whose wordless suspicion as Banquo dominated the stage and made the man for one brief immobile moment in the murder scene the centrifugal point of the drama. Unfortunately he was unable to give us a touch of his quality as the Ghost, since Henry Cass's matter-of-fact production excluded him and forced Macbeth to direct his jibberings at an empty joint-stool. I cannot believe that Shakespeare, who was not niggardly with ghosts, intended this ; especially since the dramatic irony of Macbeth's—

> Here had we now our country's honour roof'd
> Were the grac'd person of our Banquo present—

is lost if the murdered Banquo is not already sitting, an avenging apparition, at the banquet table.

THE SCHOOL FOR SCANDAL: ST. HELENA

"A M I D S T the mortifying circumstances attendant upon growing old, it is something to have seen *The School for Scandal* in its glory" wrote Charles Lamb, his pen urgent to capture for posterity the dying flame of the great acting performances of his youth. Perhaps in our own time, as in the latter days of Charles Lamb, Sheridan's masterpiece has never been seen in its full perfection, and the Old Vic production at Christmas in 1935 only chipped off a bit of the play here and there, as Hazlitt said of Kean's Lear. There was no performance to outshine the style and wit, the subtle and supple innuendo, of John Gielgud's later brilliant portrayal of Joseph Surface at the Queen's Theatre, and Leo Genn's black-suited, sombre Joseph was a patch of oil which, although highly polished, tended to weigh a trifle heavily on the rippling waters of the play. It was an excellent performance within its limits, but lacked the *élan* of the born actor of artificial comedy, and brought that touch of the realistic villain Lamb so hated to see introduced among the airy unmoral butterflies of the world of Congreve and his fellows.

Not that *The School for Scandal* moves entirely in that world, and Lamb blames the author for it. "The comedy is incongruous; a mixture of Congreve with sentimental incompatibilities." It belongs, in fact, to a later period, which retained the elegancies and manners of the Restoration comedy while absorbing something of the moral feeling and common humanity of its own time. Many people prefer it for this reason. For all its wit, its ribaldry and its sparkling artificialities, a warm heart glows at the core, and the flaying of those who "murder characters to kill time" is backed by a genuine indignation. The politician in Sheridan, as in so many of his plays, peeps through here, and the plea for legal action against libel is marked.

Sheridan was, however, too true a dramatist to make the common present-day mistake of turning his play into a pamphlet. The edge of the comedy is sharpened, not blunted, by the tart social comment beneath the surface, and Sheridan never falls into the error of subjecting his characters to the cold moral light of pure reason. He shows us in brief flashes the warm contempt of Maria and Sir Peter, the liberality behind Charles's gay profligacy, the natural candour and good humour (which so exasperates her irate husband) beneath Lady Teazle's wilfulness and giddy pursuit of fashion ; but for the rest he lets the fun wave through the action like a banner, and sees to it that we laugh with the characters as well as at them. He knew himself too well " the social spirit of raillery that used to mantle over a glass of bright Burgundy " to attempt to dim the brightness with sophistry.

Not until the advent of another Irishman, Shaw, did the English stage see again a flow of wit so continuous, brilliant and unforced, and it still awaits a comedy scene to compare in construction with the justly famous " screen " scene in this play. It is a masterpiece of plot, counterplot, suspense and revelation, in which each trick of technique is constantly being capped with another even better than the last. The invention is inexhaustible, and there is just enough undercurrent of serious implication beneath the hilarity to make the sudden gravity of the dénouement seem a natural progression of what has gone before—not an incongruous addition to the structure, like the Widow Ochre's face upon her neck.

Too often this grace-note of genuine feeling is lost in performance, but at the Old Vic it was realised both in Vivienne Bennett's contrite Lady Teazle and Ion Swinley's reaction as Charles Surface. The actor's impeccable style and refinement prompted him here to suppress the usual levity, and his reserved, quiet bow on retirement was beautifully " placed." In an earlier production Swinley had played Joseph and some people regretted he did not repeat this performance, which must have been an outstanding one. I should, however, have been sorry myself to miss a performance of such charm, elegance and natural sincerity as his Charles.

The most stylish performance apart from Swinley's was the Lady Sneerwell of that fine actress, Helen Haye, who gave the malice a " delicacy of tint, and mellowness of sneer " that fully corroborated Snake's commendation. Like Swinley she conveyed always a sense of the born aristocrat and not just a " stage " one : both were players who seemed in plays such as these to move in their natural social circle, a gift denied to most modern actors and actresses who lack, perhaps, the necessary training and background. Vivienne

Bennett was a wholly charming Lady Teazle, who did not lose sight of the unaffected country-bred girl beneath the spoilt airs and teasing graces. This is as it should be, for Lady Teazle, whatever her other faults, is no snob and never seems in the least desirous of concealing her origin or disarmed by references to it.

As Sir Peter Cecil Trouncer was passionate rather than irritable—an interpretation I prefer—and there were nice sketches of Old Rowley by Christopher Casson and of the supercilious Trip by Alec Clunes.   Modern small-part actors are not likely to challenge Lamb's Parsons and Dodd—" the wasp and the butterfly of *The School for Scandal* "—in the parts of Crabtree and Sir Benjamin Backbite, but Keneth Kent's Sir Oliver I cannot imagine bettered in any age. The part is usually grossly overplayed, but this performance avoided farce and stressed the humanity without losing a jot of the fun.

The production was by Michael MacOwan, later responsible for many fine productions, including *Mourning Becomes Electra*, at the Westminster Theatre, but at this time director of the students in the Old Vic Dramatic School.   He gave the play pace, spirit and a neat balance of manners and feeling.   The settings and costumes of the inevitable gemini, Bagnall Harris and Betty Dyson, glittered like a Christmas tree, and Charles Surface in cream satin and Lady Teazle in ivory outshone even this jewelled constellation.   Not for some time had the Vic audience been dazzled with such lustre, and there was general debatement as to which, if any, of the diamonds were real.

St. Helena, a play about the last years of Napoleon by Jeanne de Casalis and R. C. Sherriff, was the only other non-Shakespearean play to be performed this season and one of the Old Vic's rare productions of a new play. It was produced, following the run of *Richard III*, on 4 February, 1936, and subsequently transferred to Daly's Theatre with a slightly altered cast.

Biographical and historical plays, unless the author is a poet able to transform his material as Shakespeare transformed his, rarely achieve any quality beyond the ephemeral, and the main interest of *St. Helena* to-day is in the fact that it put Keneth Kent on the map as a character actor of the front rank.   The play was an episodic history of the Emperor's last years on the island, but within the limits of its construction it was an admirable picture of the slow disintegration of defeat.   Although the supporting characters were never more than subsidiary they were quietly differentiated, the writing was sober, factual, yet sensitive to atmosphere, and the sudden little flaring dramas and conflicts, reaching a momentary heat at the arrest of Las Cases and the faithful Cipriani's attempt to assassinate the English Governor, kept the play alive and avoided monotony.

The opening was excellent. In the turmoil of redecorating Longwood House Napoleon enters with his staff, who have come to share his exile, and from the first we see the feverish and futile attempts, even in this living prison, to gather together the scattered dregs of Empire, and to maintain a petty Court with all its official distinctions and jealously-guarded privileges. The envious, temperamental, difficult General Baron Gourgaud, the suave, handsome Montholon, the ambitious secretary Las Cases, are squabbling over positions at table within a moment of entering the house, and in the years that follow they chafe against each other until only Montholon, ill and tired, remains to see the Emperor into his grave.

Napoleon himself begins with an unconquerable conviction that he will be out of St. Helena within six months, and ends by planning an orchard and garden with the imperious energy he once bestowed on the conducting of a military campaign. But he, too, is ill and tired, the long years of bitterness, regret, and petty contrivance against English authority have taken their toll. The total sum of *St. Helena* is a kaleidoscope of a wasting former greatness, illuminated by a birthday party and earthquake, the dictation of memoirs, the exchange of New Year gifts and the arrival of a bust of Napoleon's son. This last was the most moving little scene in the play. It was a sympathetic though not sentimental study, and if Napoleon's dream of the benefit of a United States of Europe (under French dictatorship) has to us now a hollower ring than in 1936, the merit as a study of character, dwarfed by descent from power to domestic trivialities, is still potent when one re-reads the play.

Keneth Kent achieved a triumph as Napoleon, suggesting both the greatness and the disintegration, and achieving pathos and dignity without shirking the irritabilities, the obstinacy and the childish uncompromising pride. It was a performance that tended to overshadow the whole play, but Clement McCallin's rough and vivid Gourgaud, Alan Wheatley's complacent but easily broken Las Cases, Alwyn Whatsley's Cipriani, Leo Genn's Montholon and Cecil Trouncer's steely-eyed Sir Hudson Lowe all had their moments, and as the " paralytic, the cretin and the lout " of a later scene

Charles Doe, Christopher Casson and Alec Clunes gave admirable sketches of inept priesthood and uncouth medicine.

RICHARD III

PRODUCED on 14 January, 1936, *Richard III* was notable for the remarkably sustained performance of William Devlin in the title rôle.

As a play *Richard III* is, perhaps, more dependent on the actor playing the leading character than any other tragedy of Shakespeare. It is an early play, in which other hands than Shakespeare's (including Marlowe's) have been suspected, and its mixture of bombast and curses, typical of its age, is held together mainly by the integrating force of this one character. In him we see Shakespeare feeling his way towards greater achievements of character, and although he shows nothing of the imaginative power and psychological conflict of Macbeth, in whom we sometimes recognise echoes of Richard, he is still a superlative study of villainy " in the round." He is the melodramatic villain *par excellence :* yet something more besides. He is the creation of a great dramatist and poet in the making, and distinguished by a sheer gusto in evil, shot with bolts of wit, that has kept his popularity with audiences burning bright through four centuries.

This argues, I think, a certain charm in Richard and charm, when he cares to use it, he certainly has. Witness his wooing of Anne, where his insinuating passion and remorse have a success startling and exhilarating even to himself. Elsewhere charm, perhaps, is too strong a word for it : fascination would better meet the case. He has the fascination of the diabolical and the witchery of all evil. He is, as Max Beerbohm wrote of Irving, " multi-radiant," and the jumbled facets of his royalty, his force, his glittering irony and his buoyant jubilation keep the play in a continual ferment of light and heat and sudden darkling shadows. Kean with his " glancing lights " must have translated this turmoil admirably, and perhaps if one had seen him one would have disagreed with Hazlitt that he needed fewer of them.

I should say that, short of total incapacity in the actor, it would be impossible to fail in Richard completely. The five I have seen—William Devlin, Emlyn Williams, Donald Wolfit, John Laurie and Laurence Olivier—were all first-rate, and in certain differing aspects of the character all touched the hem, if they did not grasp the whole garment, of greatness. And one makes this reservation

XI.—*The Winter's Tale* (1936). William Devlin as Leontes and
Dorothy Green as Paulina

XII.—*King Lear* (1936). "Hear, nature hear . . ." William Devlin
as Lear and Dorice Fordred as Goneril.

XIII.—*As You Like It* (1936). Michael Redgrave as Orlando and
Edith Evans as Rosalind.

XIV.—*Love's Labour's Lost* (1936). Group including Margaretta Scott, Rachel Kempson, Alec Guinness, Michael Redgrave and Alec Clunes. Costumes by Molly MacArthur.

XV.—*Love's Labour's Lost* (1936). Setting by Molly MacArthur.

XVI.—*The Country Wife* (1936). Ruth Gordon as Margery Pinchwife
and Ursula Jeans as Alithea.

XVII.—*Pygmalion* (1937). Diana Wynyard as Eliza Doolittle.

only because the descriptions of Kean and Irving in the part suggest
—rightly or wrongly—a heady intoxication of genius which seems
to us to-day scarcely mortal, and certainly outside the scope of a
living actor.

Of the five Devlin was the least humorous, but the most powerful.
There was no lack of maturity in this actor, who was old in looks
and mentality beyond his years, and he carried the final scenes with
a concentration of passion, organ-voiced, that attained a symphonic
splendour of reverberation.   There was swell of voice and swell of
soul, and like Kean this actor " fought like one drunk with wounds."
His kingship, a natural acceptance of his heredity, was never in
doubt ;   and this scion of royalty stepped through blood to the
throne with the ruthlessness of a right sustained, if not by God,
then by the Devil.

Like Irving, with his "merely rounded shoulders and halting
walk," Devlin did not stress the deformity, and if one lost thereby
some sense of the psychological roots of his egoism it made this
actor's performance of the wooing of Anne the most plausible
within memory.   Devlin's fine rugged head, with its high cheekbones and strong, wide mouth devoid of obvious make-up, had a
harsh attractiveness that could easily pierce the smouldering mask
of hate, and in this scene its effect was considerable.   The actor
was too intelligent to miss the sardonic completely, or indeed any
intellectual facet of the character.   He made his points and got
his occasional laughs ;   but there was iron in his humour, it lacked
buoyancy, and although there was plenty of surging emotion and
restless vigour one missed Richard's confessed " alacrity of spirit."

This was a fuller version of *Richard* than one usually sees, and it
included relentlessly all the curses of the three outraged queens
(a study in reiteration intensely trying on the players), as well as
that rather repetitive scene in which Richard woos the wronged
Queen Elizabeth for her daughter as he had previously wooed the
wretched Anne.   The last scene between Richard and his mother,
the Duchess of York (also often " cut ") was however revealing.
Richard's—

> Madam, I have a touch of your condition,
> That cannot brook the accent of reproof—

illuminates the corrosive temper of the relationship, and his savage
drowning of her taunts with drums, and momentary quail of
premonition at her curse, were finely played.

Of the queens Vivienne Bennett's Anne had a pale and fated beauty and Helen Haye's Margaret a malevolent grandeur, terrifying of mein and searing of tongue.   Hooded in black, she was like a nun satanically possessed.   Esmé Beringer as the Duchess of York and Ursula Granville as Elizabeth added due measure to the curses and lamentations, and Cecil Trouncer's bouncing Buckingham, less deep-revolving than witty, reversed the scales with a lightening cheerfulness.   The scene in which Buckingham recounts to Richard his ill-success with the burghers was genuinely funny.   There is more to Buckingham than this, but the unscrupulous relish of this actor had an invigorating effect on the play.

Ion Swinley played the small part of the dying Edward IV with an exquisitely detailed and moving perfection, and another outstanding minor performance was Leo Genn's Tyrrel.   That subtle, testing flash at Richard—" But I had rather kill two enemies "— and his revulsion after the murder of the Princes, silently ignoring Richard's proferred hand, were beautifully marked.   Alec Clunes was the Clarence, bound in the spell of Shakespeare's underwater dream-magic, and Clement McCallin as Richmond distinguished himself by the aplomb with which—Richard's crown having disappeared into the wings during the fight—he finished the play uncrowned.   The production of Henry Cass was competent, no more, and almost the only costume I remember is Richard's striking gown of bottle-green velvet with a leopard-skin collar.   This adorned many a happy student and small-part player in succeeding Old Vic productions, and was always recognised with joy and affection by the audience.

George V died during the run of this play, which was partially suspended in consequence.

> The king is sickly, weak and melancholy,
> And his physicians fear him mightily.

It was a strange experience to listen to these lines in the theatre and to go home the same night, switch on the wireless and hear their modern echo : " The king's life is drawing peacefully to its close."

THE WINTER'S TALE

THE WINTER'S TALE is not a favourite play with critics, and for this the early scenes are largely to blame.   There is something peculiarly distasteful in the spectacle of Leontes' reasonless and morbid jealousy, a kind of sexual corruption with a viciousness in revenge one never feels in the same degree in *Othello*. The scenes are full of drama, but lack psychological plausibility owing to the fact that we are never, as in the case of *Othello*, aware of the mine (if indeed there is one) that sets Leontes' fury in motion. An innocent, jesting verbal interchange between his wife and friend, affectionate and friendly yet never more than platonic, suddenly begets in the watching husband a black pall of putrefying suspicion that distorts his whole vision and so clouds his reason that he is incapable of direction or persuasion.   He is a pathological study, and an unconvincing one since there is no indication in the play that he was subject to such passions.   Even in the Trial scene, for all his obduracy, his feeble clinging to a form of justice does not suggest the natural tyrant.   His Court followers are devoted to him, never cease to plead with him as a reasoning human being and do their best to soften, without words of blame, the terrible grief and remorse that succeed his realisation of the truth.

It is at this moment that the part and the play suddenly dissolve in magic.   Leontes' suffering is suggested by the dramatist with a skill and restraint that win our minds from the past and our hearts to pity.   The veil lifts from the drama of passion and reveals a pastoral fairy tale, in which rustic humour and young love sport in an idyllic Spring.   Evil is purged by innocence, and the tragic dissonance of the elders dispelled by the radiant harmony of the young.   *The Winter's Tale* is, at the last, a *Romeo and Juliet* in which the Montagu and Capulet, Leontes and Polixenes, are brought together by an alliance as free from tragedy as the Spring air.

The Winter's Tale is one of the last plays of Shakespeare, written during, or while he was contemplating, his retirement at Stratford-on-Avon.   In it certainly is something of the lyrical sensitivity to nature of his youth, and not even *A Midsummer Night's Dream* can produce lines to match Perdita's peerless—

> daffodils,
> That come before the swallow dares, and take
> The winds of March with beauty : violets dim,
> But sweeter than the lids of Juno's eyes
> Or Cytherea's breath ; pale primroses
> That die unmarried ere they can behold
> Bright Phoebus in his strength . . .

The flowers of Warwickshire and the Avon blow through the verse like the winds of March through the gardens of New Place, and in

Florizel's description of Perdita's hand, white as " fann'd snow,"
we catch the echo of Romeo's bemused " white wonder of dear
Juliet's hand." Can anything even in Romeo surpass his—

> when you dance, I wish you
> A wave o' the sea, that might ever do
> Nothing but that ?

The jewels are scattered, and the passion of these two, Spring-
touched though it be, never attains, or is intended to attain, the
burning ecstacy and maturity of the earlier star-cross'd lovers.
It is a love contemplated from the gentle distance of advancing
age, not felt coursing through the fiery veins of youth. But its
magic transforms the play, and perhaps it is true that in Perdita
Shakespeare was drawing a loving picture of his enchanting younger
daughter Judith, now blossoming into young womanhood. If this
is so little Mamillius—that gallant child that makes old hearts
fresh—almost certainly owes something to Shakespeare's memories
of his own son Hamnet, who perished like this boy in the flowering
promise of childhood. Shakespeare's portraiture of small boys is
invariably sensitive and understanding : there are many such in his
plays, bright with childish logic and wit, and presented with a
rueful humour and pathos in which we may, if we will, read the
echo of the writer's own loss. Mamillius, with his sad tale of winter
dying on his lips unsung, is the last of them, and not the least
poignant.

The production of Michael MacOwan at the Old Vic was one of
the best I remember in these earlier years. The emphasis was
Renaissance rather than Greek, and in the sudden darkening thunder
at the Oracle's words in the Trial the play leapt to drama. The
producer was helped by Bagnall Harris's setting of the Court of
Sicilia : with its bold check-patterned floor, simple throne, and
glimpse of a turbulent copper landscape beyond classic marble
columns, it had the glowing spaciousness of a painting by Veronese.
Betty Dyson's costumes, setting Leontes in black and Hermione in
white against a richly coloured Court, had dramatic as well as
pictorial beauty, and the final statue scene a cool simplicity in
which blue and amber light softened the cold edge of white marble.
A diaphanous drop curtain served for the sea-coast of Bohemia, and
with the great shadow of the bear that destroyed Antigonus gave
us our first suggestive glimpse of fairyland, our last of horror.

Only the sheep-shearing scenes failed : the inspiration was the Botticelli " Primavera " but an ugly pink lighting gave the scene too naked an air of improvisation.

The acting was quite superlatively good. William Devlin gave Leontes from the first a raging disgust which suggested a jealousy deep-rooted, and perhaps springing from something that had happened prior to the action of the play. All his early comments to Hermione, therefore, had a note of testing irony, and if this did not " explain " or excuse Leontes it gave the part a certain dramatic solidity and at least superficial plausibility. In the final scenes of remorse his aching stillness was most moving. Vivienne Bennett's Hermione had a wounded majesty, a sense of grief dissolved in forgiveness, that were infinitely touching, and Dorothy Green, who had been leading lady to John Gielgud at the Vic some years previously, returned to vitalise the part of Paulina with a lashing loyalty of tongue and heart. Her accusation of Leontes was stamped with fire and in the last scenes, her riot stilled by age into a new kindliness, her playing was quite exquisite.

Shakespearians will probably never see two more perfect character clowns than Morland Graham and Andrew Leigh in the parts of the Old Shepherd and his son, and Alec Clunes won his first real triumph as Autolycus. Unlike Donald Wolfit, who in a remarkable performance shortly afterwards at Stratford gave the pedlar the dusty bulbous raggedness of true roguery, Clunes played for youth and a picturesque gypsy flamboyance. He was a vagabond of colour and roaring impertinence, and his *joie de vivre* " lifted " the play. Geoffrey Keen, the young son of Malcolm Keen, made an impression in his début as Florizel, but Ann Casson, daughter of Sybil Thorndike and Lewis Casson, seemed to me to miss something of the enchantment of Perdita. Both young players a little lacked lyricism, and Ann Casson has since developed, not into a romantic but into a character actress, with something of her mother's force and emotional depth. Her Perdita gave no hint that she would one day, as Electra, stand up magnificently to her mother's Clytemnestra.

The Casson family were prominent at the Vic at this period, as Sybil Thorndike and Lewis Casson had always been in the early days of Lilian Baylis's direction during the last war. William Devlin about this time became a Casson at second remove, as it were, by marrying Ann's elder sister Mary, and the girls' brother

Christopher played many minor parts throughout the season with a certain quiet skill. In this production he was an excellent Antigonus, a delicate reed beside the burly oak of George Woodbridge's forthright Camillo. The Mamillius was Tony Wickham, a boy actor who played a number of parts at the Vic this season, including young Macduff and one of the Princes in *Richard III*. Ion Swinley contented himself with intoning the Chorus, Time, through a mask with his usual noble resonance, and the dances were arranged by Sheila McCarthy, then a notable small-part character dancer with the Sadler's Wells Ballet.

KING LEAR

KING LEAR, the final Shakespeare play of this season, was produced at the Old Vic on Friday, 24 April, 1936, and enabled William Devlin to be seen in the title rôle, which he had played with such remarkable success at the Westminster Theatre at the age of twenty-two.

" *King Lear* is too huge for the stage," wrote Bradley, and Lamb and other littérateurs have made similar remarks. Such comments have, I think, been repeated too glibly and too often by people who have themselves little feeling for the stage, and who do not always realise that the only stage performances of *Lear* seen in Lamb's lifetime were not of Shakespeare's original text but a free adaptation of it by the third-rate poet Nahun Tate. Nevertheless Bradley's assertion is not totally without force and foundation. Whole scenes in the tragedy leap to life at the actor's touch, the purely human values are intensified by strong and subtle details of visual interpretation ; but the sum total of the play, its extraordinary sense of man's life pitched against a dark and inscrutable fate, may be easily dwarfed if the producer and actor of *Lear* hug the human too closely and fail to whet our imagination with a glimpse, however brief and blinding, of the unseen forces beyond. It is, as Swinburne noticed, Aeschylean in scope, and the value of Devlin's Lear was in its realisation of a certain supernatural grandeur in moments of great stress.

This Lear had a head like the Job of Blake, and his features seemed hewn out of the Druid pillars of Stonehenge. In voice and physique it appeared more than life-size, and if this a little limited its humanity and range it gave a livid power and anguish to the

scenes of the storm, and a royalty that was far from the merely
senile. " The keynote," wrote Devlin himself of the first scene
in an article in the *Old Vic Magazine*, " is unbending pride—this
demands that his abdication be no hole and corner business swiftly
pushed through in the council chamber, but an imposing public
function ; secondly as he was no beaten tyrant but still a great king
and proud in his strength, his gifts must be humbly sought, the
beneficiaries, his daughters, must beg their legacy on bended knee
and then, and only then, will it be right and proper for Lear in his
joint position as King and *pater familias* graciously to grant it."

It is interesting now to see how much this interpretation of the
difficult opening scene, which Devlin conveyed on the stage with
incisive strength, tallies with that of Laurence Olivier ten years
later ; and in his article at the time—though not to my memory
in his performance—Devlin also noted that possible " glint of
humour " in the line " unburthened crawl towards death " that
Olivier made later a dominating motive force in the scene.

Kean's famous action in the delivery of the Curse, throwing
himself on his knees and lifting up his arms " like withered stumps "
to the sky, Devlin reproduced with effect. The lines to Regan—

> Dear daughter, I confess that I am old—
> Age is unnecessary—

obviously sardonic in intent, he delivered in the earlier performances
with too natural a sincerity and one missed the old man's sting of
irony. Nor was he, perhaps, sufficiently crazed in the mad scenes ;
something in that noble and intellectual head defied the impression
of mental distraction. The main portrait was one of dignity and
passion, not of pathos ; but there was plenty of indication that
the actor knew where the pathos should occur, even though he
could not as yet always wring our hearts with it. Pity there was
undeniably, and the fiery tumult of the king's tyranny subsided
into a quiet but regal calm. The heart that cracked was a king's
heart, the man a giant to the last.

Dramatically this Lear was superbly backed by his Goneril,
Regan, Cordelia and Kent. Catherine Lacey's Regan, red of hair
and emerald of dress, had a livid Renaissance cruelty, and Dorice
Fordred's plump and pasty Goneril a contrasting sogginess in
evil. The pair in ringing concert made one understand Bradley's
imaginative allusion to " the iron voices " of Lear's daughters.

Vivienne Bennett's Cordelia was sympathy and candour personified, yet with enough inner strength to explain that inflexible resistance to Lear's imperious demands on her love in the opening scene. Ion Swinley's Kent I have not seen surpassed anywhere, although I have seen several fine ones, notably that of Donald Wolfit in the Komisarjevsky production at Stratford the same year. Christopher Casson's Gloucester was beautifully played, and Alec Clunes as Edmund and Geoffrey Keen as Edgar both showed eager promise, though their method of showing it took the disconcerting form of almost lifting the roof with their combined vocal efforts. (Nevertheless too much fire in a young actor is always a better sign than too little : the first may be reduced to the glow of genius, the second rarely stoked to a comparable heat.)

The most serious piece of miscasting was that of Morland Graham as the Fool, that tender shadow of Lear whose frail wit is quenched in the drenching fury of the storm. This lovely actor did his best, but an aged Fool is unthinkable if one examines the text : one must feel the pathos of youth under the wry shafts of the jester, and Lear's care for him in the storm is the care of an old man for a child.

Henry Cass's production set the play back in time to a barbaric Britain of crude boulders and arid landscape. It was a fairly neutral background that gave the drama scope, and caught something of what Bradley visualises as " the strange atmosphere, cold and dark, which strikes on us as we enter this scene, enfolding these figures and magnifying their dim outlines like a winter mist."

This was Ion Swinley's last season at the Old Vic, and many will remember his generous gesture on parting : that tribute to Devlin's Lear which he spoke from the stage with such spontaneous sincerity and grace. He died on 16 September, 1937, at the early age of forty-five, and the obituary in the *Old Vic Magazine* made reference to his splendid Old Vic performances as Hamlet, Orlando, Othello, Proteus, Orsino, Buckingham, Coriolanus and Troilus, and to " his other-world personality which made him one of the finest Oberons we have yet seen." He had the large melancholy eyes, noble brow and sensitive mouth and features of the natural poet, and the expression was one of intelligence and sweetness. His voice and elocution were of unique beauty and made him much sought after as an actor and poetry-reader on the wireless, where his performances as the King of the Beggars in *Hassan* and as Conway in *Lost Horizon* were memorable. Only a faulty memory and rather tragic personal history (precipitated by shell-shock in the first World War) prevented his taking the major place his gifts deserved in the theatre of his generation.

CHAPTER III

GUTHRIE AND SOME VISITORS

LOVE'S LABOUR'S LOST

T H E reopening of the Old Vic for the new season on 14 September, 1936, marked a change of policy under the direction of Tyrone Guthrie, who now returned to the theatre as resident producer. Feeling the limitations of the three-week run, which often meant a play had to be taken off just as it was beginning to make money, and the disadvantages of casting from a stock company, Guthrie proposed that the plays should run as long as they could attract up to a maximum of eight weeks, and the best available cast should be engaged for each production. This meant in effect the abandonment of the stock company principle, and only a nucleus of permanent players was retained throughout the season.

The guest artists to be seen in individual plays during the following two seasons included Edith Evans, Laurence Olivier, Ralph Richardson and Emlyn Williams, and of these Laurence Olivier appeared so regularly during the next two years, and made such remarkable progress as a Shakespearean actor, that I propose to deal with the productions in which he appeared in a separate chapter. The present chapter therefore comprises studies of all the remaining plays and performances seen at the theatre during the two seasons beginning in the Autumn of 1936 and 1937 respectively.

In *Love's Labour's Lost*, that charming, dated and rarely played first comedy of the young Shakespeare, which opened the present season, the visitors were Ernest Milton (a famous Old Vic actor of previous seasons) as Don Armado and Margaretta Scott as the dark and taunting Rosaline. It is a play, however, in which the leading parts are very equally balanced and adjusted, and neither player can be said to have given a greater lustre to the production than such young and lesser-known artists as Michael Redgrave, Alec Clunes and Rachel Kempson, who appeared in the romantic rôles of the King of Navarre, Berowne and the Princess of France. The Old

Vic, therefore, seemed likely still to create its own future leading players, as well as bring them in from outside, and the fact seemed recognised by Guthrie himself when he wrote of both Redgrave and Clunes as young actors with " the equipment of a potential star."

The enchantment of this particular production rested in a perfect fusion of team acting, decoration and artistic direction. *Love's Labour's Lost* is a play written for the young gallants of the day by a youthful poet who wished to delight them with a reproduction of their own aristocratic grace and bright crackle of repartee. It is a play young at the heart, mocking at pedantry, mocking even at love, but with the glancing gravity under the wit that can melt into lyricism at a touch. The pedantry drags and dates, and the wise producer will know how to prune its obscurities ; but the romance flings free, and suddenly bursts into song when Berowne, the commonsensical *railleur* at affectation and sentimentality, yields to the caressing brush of blind Cupid's wing :

> But love, first learned in a lady's eyes,
> Lives not alone immured in the brain,
> But, with the motion of all elements,
> Courses as swift as thought in every power,
> And gives to every power a double power
> Above their functions and their offices.
> It adds a precious seeing to the eye :
> A lover's eyes will gaze an eagle blind ;
> A lover's ear will hear the lowest sound,
> When the suspicious head of theft is stopp'd ;
> Love's feeling is more soft and sensible
> Than are the tender horns of cockled snails ;
> Love's tongue proves dainty Bacchus gross in taste :
> For valour, is not love a Hercules,
> Still climbing trees in the Hesperides ?
> Subtle as sphinx ; as sweet and musical
> As bright Apollo's lute, strung with his hair ?
> And when love speaks, the voice of all the gods
> Makes heaven drowsy with the harmony.

This is rarest music, and the sensitive Elizabethan might in the last four lines have foreseen Romeo. The masque—the play is little more—fades out in magic : at the sudden icy breath of death —and how economically Shakespeare handled this tiny scene in which the Princess learns of her bereavement—the gaiety evaporates like a mist, and we leave the theatre with Moth's song of Spring and Winter, and Armado's brief strange epilogue, ringing plaintively in our ears.

The words of Mercury are harsh after the songs of Apollo.
You that way ; we this way.

There is something of the spirit of the *fête galante* in this play,
and the young producer Peter Brook at Stratford-on-Avon recently
aptly translated its action into a series of pictures that might
have been painted by Watteau or Fragonard. Costard in this
setting became a comedian of the Commedia del' Arte, the Princess
an eighteenth-century French marquise attended by a melancholy
zany : only the transformation of Dull into a modern policeman
à la Komisarjevsky broke the pattern of Gallic taste and elegance.

Yet there were false notes in Brook's production that Guthrie,
with his greater experience, avoided : a ballet of sluts shaking their
fists at Navarre's proclamation, some artificial trumpeters in fantastic towers, far too solemn a respect for the gabbling pedantries
of Holofernes and Sir Nathaniel. The sky clouded with poetic
sensitivity at the appearance of the messenger of death, but there
had been too little laughter to quench : the scene, rich in beauty,
lacked sparkle, and that light and shade of voice and intonation
that come from experienced direction of acting as well as movement.

This opinion was, I am aware, not shared by numerous critics
who rightly emphasised the young producer's brilliant promise ;
but how many of them, I wonder, remembered Guthrie's production
of ten years ago ? This had an iridescent lightness that kept the
wit buoyant, mobile as quicksilver ; and the gay-patterned movement flowed through the play with a stylised grace that avoided
artifice. Armado, it is true, was a more fantasticated portrait
than the superb Velasquez of the remarkable young actor Paul
Scofield at Stratford : but parody is a legitimate element in this
part, and Ernest Milton, in a dazzling enlargement of his own
idiosyncracies, did not fail to reveal the man's rather touching
pride in poverty at the last.

The design was indefinite in period and locality but a triumph
for Molly MacArthur, who set costumes in pastel shades of pink,
green and cream against a delicate scene which comprised only
a fountain, two tents on either side of the stage, and a wrought
iron gate, topped by an arc of fresh leaves, leading into the domains
of Navarre. Beyond the gate were simple curtains. The clear
space and unobtrusive background, beautifully lit, accentuated
the splendour of the figures of the Court, and Moth sang his final
song in a twilight illumined by the glow of torches.

Michael Redgrave and his wife, Rachel Kempson, had come from the Liverpool Repertory to play the parts of the King of Navarre and Princess of France, and their blonde physical beauty and fine speaking gave them romantic distinction. Berowne, however, is the better part, and the only one in the play that suggests true character development. Alec Clunes in this scored a palpable hit, showing a new lyrical feeling and delicacy of touch in the great speech on love, and riding the wit with vitality and great charm.

Margaretta Scott was a Rosaline of intelligence and verbal resource, and there was a perfect and stylish cameo of the middle-aged courtier, Boyet, by a new young actor Alec Guinness. Guinness at scarcely twenty had played Osric to John Gielgud's Hamlet at the New Theatre, and in another two years' time was himself to be the Old Vic's first Hamlet in modern dress. Frederick Bennett, to prove a valuable comedian in many future Old Vic productions— in personality he had something in common with Andrew Leigh— was an excellent Costard, and John Abbott and Evan John, a rising actor and historical novelist respectively, made the parson and the schoolmaster as little dull as they are ever like to be. The pert page Moth was nicely played and charmingly sung by a boy actor Gordon Miller, who later played Richard, Duke of York, in *Richard I I I* and Puck in *A Midsummer Night's Dream*. Possibly few Old Vic casts have contained so many artists hall-marked for future distinction.

This was Rachel Kempson's first and only performance at the Old Vic, if one excepts an appearance as Imogen in scenes from *Cymbeline*, with her husband as Iachimo, at the Shakespeare Birthday Festival the following Spring. Her daughter Vanessa was born later in the season : thus following the precedent created by Ann Casson, who also timed her entry to coincide with her parents' appearance as leading players at the Old Vic.

THE COUNTRY WIFE

T H E production of Wycherley's *Country Wife* on 6 October, 1936, provoked a minor storm of criticism. It was presented in association with Gilbert Miller, who wished later to transfer the production to New York, and a good deal of ink was spilled on the question of the suitability of the play for presentation at the Old Vic : a theatre which was allowed freedom from entertainment tax on the grounds that the plays produced were of educational value. The management's view was apparently expressed in a statement which appeared shortly afterwards in the *Old Vic Magazine* : " The Old Vic is exempted from entertainment tax because it takes the place of a National Theatre . . . It is the duty and mission of a National Theatre to revive occasionally those works which have their place in our dramatic history, but none, surely, in the commercial theatre."

I think there is something to be said for this last remark, though if the phrase " educational value " had been used one might pardon-ably have sensed chop-logic. *The Country Wife* has no cultural value in the sense that Ford's *'Tis Pity She's a Whore* and Shelley's *The Cenci* might be said to have cultural value, through the beauty of the verse the plays contain ; though such is the nature of the Censorship in England that I suspect the Old Vic would find it more difficult to present the last two plays, which deal rationally and with a certain moral pity with the subject of incest, than Wycherley's frankly unsavoury comedy of amorous intrigue and sexual impotence.

There is, of course, no verse in *The Country Wife* and the standard of its wit and prose is not comparable to that of Congreve. But it does take its place as a representative play of a particular period in the history of the English stage, and although the concentration on one salacious joke, not always wittily expressed, makes for heavy reading, many of the scenes are eminently " playable " in the theatre. The " letter " scene, the scene in which the country wife, dressed as a boy by her jealous husband, is kissed and enticed away under his nose by the young gallants of the town, the rowdy complications of intrigue at the last—these are the work of a born dramatist.

Wycherley has undeniable gusto, and he was certainly influenced by Molière to some extent. " He set himself," wrote Edmund Gosse in an admirable critical analysis, " to create scenes of current social life as he cynically saw it, in a state of decomposition. His diagnosis of vice was scandalously farcical, and his picture of society under Charles II was too heartless and too violent to be anything but a caricature. Nevertheless, Wycherley has vitality, and while we cross his vociferous stage, the curious and unholy men and women who hurtle against us seem living beings. His plays were closely adapted to the tempo of the times, and their coarseness, which is offensive to our taste, was not apparent to his immediate contemporaries."

It is obvious that a Restoration play needs perfection of acting if one is to appreciate any wit and style in the characters apart from their grossness of physical appetite. In a vicious but artificial age they carry off their vices with a polished elegance ; if they lack morals they do not lack manners, and manners are not something the modern actor or actress will be frequently called upon to depict. The Old Vic was fortunate therefore in the return of Edith Evans, past mistress of the art of acting Restoration comedy, to play the part of Lady Fidget, and her delivery of the line " Nay, fy ! let us not be smutty " raised the biggest laugh in the play.

The brilliant casting of the part of Margery Pinchwife, the Country Wife, was also in itself a justification for producing the play, since it enabled us to see a performance of enchanting ingenuousness by the young American actress Ruth Gordon. It is impossible to imagine any other actress tackling this character with such wit and hoydenish charm, such shy, awkward grace and such a delicate suggestion of growing, yet essentially innocent, slyness. I would rank this as one of the few great performances of comedy the contemporary stage has seen.

Almost as much controversy as attended the production of the play was aroused by the casting of Michael Redgrave in the part of the deplorable Mr. Horner. Since there is considerable reference in the text to the young gallant's personal attractions there is no need to expect Mr. Horner to appear a monster in physique as well as vice, but Redgrave's debonnair charm had a natural pleasantness about it that made it difficult to associate him with the immoralities and intrigues of the part. The suggestion that this playing made the play more palatable can be dismissed surely as wishful thinking. An excellent cast included Richard Goolden as Sir Jasper Fidget, Ernest Thesiger as Mr. Sparkish, James Dale as Mr. Pinchwife, and Iris Hoey, Kate Cutler and Eileen Peel as Lady Fidget's dubious associates. The two more pleasant lovers, Mr. Harcourt and Alithea, were played by Alec Clunes and Ursula Jeans, the last proving herself an actress with a perfect command of eighteenth-century style. Guthrie's production had his usual ingenuity and zest and the exquisite costumes of Oliver Messel threw a gloss of fashionable elegance over the whole play.

AS YOU LIKE IT

AS YOU LIKE IT, produced on 10 November, instituted the new practice of including guest producers as well as guest artists at the Vic for certain plays. Esme Church, who produced this comedy, was not a guest in the widest sense, since she was already connected with the organisation as Director of the Old Vic Dramatic School, in which position she had succeeded Michael MacOwan. Her production was an outstanding success, and early the next year was transferred to the New Theatre with Edith Evans, Michael Redgrave and several others of the original Old Vic cast.

The lovely idea of producing the play in Watteau settings and costumes alarmed a few critics, who suddenly perceived in the play a rampant Elizabethanism alien to eighteenth-century manners. This surely is robbing the pastorale of its essential timelessness ? The key to the whole play is Rosalind's love, as ardent as Juliet's for all its superstructure of comedy, and as applicable to women in any period. What woman does not recognise from her own experience—her own or that of others—the sudden depth and abandon of that " O coz, coz, coz, my pretty little coz, that thou didst know how many fathom deep I am in love ! But it cannot be sounded . . ." ? The relief of dispraise in " His very hair is of a dissembling colour," and immediate reassertion of loyalty when someone else takes up the tune, have a universal psychological truth as well as a charming humour. And although the Forest of Arden may be as English as Shakespeare's " Wood near Athens," its true locality, after all, is France, and the Court of the usurping Duke not so far removed in its manners from Versailles—or indeed any Court since Jove was a bachelor.

Except where the play is obviously historical, most disputes on period costume and setting in Shakespearean productions tend to be over-nice. If the acting is good and the background attractive few of the average audience are likely to sense anything wrong, for Shakespeare's humanity is not bounded by time or place and visual beauty creates its own standards in any form. The bright and melancholy autumn woods and marble terraces Molly Mac-Arthur designed for this play seemed the perfect setting for its tendernesses and humours, and for the mellow yet bitter-sweet nostalgia of its songs. At the last, the singing and dancing and procession of Hymen caught the true essence of the masque.

XVIII.—*Measure for Measure* (1937). Marie Ney as Isabella and
Emlyn Williams as Angelo.

XIX.—*Richard III* (1937).   Angela Baddeley as Anne.

XX.—*Richard III* (1937). Emlyn Williams as Richard

XXI.—*A Midsummer Night's Dream* (1937). "Seest thou this sweet sight . . ." Scene with Ralph Richardson, Vivien Leigh, Robert Helpmann and Gordon Miller. Setting and costumes by Oliver Messel.

XXII.—*A Midsummer Night's Dream* (1937-38). Robert Helpmann as
Oberon.

XXIII. — *A Midsummer Night's Dream* (1938). Scene with ballet and Dorothy Hyson as Titania. *Décor* by Oliver Messel.

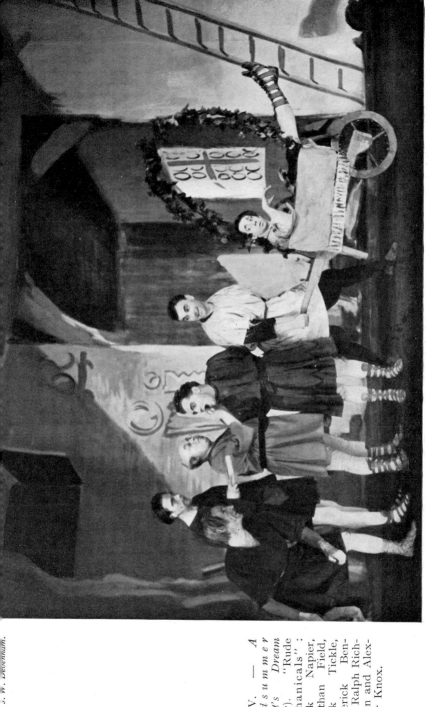

J. W. Debenham.

XXIV. — *A Midsummer Night's Dream* "Rude Mechanicals" (1937). Frank Napier, Jonathan Field, Frank Tickle, Frederick Bennett, Ralph Richardson and Alexander Knox.

J. W. Debenha[m]

XXV.—*A Midsummer Night's Dream* (1937). "Out of this wood
do not desire to go . . ." Vivien Leigh as Titania.

The small jars were entirely of costume, and most of these dis-appeared before the production was transferred to the West End. Among them were Rosalind's upswept hair-style (authentic Watteau but unbecoming to this particular actress) and the black Puritan costume for Jaques which a critic aptly designated as a " Richmond Gem." Certainly the full flower of the production's beauty did not bloom till after a short " settling " period : Jaques gained by a change of actor as well as costume, and even Edith Evans's heavenly Rosalind matured, like good wine, with keeping. In the end the enchantment was complete : there was magic in the very web of it.

Edith Evans's Rosalind has set a standard for our time : for me (such judgments must be purely personal) it remains the loveliest Shakespearean performance by an actress in approaching twenty years of playgoing. What other actress could wring such wit out of the mere comment " So this is the Forest of Arden ? " Her " Alas the day ! What shall I do with my doublet and hose ? " and " Come, woo me, woo me ! " were the very essence of comedy, and at Celia's discovery of Orlando her breathless stream of in-terrogation, the words dancing tip-toe in eagerness, had in it the tingling ecstasy of love. Yet how exquisite the tenderness too ! That sudden touching—

> Alas, poor shepherd ! searching of thy wound
> I have by hard adventure found mine own—

was like a cloud across the sun, and in all the teasing of Orlando one never lost sight for one moment of the reserves of feeling beneath.

This Rosalind was all woman, from her preposterous untruth " He calls me back ! "—a transparent device to get another word with Orlando—to the genuine swoon at the thought of her lover's danger, when Juliet, star-cross'd, for a moment stepped out of the shadows to touch the hand of Rosalind. She was wayward and gay, grave and loving, in an instant ; as changing in moods as an April day, yet with a glow at the heart as bright as Juliet's own. I do not know Edith Evans's exact age when she played this part, but certainly she was not young. Nor has she ever been beautiful in the accepted sense, although she is an actress who can assume beauty at will on the stage. I can only record that as Rosalind she had a radiance that seemed to proceed from beauty, youth and all the bewitching graces of feminity : she was young love incarnate.

If any Orlando could be worthy such a Rosalind (the character is no Romeo) Michael Redgrave might come near the ideal. He made the youth a handsome, well-spoken stripling, with a strong measure of charm and enough virility to force one to believe him when he said he felt the spirit of his father grow strong within him. (Like the " old religious man " who so spectacularly converts Duke Frederick, the deceased Sir Rowland de Boys is one of those Shakespearean characters, mentioned but never appearing in a play, who provoke one's curiosity). Milton Rosmer, perhaps not quite happy in his Italian comedy costume, was a rather melancholy Touchstone, and as Jaques James Dale lacked the silken beauty of tongue Leon Quartermaine so conspicuously brought to the part later. Dale is a good character and even Shakespearean actor, but by voice and temperament deficient in poetry, and Jaques' " All the world's a stage " is poetry or nothing. Eileen Peel was a charming Celia, if without the experience that enabled Marie Ney to give such an enchanting performance afterwards at the New Theatre. Alec Guinness cleverly doubled Le Beau and the rustic William, and Freda Jackson attracted attention as Audrey, though without reconciling me to the ill fate which links me to my only Shakespearean namesake.

Frederick Bennett was an excellent Corin and Daphne Heard a pretty Phebe, but it was sad to see William Devlin, the Lear and Richard III of the previous season, return to play such an unrewarding part as that of Duke Frederick. His fate in the following play, *The Witch of Edmonton*, was no better, and in spite of a fine performance as Clemenceau in a play at the Embassy Theatre he never achieved, before the War, the London eminence his gifts deserved. He became, perhaps, too completely associated with old men's parts. After a long period of war service he is, at the time of writing, remaking his career with the Old Vic company at Bristol, where his King Lear, now a fully mature performance, has been very highly praised.

The wrestling match in this production of *As You Like It* was the most exciting and realistic I have ever seen on the stage. The Charles was Stefan Schnabel, son of the pianist, who had been a student and small-part player at the Vic during the Maurice Evans season, and he and Redgrave provided a magnificent contrast of power-driven brawn and lithe, steel-tempered agility. One had an alarmed momentary doubt as to whether the right man would manage to win.[1]

THE WITCH OF EDMONTON

A N O T H E R distinguished visitor, Michel St. Denis, was invited to direct the following production, *The Witch of Edmonton*. St. Denis was already well-known in England through his work for the famous Compagnie des Quinze, in which Marius Goring, the leading actor in *The Witch*, had some early experience. He had also produced the English adaptation of Obey's *Noah* for John Gielgud in 1935, and at the time was director of a theatre school, the St. Denis Studio, in which some of the best young actors of this period graduated. The end-of-term public performances by the students of this Studio were distinguished by quite exceptional taste and professional finish, and it was in the tiny St. Denis studio theatre that I saw performed, under the direction of Marius Goring, the only pre-War production of scenes from Thomas Heywood's *A Woman Killed by Kindness*.

This awareness of the Elizabethan drama was shown also in the choice of play for the French producer's début at the Old Vic. The author of the strange play of *The Witch of Edmonton* was named on the Old Vic programme as Dekker, but Ford is also recognised by most authorities to have had some hand in it. Certainly we can trace in the play that instinct for painting the everyday life of the artisan and common people that marks all Dekker's work, and makes his *Shoemaker's Holiday* the most genial and democratic of Elizabethan comedies. The pity of poverty springs, one senses, from a grim personal experience, and if in some few flashes of poetry one recognises the hand of the author of *'Tis Pity She's a Whore*, it is difficult to evade the conviction that Mother Sawyer, the Witch, is almost wholly Dekker's creation.

The most interesting thing in the play, to a modern audience, was the drawing of character, for it showed a certain pity and psychological awareness in advance of Dekker's own age. Mother Sawyer, significantly, does not begin as a witch : she is the prototype of those many old women of the time, ugly and poor, who

---

[1] This reminds me of that good Old Vic story (probably, alas, apocryphal) of the person who had to be posted in the wings during Laurence Olivier's last scene as Macbeth in order to hiss the warning "Hey, Larry ! You've got to *lose* this fight !"

were believed by the ignorant to be witches and ill-treated accordingly. It is her resentment at this slander and brutality that drives her, in revenge, to seek supernatural aid.

> And why on me ? why should the envious world
> Throw all their scandalous malice upon me ?
> ' Cause I am poor, deformed, and ignorant,
> And like a bow buckled and bent together
> By some more strong in mischiefs than myself,
> Must I for that be made a common sink
> For all the filth and rubbish of men's tongues
> To fall and run into ? Some call me witch,
> And being ignorant of myself, they go
> About to teach me how to be one . . .

Many modern authorities on witchcraft would confirm the psychological truth of this : half the supposed witches of the Middle Ages were deluded into believing themselves so by the calumnies of their superstitious neighbours, or their own incentive of spite against those who had injured or slighted them. Mother Sawyer gains her desire, and is helped by a " familiar " in the form of a dog : but a programme note warned us " The dog should be accepted as the symbol of mental and emotional conflicts which can still torment us to-day," and this reading of certain scenes of the play distorts Dekker's intention less than one would think.

The dog, one fears, to a modern audience is more charming than diabolical. Mother Sawyer's own affection for him borders on domesticity, and the brilliant miming of the part by Hedley Briggs in this production gave him an irresistible fascination. The macabre terror of the tale was centred far more in the human motives of the young murderer Frank Thorney, and the drama of his spiritual downfall, partly owing to the acting of Marius Goring, was considerable. The daemonic influence is a bare excuse here, and Frank's psychological problem, like Macbeth's, hinges on his own character.

> On every side I am distracted ;
> Am waded deeper into mischief
> Than virtue can avoid ; but on I must :
> Fate leads me ; I will follow . . .

The similarity to Macbeth's " I am in blood stepp'd in so far Returning were as tedious as go o'er " is striking, and the talk of Fate without conviction. Frank's fate is within himself, and his spiritual unease, so touchingly sensed by the young wife he plans

to murder, shows he still has the chance to retreat.   For a moment
he almost wavers :

> Prithee, prithee, talk not
> Of deaths or graves ; thou art so rare a goodness
> As Death would rather put itself to death
> Than murder thee.

But it is a moment only, and when he comes to strike the blow it
is with a cruel, blunt, curt " I must kill you."

The rest of the play—his clumsy and surprisingly successful
attempt to shift the blame, and his final delirium and unmasking—
has not the same cumulative force, though there remains the moving
loyalty of the first wife Winnifred, for whom he committed the
murder though without her knowledge or will.   Her comment on
his death at an offer of 1,000 marks to help her—

> Sir, 'tis too great a sum to be employed
> Upon my funeral—

has a spare dignity.   The selfless devotion of women for the man
they love is beautifully delineated all through, and becomes irksome
only at the murder of Susan, whose moralising at the point of death,
running to several long speeches and a remarkable reserve of lung
power, is ludicrous in performance.   But to her, earlier, is given
the most melting love poetry in the play :

> You, sweet, have the power
> To make me passionate as an April day.
> Now smile, then weep ; now pale, then crimson red.
> You are the powerful moon of my blood's sea,
> To make it ebb or flow into my face
> As your looks change.

Edith Evans, sinking the poetry and wit of her Rosalind into that
bag of rags and bones Mother Sawyer, acted with the cankerous
malice and glimmer of pity the part demands.   At the early performances she tended to shout, but later adjusted her voice to
this theatre's crystal-clear acoustics.   Anna Konstam played the
ill-fated Susan with a candid sweetness that almost retained our
patience during the unconscionable long time she was a-dying,
and Beatrix Lehmann, with her strange suppressed power, brought
a watchful intelligence and compelling mask of grief to the earlier
wife Winnifred.   George Hayes, always a striking actor in sinister
parts, returned to the Vic to play Sir Arthur Carrington, a part which
begins well as a subtle and dashing villain but peters out as the
play proceeds.   The scenery and costumes were by Motley, and

the production caught something of the grey sordidness and in-tolerance of sixteenth-century village life, as well as the sharp fantastic flare of contemporary daemonism.

" There is a Hell named in our creed and a Heaven, and the Hell comes before ; if we look not into the first, we shall never live in the last," wrote Dekker in *His Dream*, and in *The Witch of Edmonton* the embers of Hell smoulder even in the scenes of comedy. But the Hell is a Hell of the mind, far more than a Hell of superstition, and that Dekker himself was fully aware of what he was doing here is proved, I think, by the above quotation. No modern philosopher could have expressed a spiritual truth with a darker penetration.

PYGMALION

HAMLET, *Twelfth Night* and *Henry V*, with Laurence Olivier, followed *The Witch of Edmonton* in the New Year, and terminated the 1936-37 season. The 1937-38 season began on Tuesday, 21 September, 1937, with a production of Shaw's *Pygmalion*. Tyrone Guthrie remained as principal producer and Diana Wynyard and Robert Morley appeared as guest artists in the parts of Eliza Doolittle and Professor Higgins.

It was still unusual for the Old Vic at this time to commence a season with a non-Shakespearean play, but Shaw had long since been established as an " Old Vic " dramatist and a great deal of interest attached to Diana Wynyard's first appearance at the theatre. Robert Morley, replacing Cecil Trouncer who was obliged to re-linquish the rôle through illness, was not at this time so generally known, although his performances as Oscar Wilde and Alexandre Dumas had already marked him out as a character actor of future distinction. Most of the other artists were completely new to the Old Vic but Stephen Murray, who played Freddy, had won some notice as the Dauphin in *Henry V* at the end of the previous season.

The atmosphere of Shaw's opening scene at Covent Garden, with its huddled crowd of opera-goers waiting for cabs in a confined space swept by rain and illumined by foggy lamplight, was excellently conveyed in Guthrie's production : but it is by the acting that this play must live and its richness of character, in the main quite uncaricatured, has a warmth and vitality that give the two leading players in particular full scope. Eliza has, indeed, for Shaw, unusual tenderness : a kind of innocent candour that is apparent and touching from her first entrance, and a bedraggled dignity that struggles through the awful dialect and battered clothes and makes the subsequent transformation just possible. Shaw himself in the next scene, when Eliza visits Higgins with her scrap of money and demands to be coached in pronunciation (" I want to be a lady in a flower shop instead of selling at the corner of Tottenham Court Road ") refers to " the pathos of this deplorable figure, with its vanity and consequential air." He has already shown something of that pathos through the unspoken social comment of Eliza's fear of the police. The distress of the poor at the possibility of " losing character," the fear of being driven on the streets, the despairing clutch at " respectability " : Shaw, through his Fabian and Borough Council work, knew too much about this to draw a comic " stage " character without any sense of the lurking tragedy under the humour of the Cockney.

In this part of the play Diana Wynyard was wholly enchanting : she sketched the guttersnipe with unexpected veracity but without losing the wistful hopefulness that is Eliza's own. And although in the last part of the play one missed the dark fire that must have leapt into the angry eyes of Mrs. Patrick Campbell, and which Shaw has imagined so vividly in his stage directions, her new dignity and flare of emotion were never in doubt. It was a paler flame, but an authentic one.

Higgins is in some ways a tougher nut to crack than Eliza ; for we must feel, under his monstrous selfishness and insensitivity to the feelings of others, the fanatical absorption of the genius in his work, as well as the contradictory lovableness of the spoilt child that is so often the corollary of genius in the artist. Higgins is an artist—an artist of science if you will—with a single-track mind. Eliza has the extreme sensitivity of the respectable poor ; he the bludgeoning lack of imagination of the intellectually dedicate. In the conflict of spirit it is she who gets hurt, as so many get hurt in their devotion to genius, and her flinging of the slippers at Higgins's head is a reaction of which Higgins himself, with his masculine self-absorption, would never for one moment be capable. He is dumbfounded when it occurs, and remains blind to Eliza's feelings to the last. Yet he has charm, as such men nearly always have, and Morley, plump, puppyish and absent-minded, brilliantly suggested this charm through the slovenliness of habits and meticulous tidiness of mind.

Mrs. Higgins's dry wisdom was perfectly conveyed by Jean Cadell, and as Doolittle Jay Laurier, deserting the music hall for Shaw and Shakespeare, caught something of the magisterial logic and independence of that dusty spokesman for the "undeserving poor." Dora Gregory, like Jean Cadell a character actress of many years' distinction, played Mrs. Pearce, with Mark Dignam as Colonel Pickering and Frances Waring and Sylvia Coleridge as those rather pathetic remnants of the genteel-poor, Mrs. Eynsford Hill and daughter.

MEASURE FOR MEASURE

MEASURE FOR MEASURE was one of the plays performed during the summer drama festival at Buxton, where the Old Vic company played for the first time this year. It was produced at the Old Vic on Tuesday, 12 October, 1937, with Marie Ney and Emlyn Williams in the leading rôles of Isabella and Angelo, which had last been acted at the Old Vic by Flora Robson and Charles Laughton in the Tyrone Guthrie season of 1933. Guthrie again produced, setting the play in a heavy stone Gothic scene by Frank Scarlett, A.R.I.B.A., with costumes by John Armstrong.

There was some attempt at choreographic pattern in the grouping of the nuns, and there were enough steps to give a certain architectural force to the staging throughout. But in spite of a few splashes of colour the general effect was grey, clammy and cold, as if the very atmosphere had become infected by Angelo's ice-bound puritanism.

It is interesting now to compare the production with two later ones at Stratford-on-Avon by B. Iden Payne and Frank McMullan (lecturer in drama at Yale University) respectively. In 1941 Payne produced the play in a picturesque setting, consisting of a vaulting arch of stone through which one glimpsed a colourful perspective of roofs and buildings. He chose a young Isabella, Peggy Bryan, who acted with the passion and burning idealistic integrity of youth. As a result the part assumed an unexpected pathos, the pathos of youth passing through a romantic religious phase, and the fire of experience, to a new acceptance of life and, perhaps, a broader morality. Many young girls from the time of their confirmation go through something the same experience and "see" themselves romantically as a nun, especially in Catholic

Ruled

6

A '

Trim ski suit and stocking cap for Vivien Leigh—Lady Olivier
—for her role as Hester in the screen version of
gan's stage success "The Deep

T̲H̲E̲
of
cheerful
is no l
Sydney
years-c
a littl

One
Thornto
and the
home at

This
paign fo
arose wl
mean an

So the
down at
and five
councillo
protest
which fo

Only Mr.
man, was l

l Oppose
l Centre

EST MEETING

" Star" Reporter

meeting is to be held by Ray-
sex, residents who object to a
Borstal girls being established

was passed earlier demanding an in-
gh the Prison Commissioners' plans
en completed, the Housing Minister
ene.

re—the Commissioners have openly
hief characteristic will be security—
d in a 20-roomed modern mansion
iles from Southend.

Essex County Council,
being assured that escapes
would be virtually impos-
sible, offered no opposition
to the scheme when ap-
proached confidentially by
Whitehall.

But other authorities, especially Rayleigh Council, objected
officially on the ground that the
proposal would seriously impede
building development in the
neighbourhood and would pre-
vent people from other areas
settling in the neighbourhood.

countries. It is the only interpretation which can, I believe, make Isabella's consideration of marriage with the Duke even remotely acceptable to the audience. The fact that Isabella is nearly always played by a mature actress on the stage has made the incredibility of Shakespeare's ending too glaring to be ignored : if one senses mature opinion and a deep-ingrained monasticism the woman's sudden response to the call of the flesh is inconceivable. Payne's production also contained in Donald Layne-Smith the best Claudio I have seen or could imagine : touched with shame and bitter pride, and with the awe of death beating like invisible wings about him.

McMullan's production in 1946 worked miracles of unobtrusive beauty by means of simple expressionistic settings and an imaginatively lit cyclorama ; it was stylised but not too fantasticated, and the atmosphere of a lively, sensual Court continually erupted through the surface of enforced prudery. Both Stratford productions were lighter than Guthrie's, more flexible in feeling, and gave greater stress to the young blood and Italian gallantry. At the Old Vic, on the other hand, one had a stronger sense of that bitter corruption that seeps darkly through the scenes of bawdry and puts this play, like *All's Well That Ends Well*, into that grim class of later comedy in which Shakespeare has neither shaken off the black fatalism of *Timon of Athens* and *King Lear* nor emerged into the clear sunlight of *The Tempest*. Both Stratford Angelos (Basil C. Langton and Robert Harris) had fine moments, but it was Emlyn Williams in the Old Vic production who conveyed most vividly the man's leaping sensuality and tortured conflict of soul. One sensed here the tragic stature Angelo might have attained had Shakespeare continued with him as he began.

It is surprising how short this famous part is, and how much we learn about the character from others. But what we learn is revealing :

> Lord Angelo, a man whose blood
> Is very snow-broth ; one who never feels
> The wanton stings and motions of the sense.

The *motif* is repeated again and again, though in the Duke's " hence shall we see, If power change purpose, what our seemers be " we may, perhaps, read a hint that some people, at least, suspect Angelo to be not quite that " angel to the outward view " they describe.

Williams, in a long blonde wig, deliberately played on the angelic note : he was serene, effeminate almost ; but the poise of the head denoted pride, and the lips were sensuous. Nor did he make the mistake of understressing the man's ambition ; one felt the lust for power quiver and flash through his frame at the Duke's nomination, and at the end the tragedy of the man's fall was unmistakably marked. His temptation was the temptation of a man racked by an appetite the stronger for its unnatural suppression : there was real agony in his realisation of it, and his struggle against a growing passion, his yielding and remorse, were actually moving. This Angelo's pride was spiritual as well as temporal, and his suffering and shame the greater. The facial expression was subtle and varied throughout and for an actor new to Shakespeare Williams spoke the verse with a fine clarity and rhythmic fire. Never for one moment did he cease to dominate the scene : in flesh or spirit his strange beauty haunted the play like the image of fallen Lucifer.

Marie Ney, unlike Williams, was a highly experienced Shakespearean artist as well as an equally fine actress of certain modern parts. When I first saw her, in a play called *Thunder in the Air,* the impression she made on my fifteen-year-old mind remained vivid for many years. Williams himself wrote of her that she appeared " more like a French than an English actress, in her extraordinary combination of a battery of technical accomplishment with an inexhaustible store of real emotional power." Her Isabella, though it was what the French call *spirituelle*, was not cold and had true intensity of feeling : it was a fine performance, even though its intellectual maturity and poise made it impossible to accept Shakespeare's ending or to forgive the way in which Isabella sends a young brother to his death. That action smacks more of Christian pride than Christian charity, and to the modern mind is indefensible.

I do not think one should underrate the sacrifice demanded of Isabella in yielding to Angelo's demands : to one of her nature it would have been unspeakably repugnant. But the alternative was hideous and final, and Claudio's warm-blooded, youthful rebellion against the cold decay of death is more natural and touching than Isabella's severe honour. To him, too, with the aura of death about him, falls the most imaginative poetry of the play: and his

> If I must die
> I will encounter darkness as a bride
> And hug it in my arms

has the true Elizabethan splendour.

David King-Wood was less happy as Claudio than as the Duke nine years later at Stratford-on-Avon, where his virile yet mellow charm gave persuasiveness to a character Shakespeare made less a human being than a slightly hypocritical moralising bore. Stephen Murray, a rising young character actor, was defeated by the Duke at the Old Vic, perhaps because his middle-aged make-up seemed irrelevant. (Why should the Duke deny that he has " the aims and ends of burning youth " if he is not himself young and therefore open to the accusation ?). Jean Cadell, that perfect actress of spinsters and society matrons, was an unlikely bawd, and Jay Laurier's Pompey had the sly innocence of a " natural " rather than the uglier marks of a sensual trade. But Laurier is a superb clown, and his long passage of mime in the prison scene was brilliant enough to convince one that if Shakespeare didn't think of it first, then he ought to have done !

Richard Littledale made Lucio—that waterfly blistering of tongue but warm in friendship—a not unlikeable fantastic, and there was a sympathetic sketch by Sylvia Coleridge of the deserted Marianna, whose

> O my dear lord,
> I crave no other, nor no better man

has in it the ringing truth of feminine love and fidelity. That other Coleridge, Samuel Taylor, thought the pardon and marriage of Angelo " degrading to the character of women " ; but surely Marianna's acceptance of Angelo as he is, her forgiveness of every injury, is nearer the sublime ? One hopes, for her sake, he will in time begin to deserve her.

GHOSTS: RICHARD III

O N E of the Old Vic productions performed at Buxton had been Ibsen's *Ghosts*, with Marie Ney as Mrs. Alving and Emlyn Williams as Oswald. It was found, however, in the autumn that it was impossible to fit the play into the season at the Old Vic itself, and it was therefore produced at the Vaudeville Theatre, by arrangement with Lilian Baylis and the Governors of the Old Vic, on

Monday, 8 November. The presenter was Bronson Albery, a West End manager who was to take a very active part in Old Vic activities during the war period. Owing to Emlyn Williams's concurrent appearance as Richard III at the Old Vic the part of Oswald was taken at the Vaudeville by Clifford Evans.

It is difficult for this generation to understand the outburst of critical vituperation that greeted the first performance of *Ghosts* in England : its nearest modern equivalent is to be found in the not quite sane world of ballet, where criticism sometimes shows a similar trend of unbalanced personal malice, and where both critics and artists receive anonymous letters as abusive as Clement Scott's famous attack on this play.[1] Bernard Shaw in *The Quintessence of Ibsenism* suggested Ibsen was virulently hated by some of his critics " as all great and original artists are hated by contemporary mediocrity, which needs must hate the highest when it sees it," but there is no doubt, as Shaw himself realised, that although repulsively expressed the criticism was in many cases sincere. The critics were, in fact, genuinely shocked.

The artist who breaks new ground and overrides established rules of technique will always be hated and abused by those whose position as artists or critics is founded on those rules : but Ibsen overrode rules of social conduct and morality, not rules of technique, and used the whole established battery of dramatic technique, more brilliantly than any of his rivals, in order to do it. He was, as a result, twice as dangerous and his enemies knew it. Hence the howls of abuse which in 1891 reached a pitch of hysteria unprecedented in English theatre history.

What is this play of *Ghosts* which was the focal point of this cascade of wrath ? To us it is a great tragedy of character and its sociological premise, its exposure of the disasters which may accrue from a moral system which ties a woman to a dissolute husband, is now too generally accepted to disturb us. I doubt even so if the social indictment is totally without contemporary force : one has

[1] As a writer on ballet for a number of years I speak here from personal experience. A ballet " fan " magazine as I write dreams hopefully of the time when a distinguished English choreographer will have perished at the hands of a paid assassin, and another (honoured by the C.B.E.) will have been deported to her native Ireland. A well-known critic (of more balanced views) a few years ago had the mediaeval experience of being stoned by ballet-omanes ! Compared to this my own confinement (in anonymous letters) to Wormwood Scrubbs and the Circus seems relatively mild ! It is a sad reflection on human nature that the worst abuse is aroused by praise of an artist. not by adverse criticism.

only to look at the posters featuring venereal disease to realise that the most terrible of *Ghosts'* sociological problems remains unsolved. *Ghosts* will have contemporary relevance as long as children continue to suffer for the sins of the fathers and medical science is powerless to save them. And even if penicillin and its successors work the miracle, what then ? We still have the timeless drama of a woman who, sacrificing her life to social convention, lives to see the son for whom she made the sacrifice attacked and driven insane by an incurable disease. The study of character stands, and if one can accept the play's place in the past—as one accepts without question that of any costume drama or work of Shakespeare—the drama will live again every time it is acted. The stage technique is untarnished and untarnishable, and the revelation of past lives, built up piece by piece till the whole fabric is laid bare, as dramatic as in any play of Ibsen except, perhaps, *The Wild Duck*. That curtain when Mrs. Alving hears an echo of the past in Oswald's words to Regina, and cries " Ghosts . . . ghosts . . ." in a moment of understanding and premonition, is still the finest in modern drama. And given the actress the ending has few peers.

Esme Church in her production rightly, I think, accepted the play's period and with the help of Molly MacArthur's setting emphasised the atmosphere of Victorian respectability, airless and overfurnished, that set Oswald within two days beating as against prison bars. The small cast was well-chosen, with Sylvia Coleridge as Regina, Frederick Bennett as Engstrand and the young actor Stephen Murray, got up to look vaguely like Mr. George Bernard Shaw, as Pastor Manders. This last was an excellent character sketch made notable by a not unlovable but exasperating nervous habit of twisting pieces of string : it pointed the man's unease in Mrs. Alving's presence, and perhaps his carefully suppressed but still active presentiment that his advice had not been quite so infallible as he'd imagined.

Marie Ney's Mrs. Alving was what Eliza Doolittle would have unhesitatingly recognised as " a lady." One felt distinction of mind as well as bearing, and recognised a woman who had both suffered and thought. The emotional feeling, as in all this actress's work, was deep and moving. Clifford Evans, never less than interesting as an actor, gave Oswald a tense neurotic force ; but his pale hollow mask suggested the ascetic, and one missed the blaze of Oswald's *joie de vivre* as well as his restless morbidity. In the last scene Marie Ney played superbly, but there was no flashing emotional contact as when Nancy Price and Glen Byam Shaw played the parts in a memorable production, some years before, and ended the play on an upward wave, as it were, of nerve-racked intensity.

Richard I I I was produced at the Old Vic on 2 November and was played for the following three weeks. The production by Guthrie included the effective use of a triptych for the visitations of the ghosts, and there was commendable bustle, vitality and humour until the last scene, when the arrangement of the battle became so seriously muddled that Richard's " A horse, a horse . . ." and death on his feet were lost in the general confusion. I believe this was because another engagement prevented Guthrie from tidying up his loose ends here, but there is no doubt the production smothered the flame of Emlyn Williams's dying Richard.

The portrait till then had been life-size : more than life-size, if one adds that extra inch of royalty that enables the man who has usurped the crown to wear it as if it were his natural heritage. Williams in the Coronation Scene was superb, and seemed actually to grow in stature, as if swollen by the yeast of satisfied ambition. His sitting for the first time on the throne—delaying the moment like a child saving the jam till last—had a ghastly splendour : one held one's breath and waited for the forked lightning. Other-wise this was a short, swarthy Richard, deformed, unkempt and oily ; there was no attempt at romanticism, and the plausibility of the scene of the wooing of Anne suffered in consequence. But the figure had a darting power, enormous subtlety and humour, and the quick satiric emphasis on the line " this princely heap," flashed at the bowing courtiers, raised a laugh I have never heard equalled in the course of this play. Like Irving's, Williams's Richard had a " diabolical delight in his own enormities " : there was mockery as well as menace, and one extraordinary touch of pathos in the opening speech,

For love forswore me in my mother's womb.

This line comes from Gloucester's soliloquy in *Henry V I, Part I I I,* and was introduced here with quite legitimate psychological effect. There were several moments when for a quivering instant one sensed the loneliness of this Richard, the isolation of his deformity that marks him out from other men. Perhaps it was the actor's strain of Welsh poetry that enabled him to reveal this in almost indefinable touches. The monster was also human, and given half the chance would have lifted the play from melodrama to tragedy. I still want to see Mr. Williams as Macbeth.

Angela Baddeley, who at the age of nine had made her Old Vic début as one of the little Princes in the Tower, returned to play Anne with her natural sympathy and intelligence. One wished, though, that in one of her rare Shakespearean appearances this enchanting actress had had a more rewarding part. Peter Scott and Gordon Miller were excellent as the young Princes, parts requiring a certain power of unspoken suggestion in the children playing them, and Jean Cadell as Margaret led the chorus of queens with a vinegary malice. Mark Dignam, miscast, lacked the buoyancy and wit for Buckingham, and although Alec Clunes as Clarence spoke the dream speech with imagination he tended to overplay his pleading with the murderers. On the other hand Clunes's Tyrrel was remarkably subtle and intelligent, and the whole of his scene with Richard a masterly interplay of insinuation and reaction.

A MIDSUMMER NIGHT'S DREAM

T Y R O N E Guthrie's production of *A Midsummer Night's Dream* was produced on the afternoon of Boxing Day—which this year fell on 27 December—1937, and not in my entire theatrical experience have I attended a performance so charged with magic.

A programme note of the producer warned us that the style of the production would be early Victorian, and that it would attempt " to make a union between the words of Shakespeare, the music of Mendelssohn and the architecture of the Old Vic." It was known that Oliver Messel was to design the costumes, and Ninette de Valois to compose flying fairy ballets in the Romantic Period tradition that produced Taglioni in *La Sylphide* and Grisi in *Giselle*. Most of the Old Vic and Sadler's Wells audience had also heard, in some cases with misgiving, that a further link with ballet was to be established by the casting of the dancer, Robert Helpmann, as Oberon. What no one, I think, was prepared for was the fact that all these varied elements should be fused into an organic whole so completely drenched with the spirit of Shakespeare's fairyland. The play seemed steeped in enchantment, and the lyric verse, so far from being subdued by the accessories of vision and music, seemed to leap free of them with a new iridescence and grace.

There is, of course, still a faction that contends, with Granville-Barker, that only the refined stylishness of Elizabethan music can really fit this play. My own experience is that productions using such music tend to reduce the magic to stylisation : the music is of the right period, but the wrong atmosphere, and in Shakespearean production atmosphere wins over period every time. Mendelssohn's music is fairy music, light as gossamer, haunting the night woods like a darkened echo : in this sense it is beyond period, part of the very texture of the world of fantasy bodied forth from the imagination of the poet.

And what an imagination this is ! How delicate, yet how consistent with itself ! The swiftness and minuteness of the fairy world are established and sustained with unending resource. " I'll put a girdle round about the earth in forty minutes," " Then for the third part of a minute hence," Titania and Oberon compassing the globe " swifter than the wandering moon," the snake throwing her enamelled skin " weed wide enough to wrap a fairy in," the leathern wings of reremice which make Titania's small elves coats, fairies creeping into acorn cups, and hiding them there . . . It is a world of butterflies' wings and gossamer, ruled by a " king of shadows," dancing its ringlets to the whistling wind and entwined with the tendrils and petals of plants and flowers.

> I know a bank whereon the wild thyme blows
> Where oxlips and the nodding violet grows ;
> Quite over-canopied with lush woodbine . . .

It is Shakespeare's Warwickshire, not Theseus' Athens, but transformed in the moonlight to something rich and strange, " the fierce vexation of a dream." Even the chill and damp of an English summer proceed from fairy dissension : a touch of humour the Elizabethans, like ourselves, must have ruefully relished !

> Hoary-headed frosts
> Fall in the fresh lap of the crimson rose ;
> And on old Hymen's thin and icy crown
> An odorous chaplet of sweet summer buds
> Is as in mockery set.

The liquid phrasing gilds even this.

Ninette de Valois's white-skirted fairies, soaring and alighting like winged thistledown, seemed natural denizens of these enchanted groves, and Oliver Messel's gauze screens, painted with the calyxes of giant bell-flowers, reduced them to insubstantiality and misty grace. His was a land of insects' wings and moonlight, cobwebs and flowers ; his Oberon glittered darkly in the midnight shadows, his Titania, in white ballet tarlatan, was radiant with dew and rose petals. There was little consistency of period, even among the mortals. The Hermia of Alexis France was a tiny Queen Victoria ; but Theseus glowed like plated Mars, plumed Nubian slaves guarded his Court, and the pillars of his palace, wreathed with garlands and suffused in a flicker of coppery light, had a Grecian classicism. It was a land outside place and outside time, a land of enchantment ; and its success lay in the fact that one accepted it as such.

Yet music and design alone cannot make a fairyland : one needs also the actors. The chorus of wonder with which the critics the following morning greeted Robert Helpmann's Oberon had its amusing side : for although a dancer he had been trained as an actor, and those who followed the fortunes of the Sadler's Wells Ballet knew his powers as a mime. Now he flashed forth not merely as an actor of imagination and grace, but as a speaker of poetic fire. His voice proved musical, clear, strong enough for authority and sensitively attuned to rhythm and mood. No actor I have seen has invested with such glory the lines about the " eastern gate, all fiery red," turning into yellow-gold Neptune's " salt green streams " ; or spoken " But we are spirits of another sort " with such unearthly magic. The playing of Puck by a child, creeping in fear to Oberon's side, emphasised the note of protectiveness here.

Helpmann's Oberon was a creature of the woods and air, a shimmering night vision, never mortal. Its green sequined eyelids, its pallid mask slashed with ferns, gave it an air of strangeness and fantasy, and its silent movements seemed to lose contact with the earth. But it had royalty too, and a dark elfin gleam of mischief that justified Titania's recoil of suspicion at " How came these things to pass ? " Apart from the natural beauty and ease of movement the only concession to dance-training was in the swift pirouette at the words " I am invisible " : here Oberon did seem for the moment to whirr himself silently into oblivion. The critics were almost unanimous in acclaiming this the best Oberon of our time. When even James Agate, that seasoned enemy of the art of ballet, metaphorically threw in the sponge, Helpmann's triumph was complete.

Vivien Leigh's Titania was a bewitching partner to this Oberon : as graceful as he, beautiful as a fairy princess, silver of tongue and meltingly seductive. The Puck, Gordon Miller, was quick and elvish, and red-haired Chattie Salaman, a pupil of the St. Denis Studio, gave the fairy who accosts him a mercurial tinker-bell piquancy of her own. The acting honours, however, rested only in part with the immortals. The lovers—Agnes Lauchlan as Helena, Alexis France as Hermia, Stephen Murray as Lysander and Anthony Quayle as Demetrius—played cleverly for laughs, but they did not descend into that shrill forcing of humour that has spoiled other productions since, and Hermia's cry after Lysander in the forest, an echoing *diminuendo* through fading music, made a poignant and atmospheric " curtain." Agnes Lauchlan's Helena was in the languishing Edith Evans style and was wittily pointed : only Joyce Bland has, I think, equalled her in this part in recent years. Gyles Isham, who had played at the Vic during the first John Gielgud season, was a majestic and stalwart Theseus, and Sidney Bromley gave an amusing touch of snobbery to Philostrate.

The greatest richness among the mortals, however, was that of the clowns. These were brilliantly played in every case, and gave the " rude mechanicals," as I am sure Shakespeare intended, a living and uncaricatured humanity. Ralph Richardson as Bottom was the very clay of the urban artisan, and on that glowing, complacent moon-dial the expressions crossed like summer clouds. The pucker of thought on the brow reminded one of Lamb's description of Dodd (" You could see the first dawn of an idea stealing slowly over his countenance, climbing up little and little, with a painful process, till it cleared up at last to the fulness of a twilight conception ") ; and had the actor, like Munden, been called upon to contemplate a tub of butter (unfortunately Shakespeare did not think of it) I have no doubt it would have assumed the proportions of " a platonic idea." This Bottom had the eager and naïve vanity of the born amateur actor, and one understood why his companions worshipped him, soothed him and accepted him as their natural leader. Even in the fairy world he accepted his position of authority with dignity, and bossed the Peascods and Mustardseeds as busily as if they had been his fellow mechanicals. His waking from his " most rare vision," with the dew of wonder on him, was exquisite drollery. One longed for a Lamb to record it.

The revelation of this production, after Helpmann's Oberon, was the emergence of an unknown young character actor, Alexander Knox, in the tiny part of Snout. Knox, a Canadian-Scot, had made his first appearance at the Vic as Catesby in the Emlyn Williams *Richard III*: a secret, dour-lipped performance which left one guessing as to the actor's real capabilities. After *A Midsummer Night's Dream* one guessed no more. Snout leapt to life as a " character ": mournful of face, with a voice dripping melancholy, and a shy nervous habit of running his hand through his hair and down his side. His was the very lyricism of woe, and his frightened lisp in Wall's rhyme—

> And this the cranny is, right and sinister,
> Through which the fearful lovers are to whinisper—

has, so to speak, " dropped into the language." I have heard it repeated in at least one production since, but the personality of the actor remains unique. Frank Tickle, rubicond and Pickwickian, was the Quince, Frank Napier Flute, Frederick Bennett Snug and Jonathan Field Starveling. The fun of Pyramus and Thisbe waxed furious, but at the last Oberon's " Through this house give glimmering light " brought us back into the heart of fairyland. The lights of fairy wands danced like pattines of bright gold through the darkened palace, and Puck's " If we shadows have offended " dissolved the play like a dream. The music was beautifully conducted by Herbert Menges throughout and became a romantic part of the whole atmosphere.

A Midsummer Night's Dream, which ran until 5 February, 1938, was so successful that it was revived the following Christmas. Robert Helpmann again played Oberon and John Mills proved an acquisition as Puck: Pan-like, mischievous, and vivid with the spirit of the lines

> And those things do best please me
> That befall preposterously.

Edward Chapman was a workmanlike and genial Bottom, Peggy Livesey a good Helena and Dorothy Hyson a very pretty but rather monotonous Titania. Knox had by this time worked his way up to more important things, and was playing the Judge in the West End production of Shaw's *Geneva*. Few of the original cast remained and the magic, as so often in such cases, tended to evaporate. The first *Dream* was one of those rare perfections which are not repeated in a generation, but must be enjoyed for the passing moment. This one, I think, will live in legend.

CHAPTER IV.

OLIVIER'S PROGRESS

HAMLET

L A U R E N C E Olivier made his first appearance at the Old Vic as Hamlet in Guthrie's "entirety" production on Tuesday, 5 January, 1937. It was only his second professional appearance in a leading Shakespearean part, although history records an early début as Katharine in a school production of *The Taming of the Shrew*. Beginning as a fashionable young actor of light comedies, he had leapt early into the dramatic limelight through his audacity of attack and romantic fire, and many playgoers and critics will remember his Bothwell in Gordon Daviot's *Queen of Scots* as an early outstanding example of his promise in more serious characterisation.

John Gielgud, with that professional generosity that has marked his whole career, had on his revival of *Romeo and Juliet* at the New Theatre in 1934 invited the young Olivier to play the part of Romeo for the first six weeks of the run, with himself in the subsidiary rôle of Mercutio. The result was a portrait which looked like an Italian old master and had youth, impulse and any amount of romantic subtlety of detail. Some moments of this Romeo linger in the memory even now : notably his tender fingering of the supports of Juliet's balcony, as if the stone were a sentient part of her, and his blanched prevision of doom over Tybalt's body. The only thing lacking—and it is a large " only "—was poetry : poetry in the literal sense of verse-speaking and intonation, not in the sense of visual lyricism of which the performance had an abundance. This Romeo had the warm sun of Italy in his face and veins, but his voice still had some of the hard edge of the North. The richness was there, waiting to be mined, but entombed in clipped speech and too transient a feeling for words. Later Gielgud's own performance of Romeo, less passionate, more sensitive, but steeped in vocal music, emphasised this still further. Significantly Olivier's Mercutio, when the actors changed parts, now butchered the

82

" Queen Mab " speech, to which Gielgud had given a winged iridescent beauty ; but his characterisation, virile, bawdy and rough in cyncism, had Elizabethan force and truth.

His Hamlet showed many of the advantages and faults of his Romeo. The verse-speaking had not greatly improved ; it was a prose Hamlet throughout, with a tendency to " rush " the speeches at the expense of clarity, and at times to give a false emphasis to certain words which made one wonder if the actor really understood what he was talking about. Passion ruled intellect, and one had the impression of genius of character rather than brain. Nor did one ever (with one magnificent exception I shall cite later) quite believe in this Hamlet's physical incapability to avenge his father's murder at the first opportunity. Agate's quip that Olivier's Hamlet was " the best Hotspur this generation has seen " carried, like all half-truths, the kernel of the matter within it. For this Hamlet was more man of action than scholar, with that quickness of uptake that goes with a flashing blade and dangerous temper. One could never quote in connection with it Schlegel's interpretation of a " calculating consideration " that " cripples the power of action."

On the other hand its Renaissance drive and flexibility of mood made it a refreshing contrast to some over-sentimentalised and bowdlerized performances, and it fitted certain of those aspects of Elizabethan " melancholy " first brilliantly analysed in the character of Hamlet by Bradley. " One would judge that by temperament he was inclined to nervous instability, to rapid and perhaps extreme changes of feeling and mood, and that he was disposed to be, for the time, absorbed in the feeling or mood that possessed him, whether it were joyous or depressed. This temperament the Elizabethans would have called melancholic." This temperament also was possessed by Olivier's Hamlet in a high degree, qualified only by the fact that the brooding or quiet aspect too little appeared. The heat was too constant, and such speeches as " To be or not to be " suffered in consequence. There was, on the whole, little tenderness or sweetness, though it had what one of Olivier's actress-colleagues once described as his " oceans of charm." In a later Old Vic play, Bridie's *King of Nowhere*, the shrewd Scots doctor, looking at a photograph of the character played by Olivier, remarks " That's Hamlet's face, all right . . . It's the face of a man with bad dreams." This was literally true, and in this dark sinewy athlete one felt the beat of an anguished and haunted mind.

The dramatic excitement of such a performance goes without saying, and in the final duel and killing of the King the actor played, as it were, with all the stops out, firing the stage with Renaissance fury and revenge. I have referred previously to the one indication of that fatal propensity to delay which Bradley thought inherent in the character. This was in the " Now might I do it pat " scene, which I have never before or since seen so revealingly played (although Jean-Louis Barrault, the French actor, caught a hint of the same idea). Olivier lifted his sword at the beginning of this scene with all the demoniac intention of assassination : then his sword-arm dropped as if dragged down by some unseen leaden force, and throughout the whole of the rest of the speech—with its merest shell of excuse for his own inaction—he paced the stage with a restless and uncomprehending exasperation. The sense of a man not temperamentally inactive, but rendered impotent by a psychological restriction he cannot himself understand, was forcibly suggested, and this scene linked up perfectly with the whole Bradley analysis of melancholia.

Guthrie's production, the first of his three Old Vic *Hamlets*, matched this performance. It had pace, gusto, illuminating thought in detail, and in the last scene, emulating the drama of Marlowe and Webster, made the stage run blood. It was built up on a simple principle of bare rostrums which must have been effective later when the whole production was transferred to the court-yard of Kronborg Castle, Elsinore ; the action was able as a result to spread itself over varied levels, with some consequent gain in grouping and flow of action, and the Queen's faint from one of these high rostrums into the arms of the terrified courtiers below had a spectacular melodramatic effect. If this was not the most authentic and poetic last scene of *Hamlet* one has seen, it was certainly the most thrilling.

As always with this producer the Players had plenty of contrasting flamboyance, but even if one accepts the theory that the Players were intended as a burlesque of the Globe's rivals, Edward Alleyn and the Lord Admiral's troupe, I do not see why the First Player should appear as senile as Guthrie invariably makes him. Though out of favour, like his company, the character is obviously still able to sustain the principal parts in the great tragedies in the repertoire, and the speech given to him suggests the vigour of an actor in his prime, if not in his first youth. Apart from this over-emphasis of senility Marius Goring played the part well, and again repeated his admirable Fortinbras.

Unfortunately I missed the first performance of this production and therefore Dorothy Dix's Gertrude, as the actress fell ill (perhaps from a fear of excessive heights?) and was replaced by Esme Church early in the run. Her successor had not the dark flashing beauty the critics ascribed to Dorothy Dix : she was phlegmatic rather than passionate, and perhaps it was because of this that one missed in performance any suggestion of the Oedipus complex which Guthrie advanced in theory. It was, however, a thoroughly intelligent and capable performance from an intelligent and capable actress, and since she took up the part at a few hours' notice her fall from the rostrum showed a blood-curdling strength of nerve !

The King of Francis L. Sullivan was bold, sensual and not without the grip of conscience : I remember with particular vividness his collapse at the knees, shrunk with grief and the knowledge of defeat, at the Queen's death, and his helpless " It is the poisoned cup— it is too late." The man's whole fleshy frame seemed to cave in. George Howe was well-known at the Vic for his excellent and humorous Polonius with Gielgud, which he here repeated ; Michael Redgrave was a fine Laertes, magnificent of speech and presence and moving without loss of vitality ; and Cherry Cottrell's Ophelia was touching, easily unbalanced and authentically crazed. A beautiful and sensitive performance later as the girl Vera in Turgenev's *A Month in the Country*, at the Westminster Theatre, suggested an unusual talent and personality here of which the theatre never made adequate use.

Robert Newton, making his only Old Vic appearance before his screen successes, was the Horatio, and Torin Thatcher made a good Ghost—though less good than his remarkably fine King in Michael MacOwan's production at the Westminster about the same period. The most brilliant of the minor performances was Alec Guinness's Osric, which cleverly placed the waterfly in the treachery of the duel—after Dr. Dover Wilson's suggestion—and got his laughs easily without losing the hint of a courtier's craft beneath the mask. This extremely subtle young actor also played Reynaldo, a part not without humour and effect in an " entirety " version. Martin Battersby and Osborne Robinson were respectively responsible for the scenery and costumes, Herbert Menges for the music and Gabriel Toyne for the luridly exciting duel.

TWELFTH NIGHT

T Y R O N E Guthrie's production of *Twelfth Night* followed
Hamlet on 23 February, 1937, with Olivier as Sir Toby Belch,
Jessica Tandy as Viola, John Abbott as Malvolio, Marius Goring
as Feste the Clown, Alec Guinness as Sir Andrew Aguecheek, Ivy
St. Helier as Maria, Leo Genn as Orsino and Jill Esmond as Olivia.
Even in these days of West End popularity it is difficult to imagine
the Old Vic putting up a much better cast in this play, which
contains more good character studies, and makes bigger demands on
teamwork, than perhaps any other Shakespearean comedy.

John Masefield described *Twelfth Night* as " the greatest English
comedy " and it is easy to understand a poet's reason for doing so.
For *Twelfth Night* is compact of poetry, and for all its surface
gaiety, its brilliance of situation and character, the play carries
at its heart the ache of melancholy and the magic of word-music.
It moves in an atmosphere of sunshine and shadow, and its wit is
tinged by the reflection that youth's a stuff will not endure. Through
it all the Clown's songs, more sad than merry, sound like a bitter-
sweet comment on the transience of all mirth ; and even in the
revelry of Sir Toby and his associates one can sense, occasionally,
a desperate clinging to the passing moment, a fleeting fear of the
darkness beyond.

Perhaps for this reason it has always been a play for the connoisseur rather than for the groundlings. It was written for the
Feast of the Purification and we know from John Manningham's
journal that it was performed probably for the first time in the
Middle Temple Hall on 2 February, 1602, with Burbage as Malvolio,
the brilliant new young comedian Robert Arnim as the Clown and
(by tradition) Shakespeare himself as the Sea Captain Antonio.
(It was John Laurie who first pointed out to me that hereby Shakespeare, whose distrust of comedians' licence was soon to be forcibly
expressed in *Hamlet*, enabled himself to keep a firm personal
hold on the comic business of the duel and to end it at the right
moment with his " Put up your swords ! "). Many years passed
before the play was published, and there are few records of performances either in Shakespeare's own time or for centuries afterwards. Lamb's Bensley, throwing over the part of Malvolio " an
air of Spanish loftiness," gave the play some fame in the eighteenth
century ; but Irving's elaborate revival at the Lyceum in 1884,

with Ellen Terry as Viola and himself as a Malvolio in the Bensley
" old Castilian " tradition, was mainly notable for some decided
First Night " booing ", which evoked from the actor a frigid " front
of curtain " rebuke. In more recent times Tree's fantastic portrait,
with its red moustachios and forelock and impertinent quizzing-
glass, gave the comedy a new lease of popularity, in which farce
has tended to be stressed at the expense of poetry and the play's
glancing gravities.

Guthrie's production was a creditable attempt to restore the
balance. The scenery and costumes by Molly MacArthur gave
the whole play, with the aid of subtle lighting, the subdued beauty
of a living tapestry, and in the candlelight of the cellar scene the
faces of Sir Toby, Sir Andrew and the Clown moved at times with
a strange ghostliness against the dark. The fatality was emphasised
most of all in Marius Goring's Clown : a death's head framed in
black, singing his songs of mortality in a voice as soft and dark as
the surrounding twilight. Perhaps this was overdone : one missed
the " glad heart " of a Dicky Suett, the resilient wit of the jester
that gilds the philosophic undercurrents. But in his dazzling
Sir Topas scene the actor made amends, and gave us the joy and
crackle of the natural mimic.

Something of the same plaintive echo was caught in Alec Guinness's
Sir Andrew : a wistful flaxen gull with the sad ingenuous eyes of a
Dan Leno, and the same upstanding quiff of hair on the forehead.
The character had a harmless, amiable silliness that was likeable
as well as funny. His " I was adored once too " was perfect in
its mixture of nostalgia and naïve pride. Leo Genn gave Orsino's
moody passion a certain dignity and Italianate virility that fitted
that sudden dark flash at the end about killing the thing he loves,
and Jessica Tandy's Viola, softly spoken, brought to flower much
of the rare regretful beauty, the inescapable heartache, of the
speeches about unrequited love. Her wit was grave, girlish and
pretty rather than dry and sparkling, as the wit of this remarkably
resourceful and varied heroine should be.

An innovation in this production was the casting of the same
actress for Viola and the twin brother Sebastian. Visually this
worked well, but the casting of Olivia tended to throw the youthful
femininity of this Sebastian too much into relief, for Jill Esmond
played Olivia (very well) along the traditional lines of a woman in

the prime of her beauty and nobility.   At Stratford just before the War the part was played by a young actress, Lesley Brook, who looked like an adolescent Tenniel " Alice," and had the air of a young girl savouring her first authority but pitifully, half amusingly, lost in the thrall of her first passion.   This performance made one wonder why the tradition of the mature " great lady," at the expense of what is obviously a youthful impulsiveness, has persisted on our stage so long.   With a very young Olivia (there is no need to imply by this a lack of natural dignity), the whole Olivia-Cesario relationship gains in credibility.

The most original casting in this production was that of Malvolio.   Played by John Abbott as a slim young man of student-like aspect, with a devotion to Olivia inspired by real regard as well as ambition, the character lost all sense of caricature and became a flesh-and-blood part of the play.   This gave Malvolio's final discomforture that touch of tragedy many have felt the part needs, and the prison scene was actually moving.   On the other hand I suspect the actor weighted the scales too much on the side of gravity :   there seems something inevitably " right " about Bensley's " swell of soul," and his fall must have been Olympian. There was too little true comedy, although what there was was nicely pointed and balanced.

I have deliberately left to the last the two performances that gave the comedy its full brightness and hilarity and counter-balanced richly the sombre tones of the rest of the production. Ivy St. Helier's Maria was a tiny parcel of high spirits and knife-edged wit—a dancing flame among the dying embers—and Olivier's Sir Toby Belch had all the bustling ebullience of a Falstaff in embryo.   Riotously convivial, it yet had a disarming lovableness, and the actor accepted Olivia's rebukes with the chastened air of a small boy who has been caught stealing the jam and will repeat the operation at the first available opportunity.   Perhaps it was as well for the actor that Will Shakespeare was not on this occasion playing Antonio !   But though the mime held up the action and embroidered the lines, it was performed with immense inventiveness and fun, and the actor, flushed and fruity like an over-ripe pome-granite, never quite lost the character beneath the clown.   Coming after Hamlet this performance established Olivier's versatility and hinted at remarkable things to come.

HENRY V

T H E unwavering popularity of *Henry V* provides something of a poser for the present-day observer. The corrupt politics, the drive for an Empire with a cynical disregard for justice, the welter of conquest and shifty argument, are obviously shameful if one stops to analyse them in the light of modern political morality ; and the weighing in of those two wily customers, the Archbishop of Canterbury and Bishop of Ely, on the side of a war of aggression is not made more palatable by the Archbishop's serpentine twisting of the Salic Law to force the issue. On the other hand there is in this play all the bright blaze of English honour (honour in the field and not in the Council Chamber), and the love of country sweeps through it like the fresh wind of an English Spring. For this play does not deal only with princes : it deals with the cut-purse of the London taverns and the sturdy English yeoman, the independence and logic of the " common man " uncowed by authority, un-afraid to criticise, but fighting with stolid obduracy in the face of overwhelming odds. It is a play about Williams and Bates and Fluellen and Captain Jamy, about Nym and Bardolph and Mistress Quickly, about the boy who dies among the luggage and the happy few who fight and win on the field of Agincourt. The King is its figurehead but not its blood and heart : for its heart is the British character and the King merely the highest outward representative of British pluck and British good fellowship.

It was William Poel who first revolted against the type of specta-cular production which twisted the whole point of the play by bedecking the English side with all the glittering pageantry of overwhelming numbers and equipment. " The interest of this drama, to the Elizabethan playgoer, depended on the knowledge that a handful of starved and ragged soldiers had won a decisive battle over an army which was its superior in numbers and equip-ment, and contained all the pride and chivalry of the French nation. And the stage direction in the Folio indicates the contrast thus : ' Enter the King and his poure Souldiers ' ". The effect of Guthrie's production at the Old Vic was due to the fact that it observed this balance, and never overweighted the play with a panoply of steel. Yet it did not lack the picturesque, and an imaginative use of banners, dipped or held aloft in glowing masses of red, blue and silver, kept the stage pictures continually mobile and striking to the eye.

Motley's beautiful costumes further decorated the scene, which was simple and suggestive as regards background and relied on curtains or lighting to offset the movement and clash of war. In the scene before Harfleur a continual flux and flow of unattached soldiers gave a wonderful impression of the bustle and stir of an army breaking camp in the night : with only a handful of actors, a shifting light and no visible scenery Guthrie suggested a whole body of men on the move. His eye for choreographic effect had never been more successfully used, and the whole production bore the imprint of a quick and graphic mind.

In this nervous atmosphere of armed combat, the tension before the blow, the Chorus remained a detached observer. Simply dressed as a citizen, not as a soldier, he expressed the pride and excitement of the civilian in national events, the poetry and fire of the commentator struck with the sense of marching history. Both Marius Goring and later Michael Redgrave in this part achieved authentic passion of voice and soul, and ranged easily from the still, persuasive warmth of " a little touch of Harry in the night " to the flash and swell of lyrical description.

> Behold the threaden sails,
> Borne with the invisible and creeping wind,
> Draw the huge bottoms through the furrow'd sea,
> Breasting the lofty surge.

If King Henry is the part for the actor of royalty and rhetoric, the Chorus is always the part for the poet.

Laurence Olivier's Henry showed a marked advance in his powers as a Shakespearean actor. Only in one speech, that before Harfleur, did he rush the words into unintelligibility, and here there is some excuse in the stimulating excitement of effect. Few soldiers would not have plunged into the breach after this Henry. The note of majesty was struck at the start, and throughout the first scene the actor showed his increased subtlety in the watchful mask and intent brow of a considering mind. Only a tapping foot broke his control at the insult of the tennis balls ; but his " We are glad the Dauphin is so pleasant with us " was deadly. One sensed the greyhound straining at the leash, and when the cannon burst it loosed thunder and lightning.

The scenes with Williams and Kate on the other hand were played with a delightful humour, and none of the lighter touches of humanity or wit was missed. The question as to whether Olivier was truly a Shakespearean actor—still advanced a good deal by the Vic audience at this time—was finally settled by his delivery of the difficult and testing speech about " ceremony." This had everything he had seemed to lack till now : lucidity, the ability to sustain a train of thought, unstressed feeling and quiet pathos. It was the moving centre-piece of the whole performance.

After Olivier's Henry and the divided Chorus I would place Harcourt Williams's King of France. He had played it before at the Vic, and was the first modern actor, I think, to seize on the historical fact of Charles VI's madness—which Shakespeare does not specifically indicate—to vitalise the portrait of the weak old King ; wax in the hands of his courtiers and son, feebly and reluctantly advancing into war, haunted by impending disaster and the terrible ghosts of Crecy and Edward the Black Prince. Ivy St. Helier beautifully delivered the description of Falstaff's end, and the rag, tag and bobtail of the taverns were grandiloquently led by Lawrence Baskcomb as Pistol. A deep-voiced young actor new to the Vic, but of whom more was to be seen and heard—Stephen Murray—played the Dauphin, and Leo Genn lent his suave irony to the Constable of France and Duke of Burgundy, here boiled down from a double into a single gentleman, like the Duke of Plaza-Toro in reverse.

Frederick Bennett, though a Londoner born, made a first-rate job of the valiant and argumentative little Welshman Fluellen, and the prickly nationalism of the scenes with Captain Jamy and MacMorris (John Rae and James Pugh) was amusingly played. Jessica Tandy was an enchanting Katharine, with a demure humour always lurking at the corners of her mouth, and Ernest Hare, a sound small-part actor who has appeared much at the Old Vic, gave Williams a yeoman but not unresponsive independence.

MACBETH

HENRY V marked the end of Tyrone Guthrie's first season as producer on his return to the Vic, and at the beginning of the 1937-38 season in the autumn Olivier was not included in the company. He made his next appearance in *Macbeth* in November, 1937, and did not appear again until the production of *Othello* early the following year.

The superstition in the theatre that ill-luck dogs any performances of *Macbeth* was certainly not laid by this revival : two successive disasters cast a gloom over the whole production. The play was scheduled to open on Tuesday, 23 November, but owing to a 'flu cold which cost Olivier his voice it had to be postponed until Friday, 26 November. In that short interim, on Thursday, 25 November, Lilian Baylis died suddenly, and the play opened as scheduled— and as she herself would certainly have wished—in the immediate shock of that news. The performance was prefaced by a long obituary tribute spoken by Lord Lytton, Chairman of the Old Vic Governors, from the stage, and although generously deserved and perhaps necessary it naturally did nothing to raise the spirits of the audience or actors. In addition, since Olivier's physical fitness to carry the long part was still dubious, a former Old Vic actor of distinction, John Laurie, stood by throughout the performance in readiness to take over should Olivier collapse under the strain.

It was a strange and terrible production of *Macbeth*, produced by Michel St. Denis with all the macabre phantasmagoria a foreign mind may bring to Shakespearean tragedy. We have seen some curious examples of this in the past, but I think in this case the treatment yielded results. Motley designed the *décor* and costumes, and with the aid of the producer and some suggestive lighting did succeed in giving to the play what Bradley described as " the impression of a black night broken by flashes of light and colour."

The Weird Sisters, hideous and more than life-size in fantastic masks, glowed red as fire above their smoking cauldron, and seemed painted in the very hues of murder and hell. The predominating colours of lime green and brown cast a sickly fatalism over the scene, and nearly the whole action seemed to take place during the night : that night painted over and over again in the verse with an eerie and terrifying imagination. " Blood-boltered " Banquo in a frightening mask seemed an image struck from Macbeth's guilt-ridden brain, and the sense of the supernatural was never long absent. There were some weaknesses, among them Macbeth's skin-tight gown which seemed to hamper his freedom of movement in the Banquet Scene and made each sitting on the throne an occasion of some alarm. But *Macbeth* is one of the most difficult plays to produce and on the whole this production caught the atmosphere of the tragedy.

Olivier's Macbeth, an achievement in the circumstances, improved greatly as the run continued. It was not so complete an artistic success as his Henry V, and showed some return of unintelligibility, of sense drowned in the organ rush and roar of unadulterated sound. Nor, though enflamed with power-lust and imagination, was the actor yet ready for the bitter philosophy of " To-morrow and to-morrow and to-morrow " : this Macbeth's fire of ambition was never quite spent, his nerves and passions unblunted and un-cooled to the last. But the aim was higher than in the case of *Henry V*, and in the tragic sense the actor rose to the challenge. In patches this was the biggest thing Olivier had yet achieved.

This was no Macbeth pushed into crime by supernatural forces and an ambitious wife. His scruples were the scruples of a man already knee-deep in planned guilt, if without the absolute and unhesitating decision of one unchecked by conscience. The imagination was the imagination of a prepared murderer, never that of a naturally innocent man beset by temptation. The mask built up by the actor was one of royalty and power, the figure and tangled hair those of a warrior as hard of brain as of heart. All these things gave force to the character and tragedy, without quite losing the flashing poetry of a mind sensitive to phantoms against every intent of will.

> Light thickens ; and the crow
> Makes wing to the rooky wood :
> Will all great Neptune's ocean wash this blood
> Clean from my hand ? No, this my hand will rather
> The multitudinous seas incarnadine
> Making the green one red.

At speeches such as these Olivier seemed closed in by darkness, and one never doubted the terrible dreams that shook him nightly.

The creeping cunning of the scene with the murderers of Banquo was vividly done : and the degeneration of the last scenes un-mistakably marked. For this characterisation progressed : the actor spoiled the last scene with the Weird Sisters by shouting, but the increased ruthlessness of " But no more sights ! " quenched the last spark of conscience, and all the final scenes had the unkempt slaty edge of a tigerish ferocity. He died like Kean's Richard, " as if his will could not be disarmed, and the very phantoms of his despair had a withering power." I should like to see Olivier play this part now, with his Oedipus and King Lear behind him : it is an unfinished portrait ripe for completion.

The Lady Macbeth of the American actress, Judith Anderson, was of the Siddons strain. Nothing here of William Poel's affectionate, delicate-nerved woman ruined by the influence of a wicked husband : the woman was ruthless to the bone, eaten up with ambition, a queen in her pride. Her passion was of the dominating kind, and the main criticism of a strong performance was that it did not suggest enough nerve or heart to make the sleepwalking scene really credible. Ellis Irving was a fine, unforced and moving Macduff, and later in the run Roger Livesey took up the part and played it with a husky and rugged sympathy. Andrew Cruickshank was a good Banquo, Vera Poliakoff (afterwards Vera Lindsay) a handsome and statuesque Lady Macduff, and Basil C. Langton (later an excellent Hamlet at Stratford-on-Avon) took the eye with an extremely subtle and suspicious little characterisation of Lennox in the murder scene.

The death of Lilian Baylis made little immediate outward effect, and the productions succeeded each other smoothly until the end of the season. But it marked the end of an epoch nevertheless, and all were subconsciously aware of it. The Old Vic had passed its first necessary phase of economic planning, of careful building for the future, and in spirit if not at first in actual fact it had entered a new era with a new goal : Shakespeare not only for " the people " but for " the nation," with the best production and the best acting the English theatre could provide. Something of this new spirit had already begun to enter the theatre in Miss Baylis's lifetime : soon, under the direction of her successor, Tyrone Guthrie, and the stimulus of war, it was to become predominating, and launch the Old Vic organisation on a new phase of its history in the West End.

Nevertheless the achievement of the theatre under Lilian Baylis cannot be underestimated, and it owed its creation as a national theatre of classical drama, opera and ballet entirely to her. Like that other great and (in her sphere) not dissimilar ruler, Queen Elizabeth, Lilian Baylis was criticised for parsimony ; but that strict economy was necessary at first for the very survival of the enterprise, and in Miss Baylis's own lifetime it was already being relaxed in order to facilitate the highest artistic taste in production and the use of actors of acknowledged accomplishment. There was a new spirit in the air, and I think it should be emphasised that Lilian Baylis had already before her death shown that she was

XXVI.—*Hamlet* at Elsinore (1937). The Death of Hamlet.

J. W. Debenham

XXVII.—*Hamlet* (1937). Laurence Olivier as Hamlet and Cherry
Cottrell as Ophelia.

XXVIII.—*Twelfth Night* (1937).   Jill Esmond as Olivia and
John Abbott as Malvolio.

XXIX.—*Henry V* (1937). Final Scene : Setting by "Motley."   *J. W. Debenh*

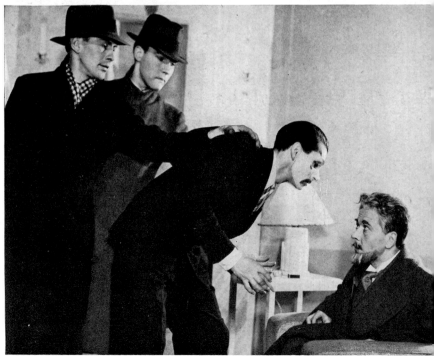

XXX.—*The King of Nowhere* (1938). Prologue : Laurence Olivier
as Vivaldi and Alexander Knox as Dr. McGilp.   *J. W. Debenhar*

XXXI.—*Henry V* (1937). Laurence Olivier as Henry and Jessica
Tandy as Katherine.

XXXII.—*Macbeth* (1937). "Give me the daggers . . ." Judith
Anderson as Lady Macbeth and Laurence Olivier as Macbeth.

XXXIII.—*Macbeth* (1937). Laurence Olivier as Macbeth.

J. W. Debenham

XXXIV.—*Coriolanus* (1938).   Laurence Olivier as Caius Marcius
and Sybil Thorndike as Volumnia.

aware of it, and had not discouraged it, even though she may not have approved of, or quite foreseen, all its eventual implications.

The most obvious loss was of the personal touch. One missed her homely but always to-the-point speeches, the sense of one figure —a " character " in the best sense—in control of the reins. Since her death the Old Vic has become more impersonal ; greater perhaps, but less marked in personality. I have referred above to Queen Elizabeth, and it was as Queen Elizabeth—in a huge ruff and horn-rimmed spectacles—that Miss Baylis, in the " frolic " that ended the annual Birthday Festival on 23 April, 1935, made one of her rare appearances " in character " on the Old Vic stage. That appearance marks better, perhaps, than anything else the " personal " nature of that past Old Vic era. The organisation is now far more brilliant, far more dignified ; it has lost something of its individuality and a lot of its fun ; but it has not lost sight of its beginnings and one hopes it never will. The ghost of Lilian Baylis is a live ghost still.

OTHELLO

A F T E R an interval during which Guthrie's *A Midsummer Night's Dream* production was staged for the first time, Olivier returned to the Old Vic as Iago in *Othello* in February, 1938, and remained till the end of the season. Ralph Richardson co-starred as Othello and both actors realised a long-standing ambition in playing these parts together.

The make-up selected by the actor is the starting point from which all performances of Othello proceed, for inevitably it has some effect on the characterisation and its subsequent development. Richardson chose that uncompromising coal-black appearance that Bradley notes was the accepted stage tradition from the time of the Restoration to the performances of Edmund Kean. There was nothing here of theatrical romanticism, no hint of that " boldly silhouetted figure of austere handsomeness, stalking nobly in profile," that Forbes-Robertson presented to C. E. Montague. The picture had one dangerous disadvantage in that Richardson's round face, blacked as if by boot-polish and surmounted by a closely-cropped frizzy wig, could not entirely avoid a " golliwog " effect and even the more fatal suggestion of the Christy Minstrel.

The height and dignity of the actor overcame it, but not without arousing some initial misgivings.

On the other hand this blackness made the Elizabethan attitude towards Desdemona's choice more plausible, and the barbaric springs of the man's passion at Cyprus were doubly stressed. White-robed like an Arab, burnt black as a Nubian by tropical suns, the figure was one of exotic ferocity, lean and trembling in a desert heat. And the very roundness of the face that detracted from its nobility made it an expressive mirror of child-like per- plexity, that slow, incredulous grasping of an idea that is the very essence of Othello's descent into jealousy. Richardson's Othello fell into Iago's trap with the look of a wondering child confronted for the first time with human perfidy ; the ensuing passion had a tattered remnant of outraged idealism as well as a foaming and restless animal frenzy.

It was a merit of Richardson's performance that one never quite forgot the dignity of the trusted general : it had been too carefully stressed in the opening scenes, and the speech to the Senate, the quiet " Put up your bright swords, for the dew will rust them," and the deadlier quelling of the riot at Cyprus, had a royal control. It was a performance that gained in authority as the run of the play continued, but unfortunately the actor's voice, which succumbed to the vocal strain, prevented its ever attaining the highest rank as poetry. One missed the sheer music of sound, the kind of lyricism that made Salvini's greeting of Desdemona at Cyprus appear to a critic " steeped in southern voluptuousness." The actor obviously knew what was wanted, but lacked the instru- ment to present it. This is I think a fairly general criticism of Richardson's work in Shakespeare ; his voice is by nature a prose voice, and when he achieves poetry (he often does) it is by the force of his will and imagination alone.

Olivier's Iago was a piece of virtuosity with one major fault : in the soliloquies he played—one would almost say literally " tipped the wink "—to the gallery so brazenly as to seem momentarily right out of character. The borderline between over-emphasis of personality and that intimacy of playing that rightfully belongs to the Elizabethan apron stage is naturally a fine one, and Olivier just overstepped it. In other respects it was perhaps his most vivid characterisation yet : full-blooded, dangerous, witty, meltingly insinuating, clever as an Italian monkey. The humour was stressed

from the start, the baiting of Brabantio and Roderigo performed
with a relish and amusement only just veiling the man's unutterable
contempt.   If this Iago played for laughs he always got them—
that checked derision of Brabantio, " You are—a Senator," was an
early example of satiric emphasis that never failed in its effect,
and reached its climax at the killing of Roderigo.

> Alas, my friend and dear countryman Roderigo ?   No—
> yes, sure—

I doubt if one would apply unreservedly to this Iago Coleridge's
description of " motiveless malignity " :   there was too much incentive of vanity, thwarted jealousy, sheer intellectual pride in
mastering and animating other human beings like puppets to his
will.   The playing on Othello's responsive mind, the sense of
theatrical timing, were superb ;   and one felt throughout the instincts of a gambler, fatally fascinated by peril for its own sake.
The man had a vulgar glitter about him, and the actor's gesture as
Othello lay senseless at his feet—his fingers flexed like cuckold's
horns upon the Moor's dark head—was magnificently in character.
There was imagination too in the speaking of Iago's lines as his
poison works :

> Not poppy, nor mandragora,
> Nor all the drowsy syrups of the world,
> Shall ever medicine thee to that sweet sleep
> Which thou ow'dst yesterday.

Olivier's growing sensitivity to the sound and meaning of words
was here well marked.

The tragedy was weakened by the fact that Desdemona was
badly misproduced, or misplayed, as a colourless pawn in the
drama.   There was no suggestion of the strength of character that
enabled this slight girl, in the face of all convention, to choose a
coloured man for husband and to give him (if we are to believe
Othello's story) a palpable hint to make the first advance.   This
was a disappointing performance by an intelligent young actress,
Curigwen Lewis.   Martita Hunt gave a fine blaze to Emilia, and
Stephen Murray's Roderigo is among the best I have ever seen.
This actor played the poor gull with an unsuspecting humour and
nervous pathos that raised the part from its usual level of *grotes-
querie* to that of a human being.   The scenes with Iago had a new
plausibility and edge in consequence.

Alexander Knox refreshingly stimulated that elderly bore Brabantio by playing unexpectedly for tragedy : his " this accident is not unlike my dream " carried a premonition of disaster, and the break in the voice at " I had rather to adopt a child than get it " was movingly done. One was not surprised to hear the old man later died of a broken heart : it had cracked before one's eyes. Anthony Quayle was a competent Cassio who grew mournful in his cups and yielded like wax to Iago's prompting, and for once Emilia's " This Lodovico is a proper man : he speaks well " did not strike one as a thumping and obvious lie. The player was no small-part nonentity but an actor, Andrew Cruickshank, who was soon to play for this company the best Claudius in *Hamlet* I have yet seen.

Tyrone Guthrie's production, picturesquely designed by Roger Furse, caught the warm glint of the Mediterranean sun : it was swift and ingenious, and only in the entrance of Roderigo at Cyprus —hacking his way out of a luggage basket—did ingenuity overreach itself.

THE KING OF NOWHERE :   CORIOLANUS

IN the two final plays of the season, which ended on 21 May, 1938, Olivier gave perhaps his two most completely successful performances. The first was a triumph of perfect casting, the second of sheer acting skill magnificently applied.

James Bridie's play, his first for the Old Vic, dealt with the psychology of dictatorship in an original way. It did not in any sense go deep into the subject and somewhere around the middle lost its hold on one's sympathy and belief ; but it had two magnificent scenes in the theatrical sense—its first and its last—and two parts which provided exceptional opportunities to the actors who played them. The dramatist was, throughout, extremely indebted to his cast and it is through their efforts that one remembers the play with pleasure at this time.

The King of Nowhere is a difficult play to read to-day, since although its underlying thesis is the essential impracticability of fascism on any humane basis, it invites one's sympathy and admiration for the idealistic woman who starts the movement in the play, using a half-mad actor as her hero and principal tool. The author fails in his object because the woman, Miss Rimmer, never for one moment convinces one (in spite of the text's constant assertions to the contrary) that she is the possessor of a first-class mind and the author of a scheme which, if it could have been practicably applied, would have been of great service to mankind. We know too much to-day of these schemes for the " service " of mankind, carried out through the suppression of individual liberty and bolstered by the waving of the red rag of anti-Communism. Some of us knew something of them even then, and not all the skill, humour and humanity of Marda Vanne's playing could quite hide the woman's essential stupidity and clap-trap patriotism.

Mr. Bridie's strength was in his portraiture of the actor, Vivaldi, in whom she sees a born leader, and the old Scots doctor Dr. McGilp, from whose mental home he escapes. The play opens superbly : the doctor has been called in by the actor's wife—a shallow woman who has her own reasons for wishing to be free—to certify her husband as a lunatic, and after a brief encounter in which it becomes clear that the actor, although not hopelessly insane, is suffering from delusions of persecution, the doctor's attendants remove him to his asylum. The actor's first entrance in this scene is a *coup de théâtre*, and Olivier, flinging wide the door and standing in all the startling incongruity of a clown's stage make-up under a trilby hat, played it to the full.

Escaping across the moors, technically cured and at the point of discharge, he takes refuge in Miss Rimmer's house and becomes the centre-piece of her wild political schemes. His actor's impressionability responds to her stronger influence, he makes a grandiloquent and passionate mouthpiece for her ideas, and only after a period does she begin to realise that her chosen instrument has a flaw in it : the flaw of the actor's unchanged egoism and malleability without conviction. At this first crack in her illusions the play switches boldly to an epilogue, two years later, in which we see the actor, apparently at the height of political responsibility, haranguing a collection of diplomats around a table. The " diplomats " prove to be lunatics, the room one in Dr. McGilp's asylum : and the surprise is brilliantly sprung. The play ends with the actor, still harried by hallucinations and conscious of a peaceful security in this retreat, baulking Miss Rimmer's plans for his release by pretending to be madder than is actually the case. The scene between Dr. McGilp and the actor in this final scene contained the best writing in the play, and the author here quietly and beautifully caught at that philosophy that was always just eluding him throughout the rest of the play.

Olivier played the temperamental actor with all the nerve-storming eloquence, the restless and haunted vitality, that one would expect from one of our greatest actors of temperament : the effect was less of an actor playing a part than of one bringing to the surface all his own instinctive stock-in-trade of emotional fire, nervous susceptibility and latent hysteria. It was a poor prophet who could not foresee in his quotations from *King Lear* some flash of the great performance we were to see eight years later. Beside this erupting volcano the old Scots doctor of Alexander Knox—limping, shock-headed, dry in wisdom—burned with a quiet flame of its own : steadier, but of equal incandescence, and matching Olivier's tart impudent wit with a cautious humour. This performance gave the actor his first big part and spurt towards fame, and it was Olivier himself, in a remarkably generous last-night speech, who acknowledged that Knox had " acted him off the stage." This was actor's exaggeration, but it was certain he had more than held his own.

Sylvia Coleridge and A. R. Whatmore got a good deal of fun out of rather obvious supporting comedy rôles, Vivienne Bennett did her experienced best with the colourless Mrs. Vivaldi, and James Hoyle distinguished himself by a delightful sketch of the family solicitor, Mr. Kitchen. Hoyle, a young actor who was stage manager at the Vic at this period and frequently seen in small parts, lost his life in the War which came so soon afterwards.

It was Lewis Casson, the producer of the Old Vic *Coriolanus*, who referred in an article at the time to Coriolanus' " arrested development." He notes his unusual reliance on and subservience to his mother, his almost schoolboy hatred of Aufidius, and the special fury at the taunt of " boy of tears " which cost him his life. This reading strikes me as perspicacious, and it was stressed in Laurence Olivier's performance. The humour of the tantrums was brilliantly revealed, but without losing a jot of natural nobility and warlike courage.

It is easy to dislike Coriolanus : for his insufferable snobbery and contempt, his glorification (which he catches from his mother) of War, his pride which seems at times on the point of cracking the whole edifice of his nature. But there are other sides too that Shakespeare, intent on producing a tragic hero, is careful to show :

the refusal to accept the " bribe " of a reward for valorous service, his natural modesty when praised, the candid affection for individuals as apart from the mob, the thought even while bleeding for an unknown old man who had " used him kindly." The pride is a patrician's pride, swollen and darkened by upbringing, but the virtues have a basis of generosity inherent in the man's nature.

As ungovernable in temper as a spoilt child, he has a child's malleability to persuasion when the persuasion comes from those he loves : when he gives way, he gives way completely and without heed to his own danger. There is a royal fatalism in that " But let it come," the four blunt words in which he shows his realisation of his own danger in sparing Rome : and Olivier magnificently caught the note of destiny as he had previously caught the " soaring insolence." In volume, rhythm and lucidity the verse-speaking surpassed anything this actor had previously achieved, and his—

> Measureless liar, thou hast made my heart
> Too great for what contains it—

had a sheer superbity probably never surpassed in this theatre. He gave the man pathos as well as a consuming passion and impatience ; his " I banish you " (nearer to Phelp's " sublimity of disdain " than Kean's " ungovernable passion ") cleaved like ice ; and the death hurtle was stupendous. The whole theatre seemed to reel at it, and the curtain fell amid the hush that precedes the most violent thunder of applause.

This was Olivier's last performance at the Vic before the War. He had come as an almost untried Shakespearean with a habit of slicing up blank verse into prose : he left as a first-rate classical actor who could give the rhetoric and prose of *Coriolanus* the music and resonance of poetry.

I do not mean by this that *Coriolanus* entirely lacks poetry : but it comes in isolated lines. Cominius'

> I tell you he does sit in gold, his eye
> Red as 'twould burn Rome :

Coriolanus'

> then let the mutinous winds
> Strike the proud cedars gainst the fiery sun :

these are flashes worthy of the later Shakespeare, master of words and of the glittering line. The rest has mastery also, but it is a mastery of prose and pungent metaphor : " the tartness of his face sours ripe grapes "—the play is littered with such phrases, mordant bitter, tanged with corruption. The darkness of Shakespeare's *Measure for Measure* period lingers on in this tragedy in a language that bites and sears, rarely blazes into the lyrical. This earthy coarseness invades the characters too : the sweating and treacherous mob, the viperish tribunes and envious Aufidius, Volumnia urging a material and blood-stained glory, Menenius the " humorous patrician," " one that loves a cup of hot wine with not a drop of allaying Tiber in 't." There is splendour in the play, as Olivier showed, but it is an earthy splendour. The only gentle touch is that " gracious silence " Virgilia, clear in her rejection of the hollow painted spectacle of War, seeing it as it really is, a ghoulish menace to the man she loves.

The Old Vic production was grandly acted, and if Sybil Thorndike's humour as the dragonish Volumnia was unorthodox—the wrangle over the number of her son's wounds was as merry a war as ever shook the Old Vic rafters—its vigour was tremendous. When emotion was needed, in the pleading for Rome, it struck deep, and both she and Olivier made their scenes together an exciting match of brain, heart and meticulously timed comedy. Menenius was played with gusto by Cecil Trouncer, and the sour and vicious Sicinius of Stephen Murray vied in perfection with John Laurie's virulent performance some short while afterwards at Stratford-on-Avon. William Devlin as Aufidius subtly conveyed the rival general's corroding sense of inferiority, and as the tribune Junius Brutus George Skillan gave ripe support to Murray's tart vinegar. Vivienne Bennett was a sweetly unassuming Virgilia and Viola Lyel made an effective fashionable butterfly of Valeria. Terence O'Brien's Cominius was a statuesque and handsome Roman of the old school, but in style a little out of key with the fresh modern attack of the rest of the company.

Lewis Casson in his production used a permanent architectural setting, with designs by Bruce Winston representing " a Renaissance view of classical costume." The action was quick and the acting co-ordinated with skill ; but the rather cramped set and predominating dark colouring gave the whole play a curious " closed-in " effect. It missed the " lift " and pictorial beauty of Iden Payne's later production at Stratford-on-Avon, where a spacious open sky, and steps up which the mob swept in massed and mobile fury, gave a surging freedom and impetus to the action. In its acting, however, the Old Vic production led all the time and Olivier's performance put him finally on the map as a Shakespearean actor of the highest eminence.

CHAPTER V

THE SEASON BEFORE THE WAR

TRELAWNEY OF THE WELLS

T H E season which commenced on Tuesday, 20 September 1938, was the twenty-fifth consecutive season of drama at the Old Vic. Perhaps for sentimental reasons the play chosen was Sir Arthur Pinero's *Trelawney of the Wells*, and the Vic therefore marked the attainment of its first quarter-century with a commemorative side-glance at the theatrical history of its sister theatre, Sadler's Wells.

Trelawney of the Wells was first produced in 1898, but even at that time it was what is called a " period " play. In a sense it was a tribute from a popular contemporary dramatist to the author, Tom Robertson, who above all others had made the modern English drama of the 'nineties possible. The Tom Wrench of this play—the unsuccessful small-part player of fustian drama who dreams of writing plays about everyday people and everyday life—is the Tom Robertson who in the 'sixties first revolutionised the theatre with his " tea-cup and saucer " comedies. Plays such as his *Caste* and *Society*, which now wear a slightly stylised period air, were actually startlingly realistic in comparison with the bombastic tragedies that had preceded them. " Windows on the one side, doors on the other—just where they should be, architecturally " breathes Tom in Pinero's play. " And locks on the doors, *real* locks to work · and handles—to turn ! " At the time that was something of a miracle—the outward sign of a new theatre—and by it we may measure both the nature of Robertson's achievement and the extent of the artificiality that preceded him.

It is a trick of time that Pinero's play—written thirty-eight years after *Caste*—seems to us now as " dated " in its charm as Robertson's comedy. Indeed, the recent revival of *Caste* at the Lyric Theatre, Hammersmith, showed Robertson's play to stand the test of time perhaps better than the one which paid tribute to it.

The great attraction of *Trelawney* to-day is in its picture of the forgotten theatrical age of the 'sixties, with its ageing stage " hams," the Telfers, being swept away by the new young actors of the realistic school, as they in their turn—Pinero hints—would be swept away by a newer style and fashion in acting and drama. Its " theatre " people are as true to their type, as abundant in vitality, as Robertson's were, and as in the case of Robertson it is the " aristocracy " who seemed stilted and theatrical. The " reality " of Sir William Gower and his sister Miss Trafalgar is as relative as the " reality " of the Marquise in *Caste :* they are stage puppets touched with sentiment, and show how much, forty years after *Caste*, the English theatre had still to learn from Ibsen.

The production by Tyrone Guthrie of *Trelawney* at the Vic rightly stressed the period charm and period stage-atmosphere : the tinsel and romance of the old " stock " theatres pervaded the whole scene, and candlelight and crinolines brushed against property baskets and dusty " flats." Avonia Bunn's padded pantomime tights provided a laugh on their own account, and the playing by Freda Jackson of this part—all heart and ripe vulgar good humour— was of immense service to the . play. This actress was known mainly at this time for her brief but incisive firework display as a temperamental prima donna in Elmer Rice's *Judgment Day*, but she played a number of minor parts at the Vic with invariable dash and resource.

The pathetic Telfers and flamboyant Gadd came sparklingly to life in the hands of Frank Tickle, Marie Tignold and Anthony Quayle, and O. B. Clarence and Nora Nicholson (later, during the War, to do some excellent character work at the Oxford Repertory Theatre) brought a faded aristocratic distinction to the Gowers. Alec Guinness, now preparing for his greatest part, did his best to breathe life into the ineffectual hero, and Sophie Stewart played Rose, the " Trelawney " of the title, with the warm humanity and independence of spirit that distinguish so much of her work. The unacknowledged hero of the play, however, is the down-at-heels Tom Wrench, and in this a new actor of rugged charm, André Morell, beautifully revealed the mask of humour and the bitter pain beneath it. His quiet pathos was spoiled only by a marked in- distinctness of diction which it took him some time to overcome : when he did overcome this defect he proved a valued Old Vic player in many important character parts.

HAMLET *IN MODERN DRESS*

T Y R O N E Guthrie's production of *Hamlet* in modern dress
at the Old Vic on Tuesday, 11 October, 1938, aroused in advance
the expected controversy : yet after the first performance few voices
were raised in dissent, and the predominant note of the critical
reviews was a surprised interest, and an appraisement which placed
more emphasis on the serious merits of the performance than on its
more sensational aspects.

The reason for this critical respect was not hard to seek. The
production had none of those irrelevancies—abbreviated skirts,
cigarettes, telephones—that have marred other modern-dress
productions of Shakespeare ; everything inessential to the play and
characterisation was avoided. The costumes had a charm which
was, in general effect, timeless : the long sweeping evening dresses
of the women, the dress-suits of the men with their Imperial sashes
and Court swords, gave an impression of a Palace levée to many
of the scenes, and made even the duelling appear spontaneous
and plausible. They filled the stage with picturesque grace and
colour, against which Hamlet's sombre black and plum-coloured
dressing jackets, and the unassuming civilian tweeds of Horatio,
achieved uncommon significance and character. For the first time
one realised how a modern-dress production may give new life and
reality to Shakespeare's characters without losing intellectual
excitement or beauty.

Beauty is, in fact, one's principal memory of this production.
Roger Furse had designed, as a permanent setting, two severely
classical pillars, but with a series of lovely backcloths which, with
the imaginative use of lighting and stage grouping, gave to the play
an artistic fascination. One remembers a tumult of pictures—
dark, thunder-charged clouds massed above the battlements of
Elsinore ; a white piazza and slender masts glimpsed from the
galleries of the Palace ; Hamlet speaking the " rogue and peasant
slave " soliloquy crouched on the floor in a golden spotlight, and
amid all the flamboyant finery of the Players ; Fortinbras, in
silver-green cloak and helmet, standing immobile against a sea-
tossed coast in the opaque light of early morning ; Ophelia's funeral,
with its dreary vista of wet umbrellas and dripping mackintoshes . .

Guthrie's sense of atmosphere was compelling throughout,
and seized and held the imagination from the first moment of the

play, when a sentry hesitated and shivered in his pacing of the battlements, to the cumulative excitement of the last scenes and the duel, fought with foils and masks and a vivid sense of the change from idle play to deadly reality. The slow encircling of Hamlet by the King's satellites after the murder of Polonius had the diabolical effect of a trap closing in on its victim. All the scenes owed much to Herbert Menges's incidental music, which beautifully caught the Fate-charged atmosphere of the production.

In the Play Scene Guthrie took the view that Claudius saw the dumb show, and placed him and the Queen in the full glare of a light which relentlessly revealed their battle for self-control. The whole scene thus centred, as in Granville-Barker's analysis, on the gradual wearing down of the King's resistance. The reading was justified in this instance owing to the magnificently sustained performance of the King ; with a lesser Claudius I doubt if it would convince one as well as Dr. Dover Wilson's alternative theory of the dumb show, which has proved both plausible and dramatic in stage performance at Stratford-on-Avon and elsewhere.

The Hamlet of the 24-year-old actor Alec Guinness fitted admirably into the production. It was essentially sane, and though the performance showed a moving pathos there was little indication of the " distracted globe." It lacked, on the whole, emotional turmoil. Intellectually Guinness showed much imagination bringing to the part many thoughtful details and a touching naturalness of gesture. Yet the performance did not lose in poetry, and besides being beautifully spoken was obviously deeply felt. It had much in common with John Gielgud's early Hamlet, a sensitive young intellectual temperamentally incapable of meeting violence with violence—an interpretation aided by Guinness's youth and fragile appearance, as well as by the curiously impotent expression with which he regarded his sword at the words " O cursèd spite ! "

The slight physique of this Hamlet had the further advantage of stressing the protective qualities of Horatio—a friend, as played by André Morell, to grapple to one's soul with hoops of steel. Apart from O. B. Clarence's excellent Polonius, the company was young and brought unusual qualities of vitality and freshness to the play. Hermione Hannen's Ophelia had a flower-like grace, and Anthony Quayle, taking an original view of her brother, brought a stricken stillness to Laertes's grief and played the duel scene with a fine appreciation of the boy's uneasy sense of guilt. John Kidd as

Osric faintly suggested a popular dance-band leader ; within its modern limits this was a gem of a performance. The Ghost, in effective modern battle-dress, was movingly spoken by Malcolm Keen, and the gravediggers of Frank Tickle and James Hoyle actually gained by the contemporary setting. Never has Shakespeare's study of the dry humour of the British workman seemed so true and observant, so applicable to our own times as well as Shakespeare's own.

The character that gained most from modern dress, however, was Claudius, and Andrew Cruickshank's acting was in many ways the most revealing in the play. This performance was a notable exposition of Stanislavsky's theory that an actor playing an evil man should look for the good in him. Granville-Barker has suggested that Claudius's speech, " But that I know love is begun by time," is a bitter reference to the fact that the Queen, since Hamlet's warning, has drifted away from him. The icy beauty of Veronica Turleigh's Gertrude helped Cruickshank to drive home this point with poignancy and power. His agony at her death was real and frightening. The whole performance realised admirably the suave and " smiling villain " of Shakespeare's text, and showed a particularly subtle and forceful understanding of the nature of ambition.

Hamlet was performed throughout the run in its " entirety ", and continued to play to increasingly large audiences for a period of six weeks.

MAN AND SUPERMAN: THE RIVALS

T H E first Old Vic production of Shaw's *Man and Superman* followed *Hamlet* on 21 November, 1938. It had been rehearsed partly because the Egyptian Government had requested it should be included in the repertoire when the Old Vic company, sponsored by the British Council, embarked on its forthcoming tour of Mediterranean countries. There had also been some early doubts that *Hamlet* would prove popular enough to justify its planned six weeks' run, although as it happened these doubts proved unfounded. *Man and Superman* was therefore staged for a limited run of two weeks only, as in the case of the following production of *The Rivals*, in which this particular company made its last Old Vic appearance prior to the foreign tour.

Shaw's play was performed in modern dress, which personally I consider a mistake since it emphasises the outmoded social conventions on which certain aspects of the plot are based. The span of centuries which divided the Elizabethan and the modern *Hamlet* seemed strangely less apparent in production than the span of just over a quarter of a century that divided the original production of *Man and Superman* and this at the Old Vic. In the same way the play of half-a-century ago often seems more " dated " than one of a far more remote epoch. We are more conscious of social changes within our own time, and feminine emancipation within living memory makes Ann's position in this play seem oddly out of key with modern dress and manners. In the dress of the period (1905) this would not worry us for an instant ; we should accept the conventions without question, and the changeless masculine-feminine relationship that is the true basis of Shaw's play would remain as pertinent as ever. For Shaw's social comedies strike too deep to " date " in any fatal sense. Only the surface conventions belong to one specific period : the fundamentals of character and philosophy apply to every generation.

Apart from this Lewis Casson's production was clear, pointed and well-cast, and presumably it had an authoritative basis since the producer had played Octavius in the original production at the Court Theatre in 1905. The third Act—sometimes now produced separately under the title *Don Juan in Hell*—was as usual omitted. This, of course, takes away the serious root of Shaw's argument, which makes the ultimate human passion not the sexual passion of man and woman but the passion of intellectual advancement, the passion for the unborn superman in the generation of which woman is merely the instrument of the Life Force. Without this Act we still have a brightly cynical comedy of the eternal genius struggling ineffectually in the toils of the eternal Eve, whose only interest in him proceeds from an instinctive urge to use him for Nature's purposes. The case is brilliantly true and brilliantly argued—especially in Tanner's great speech on the egoism of the genius that is as ruthless as the egoism of the female will for generation. And it is not damaged in the theatre by the fact that the truth is particular rather than general, and ignores those cases in which the masculine-feminine alliance represents a fusion of sympathy and intellect ; where, in fact, the genius is stimulated by the woman's love and assistance, not damaged by her selfishness and more material instinct. Male genius rises on the ladder erected by a woman's self-sacrifice as often as it is diverted by feminine irresponsibility and seduction.

Ann in this play is the seductive woman *par excellence*, able to bring every feminine wile to her aid except the slightest pretence at interest in her victim's career or intellectual processes. Even so she wins at the odds, and mainly one suspects because of that sheer physical vitality that in certain women becomes a chemical magnetism of volcanic force. "Turn up her nose, give a cast to her eye, replace her black and violet confection by the apron and feathers of a flower girl, strike all the aitches out of her speech, and Ann would still make men dream. Vitality is as common as humanity ; but like humanity, it sometimes rises to genius ; and Ann is one of the vital geniuses." Thus wrote Ann's creator, and I have yet to see the actress able to match the description. Certainly pretty Valerie Tudor did not do so ; but though she lacked the flame of vitality she commanded plenty of wiles within her limits, and twisted Tanner with neat intelligence around her precise little finger.

If Anthony Quayle was not the Jupiter of Shaw's stage direction his John Tanner, blackly bearded, came a good deal nearer than most to suggesting the author of "The Revolutionist's Handbook and Pocket Companion." There was plenty of character and elocutionary fire about this performance, and one regretted the actor's brains could not be pitted against that tougher intellectual nut, Shaw's rarely played third Act. Hermione Hannen had the right pointed chin, cool assurance and calculating edge as Violet, Andrew Cruickshank and Frank Tickle made consistent characters of Roebuck Ramsden and old Malone, and John Kidd scored easily in the dry Cockney cynicism of Henry Straker, the "New Man."

The Rivals was nevertheless the more successful production, and the Irish wit of the eighteenth century was not in the least eclipsed by the Irish wit of the twentieth. As a first play by a 23-year-old author this has boiled down, after an initial failure and some subsequent revision, into a remarkable example of play-craftsmanship and one of the most brilliant comedies in the language. It is impossible not to admire the simplicity of the device by which the various characters and sub-plots are introduced— through the conversations of Fag and Thomas and Lydia and Julia —and the way in which the plot is gradually developed and sustained. Something of the sentimental romancing against which this comedy was directed creeps, almost it would seem against Sheridan's will, into the scenes between Julia and her trying lover Faulkland ;

XXXV.—*Hamlet* in Modern Dress (1938). "Alas, poor Yorick . . ."
Alec Guinness as Hamlet

XXXVI.—*Hamlet* in Modern Dress (1938). Alec Guinness as
Hamlet and Malcolm Keen as the Ghost. *Décor* by Roger Furse.

XXXVII.—*Hamlet* in Modern Dress (1938). Andrew Cruickshank
as Claudius and Veronica Turleigh as Gertrude.

XXXVIII.— *Hamlet* in Modern Dress (1938). Play Scene : Production by Tyrone Guthrie.

Angus McBean.

J.W. Debenham.

XXXIX.—
The Rivals (1938).
Duel Scene :
André Morell,
Andrew
Cruickshank,
Meriel Forbes,
Lewis Casson,
Frank Tickle,
Anthony Quayle,
Hermione
Hannen,
Ellen Compton
and
Alec Guinness.

J. W. Debenham.

XL.—*An Enemy of the People* (1939). Roger Livesey as Dr. Stockman with Ursula Jeans, Geoffrey Holiday and David Baxter.

J. W. Debenham.

XLI.—*The Taming of the Shrew* (1939). Robert Helpmann as Gremio and Pamela Brown as Bianca.

XLII.—*The Taming of the Shrew* (1939).   Production by Tyrone Guthrie.

XLIII.—*She Stoops to Conquer* (1939). Ursula Jeans as Kate
Hardcastle and John Mills as Young Marlow.

but the other characters remain diverting figures of artificial comedy, wearing their foibles with an air and enlivened by a nice sense of romanticism-in-reverse.

Mrs. Malaprop is, of course, the gargantuan support to this brightly striped tent of wit and intrigue. She is not the first of her species—Shakespeare's Dogberry has a similar if more modest gift for " a nice derangement of epitaphs "—but she is infinitely the greatest, and quite rightly the word " malapropism " has dropped into the language. The virtuosity which Sheridan shows in the use of the device is still unapproachable, the wit consisting not only in the selection of a word of exactly the opposite meaning to that intended, but in the remarkable consistency of idea in certain groups of words so flamboyantly misapplied. " Long ago I laid my positive conjunctions on her, never to think on the fellow again :—I have since laid Sir Anthony's preposition before her ; but I am sorry to say, she seems resolved to decline every particle that I enjoin her." For sheer ingenuity this must be hard to beat. It has the type of virtuosity one recognises, in a humbler form, in that most dazzling and unlikely of all " Spoonerisms " : that in which the amiable don is supposed to have sent down an undergraduate with the indictment " You've hissed all my mystery lessons, you've tasted a whole worm, and now you're going home by the town drain ! "

Ellen Compton was a first-rate Mrs. Malaprop in the Old Vic production, and produced such jewels with a becoming dazzle. Anthony Quayle again shone as Captain Absolute, most cleverly giving his " Indeed, sir, I never was cooler in my life " a sense of suppressed but bursting temper, and playing the whole part as an obvious chip off the old block, Sir Anthony. Hermione Hannen's frail blonde beauty went well with this humorous gallantry, and her Lydia languished prettily and not without a sly touch of wit. Lewis Casson played Sir Anthony with ebullient irascibility, Andrew Cruickshank took to Sir Lucius O'Trigger in great style, and Freda Jackson as Lucy and John Kidd as Fag kept the eighteenth-century urban menial sharply in period. David's drier unromantic peasant's caution was amusingly played by Frank Tickle, and Meriel Forbes seemed to me to succeed charmingly in humanising Julia's rather studied sweetness.

Faulkland's caprice and discontent tend to make one impatient, but Julia's first speech about him shows Sheridan to have had some psychological insight into the combustible nature of inferiority

I

complex and pride. Not for the first time one is struck here by the discovery that Freud's analysis of human inhibitions is not quite as new and original as his contemporaries imagine. André Morell made Faulkland's self-torturings and uncertainties more moving than culpable, and the root of his unhappy temperament —his passionate desire for absolute love and instinctive fear that he has not the power to command it—was for once clearly and sympathetically defined.

A great deal of nonsense was written at the time to the effect that Alec Guinness was too small physically to play Bob Acres. (Actually the actor, though deceptively slight of build and thin of face, is of a good average height). I think this springs from a misconception. There is nothing whatever in the text to suggest in Bob Acres the robust, red-faced, rip-roaring countryman he frequently appears on modern stages. He is addressed on two occasions as " my little hero " or " little Valour," his timidity is frequently stressed, and Quick, the original player of the part, appears from contemporary lithographs to have been a small man. Guinness brought to the part the peaked face and sad eyes of a Dan Leno, and his shy, gauche complacency was exquisite comedy. There was a droll gravity about this performance that made one uncertain, at moments, whether to laugh or cry, and whether in hopeful curl-papers or stuck fast in the Terpsichorean difficulties of a *coupé* the actor never failed in comic invention. It was the performance of a natural clown, and looked forward to the Fool in *King Lear* as surely as the same actor's Hamlet looked forward to the more mature passion of his Ransom in *The Ascent of F*.6.

This play by W. H. Auden and Christopher Isherwood was revived at the Old Vic (though not by an Old Vic company) in July, 1939, and it was in the part originally played by William Devlin that Guinness showed the remarkable emotional strides he had made in the intervening months between his Hamlet and this play. The character of Ransom was freely based on that of T. E. Lawrence (" Lawrence of Arabia ") and Guinness was the first to bring to it Lawrence's faint hesitation of speech and nervous twitch of the face, as well as the absolute integrity of a mind fighting the temptation of its own power. There was a new fire and poetry here that but for the War we might have seen earlier come to maturity.

The scenery and costumes of *The Rivals* were beautifully designed by the American artist Stewart Chaney, and as well as being brilliantly cast Esme Church's production had every possible advantage of pace and comic ingenuity. The run ended on 17 December, 1938, and the last performance was marked by an endearing tendency on the part of the players to present each other with nosegays and sew up the fingers of each other's gloves. This added to the riot of the comedy if not to its classic dignity.

The Rivals, Hamlet in modern dress, *Trelawney of the Wells* and *Man and Superman* were among the plays included in the repertoire on the Mediterranean tour. *Henry V*, Norman Ginsbury's *Viceroy Sarah*, Priestley's *I Have Been Here Before*, and *Libel*, a play by Ward Dorane then being studied by Egyptian students, were added at the request of the Egyptian Government, who wished for a representative selection of British drama throughout the centuries. Anthony Quayle played Henry V and Cathleen Nesbitt and Curigwen Lewis joined the company for the tour—the first actress replacing Veronica Turleigh as the Queen in *Hamlet*.

The company sailed from Southampton on 20 January, 1939, and after opening their three-months' tour at Cairo appeared successively in Alexandria, Lisbon, Rome, Milan, Athens and Malta. The British Council was responsible for the itinerary, which aroused some controversy on political grounds ; but Ivor Brown was among those who put a vigorous case for the defence in a letter to the *Manchester Guardian*, and the artistic success of the company wherever it played justified the contention that appreciation of the arts may override the barriers of nationalism and political differences. The use of the arts as a propaganda force between countries—including former enemy countries—is more widely recognised to-day.

It is interesting to note that the modern dress production of *Hamlet* repeated abroad its success in England, and it aroused, in Italy especially, more critical enthusiasm than any other play. At Milan, in fact, the demand for seats was so great that special performances had to be added.

SHE STOOPS TO CONQUER

A F T E R the second Christmas revival of *A Midsummer Night's Dream, She Stoops to Conquer* opened on 24 January, 1939, with a new company replacing that which was to go abroad. This was to have been headed by Roger Livesey, Ursula Jeans and Edward

Chapman, but throat trouble prevented the first from appearing in this play. Livesey had played Tony Lumpkin with particular success in Harcourt Williams's production at the Vic in 1931, and perhaps the lack of his genial personality helped to cast a shadow on the first night. At any rate Tyrone Guthrie's production seemed at first unduly mellow and uninventive, and it was some time before George Benson really seemed at home in the part of Tony Lumpkin. This young actor had made a considerable success in the Victorian burlesque-musical, *The Two Bouquets*, and the step back from nineteenth-century dandyism to eighteenth-century hoydenism must have involved a certain effort in equilibrium. When I saw the play ten days after the first performance he appeared to have recovered his balance, and although I would not place his performance in the first class of period comedy, it had a not unlikeable awkwardness, with the toothy grin and uninhibited spirit of the natural bumpkin.

The delight of this comedy is in its plot, which Goldsmith is said to have based on an incident in his own youth, when he mistook the house of a wealthy neighbour for an inn and treated his host as landlord throughout his night's stay. Both this major plot and the sub-plot of Miss Neville's attempted elopement with her jewels provide plenty of comic situation, without counting the by-play of the abominable Tony, and the scene in which the shy lover Marlow fails spectacularly to maintain a conversation with the pretty and assured Kate Hardcastle. This last is a test for the actors, and as played by John Mills and Ursula Jeans it was infinitely the funniest scene in the Old Vic production. Nothing could surpass Mills's nerve-wracked bashfulness and tongue-tied constraint as the speechless lover, and Ursula Jeans's Kate had all the clear-minded humorous elegance one expected after her performance in *The Country Wife*. Charming apart, the two were irresistible together.

" There are things in this comedy of *Pyramus and Thisbe* that will never please " : and I incline to think there are things in *She Stoops to Conquer* which detract—let us say—from the *geniality* of the comedy for a modern audience. Marlow loses a little of our sympathy when he confronts the maid with a boldness he would have considered a discourtesy to the mistress, and his words to the disguised Kate, for whom he has shown some affection—" But to be plain with you, the difference of our birth, fortune and education makes an honourable connexion impossible "—have a sour ring to modern ears.   What to the eighteenth century seemed a natural caste distinction seems to us more like snobbery.   The real warmth of this comedy is in the character of old Mr. Hardcastle, with his comfortable eighteenth-century love of old books and good crafts-manship, his good-natured teasing affection for his daughter and his wife, his love of a good story and his unaffected hospitality. Edward Chapman, looking remarkably like Sir Henry Lytton as the Duke of Plaza-Toro, played him beautifully and gave the whole comedy the glow of seasoned oak.

Mrs. Hardcastle is far nearer caricature, and Margaret Yarde gave her the bouncing mobility of an over-painted galleon in blustery weather.   A ripe and raucous performance, if an unstylish one.   Pamela Brown, then very little known outside the Oxford Repertory, made a charming Miss Neville, with more intelligence and spirit than one usually associates with " second lead," and she was handsomely partnered by Anthony Nicholls, who had played Lysander in this season's *Midsummer Night's Dream*.   The yokels who serve at table were well produced and delightfully led by Frederick Bennett as Diggory, and the scenery was designed by David Homan.

AN ENEMY OF THE PEOPLE

T H E run of *She Stoops to Conquer* was extended beyond the two weeks originally planned, and Ibsen's *An Enemy of the People* followed on 21 February, 1939. A new translation by Norman Ginsbury (based on a literal translation by Mrs. Bolander) was used and it proved easy, incisive and packed with the right punch at moments when the doctor hits back at his enemies.

Dr. Stockman is perhaps the only Ibsen character who can definitely be indentified with Ibsen himself.   The play was written in 1882, soon after the storm aroused by the production of *Ghosts*, and there is in it the bitterness of the exile driven out of his country by rancour and misinterpretation. Dr. Stockman, too, con-templates voluntary exile at the end of this play : but he rallies just as Ibsen rallied after a period, and though we do not see him triumph in spite of his enemies, as Ibsen did on his return to Norway, we leave him with the feeling that the fight he plans for truth and self-justification will not in the end be a losing one.   An outcast in his own town, the town he loved but which he would rather see ruined than flourishing on a fraud, he has learned at the end the bitter truth which must arm him for the future :   the truth that " the strongest man on earth is the one who can stand alone."

All such spiritual discoveries involve friction and even suffering, and Dr. Stockman does not make his without the iron of disillusion entering into his soul.   The man we take leave of at the end of the play is a different man to the one we see at its opening :   convivial, easy-going, enjoying a hardly-won and retarded prosperity with his family around him.   There is a splendid guilelessness about the man that is both child-like and touching, as is so often the case with geniuses of science or mathematics ;   but when the terrible truth dawns on him, the truth that his own disinterestedness is not shared by other men but opposed by a solid phalanx of coercion and corruption, he faces that truth and fights back with all the energy and scorn of a man who will accept no compromise when justice is at stake.

Like the saint and the mathematician his only aim is the establishment of truth, and he will sacrifice everything—himself, his security, even his own family—to the cause his integrity demands he must defend.   How dear the sacrifice must be Ibsen is careful to delineate at the beginning of the play.   Dr. Stockman is not the kind of man to whom home life and home comforts mean little, nor a man to whom hatred comes easily.   He does not sacrifice the first and acquire the second without a pang :   but when the pang is past it is a new man who faces the world, a man from whose eyes the veil of trust and careless geniality has fallen, and who will fight without quarter and with fists of iron the little men who have dragged his reputation and the truth through the mud.

Does Ibsen, with his own experience of persecution still rankling, a little over-state his case ?   The issue at stake is the contamination of a Spa water supply which may result in the illness or deaths of thousands of invalids, and which cannot possibly fail to come to light at the last.   It is difficult, once or twice, to escape the feeling that the opposition to the doctor's revelation is too general and dramatically forced, even allowing for the private and financial interests at stake.   But few people watching this play will fail to realise that the Spa water is only the symbol which Ibsen uses for his true theme : the graft and avarice which will oppose any community benefit that threatens certain selfish individual interests, and which will cynically invoke the phrases " democracy " or " the solid majority " in support.

" The political truth of this picture must be recognised," wrote Shaw depressingly, " by everyone who has got as far as a seat on the committee of the most obscure Ratepayers' Association," and he was the first to demolish some possible reactionary arguments that Ibsen in this play is attacking democracy as such. He is attacking certain middle-class elements which are only too eager to press that word into their service when they actually mean something quite different : when they mean, in fact, a bureaucracy sustained for their own interests and with only the slenderest claim to represent those of the greater community. " All abstractions invested with collective consciousness or collective authority, set above the individual, and exacting duty from him on pretence of acting or thinking with greater validity than he, are man-eating idols red with human sacrifices " is Shaw's comment in *The Quintessence of Ibsenism,* and the right of the individual to think for himself outside the party machine is the quintessence of this play. That and the claim that the minority—not the majority—is right, since " the truths that the great majority accepts now are those the fighters at the outposts advanced in the days of our grandfathers. The pioneers of to-day have already discarded them." No one with any knowledge of the storm of abuse which greeted Ibsen himself—as it has greeted so many great artists with something new to give the world—and the subsequent history of his plays, is likely to contest this.

The play was well produced by Guthrie at the Vic in settings and costumes that avoided any particular emphasis on period or locality, though they conveyed a sense that the action was taking place, perhaps, some years before our own time. The shindy of the mass meeting was well depicted, and the whole play was given wit and spiritual integrity through the playing of Roger Livesey as Dr. Stockman. Livesey here was perfectly cast, and his joviality and absent-minded bustle made the doctor a living character from the first moments of the play. One never doubted the man's natural integrity or his force of brain, he retained his tang of humour to the last and carried the scene of the meeting with a rising passion.

Any normal cast of actors might seem Lilliputian beside such a Gulliver, but Edward Chapman, in a fine character study of the mean, jealous and parsimonious Mayor, managed never to be crowded out of the picture and occasionally to take a vital part in it. Frank Napier as Aslaksen, that apostle of moderation and Norwegian Uriah, and Frederick Bennett as the malicious senile Kiil, gave notable small character sketches, and Jonathan Field, in the red tie and earnest expression of a revolutionary zealot, got more fun out of Billing than one would have thought possible. Ursula Jeans as the daughter Petra, Nora Nicholson as Stockman's wife and Colin Keith-Johnston as Hovstad played the other leading parts, and the scenery and costumes were designed by Ruth Keating.

At a few performances, owing to Livesey's renewed throat trouble, the part of Dr. Stockman was played by Wilfrid Walter, a well-known Vic actor of previous seasons. But his ascetic leanness ill-suited the riper geniality of the part and one felt he was playing, intelligently but not successfully, against his personality. He was, in fact, born to play Peter, in which Edward Chapman's chubbiness would have been a handicap had he not been able, very cleverly, to suggest a fleshiness soured by mortification.

THE TAMING OF THE SHREW

UNFORTUNATELY *An Enemy of the People* did not draw large audiences and *The Taming of the Shrew* followed on 28 March. I find it intensely difficult to write of this production. Tyrone Guthrie chose to produce it as a roaring knockabout Italian harlequinade, decked out with all the Commedia del 'Arte para-phanalia of fantastic clothes, clown's make-up, acrobatic tumbling and truncheon-beating. Petruchio attended his wedding in a pair of Victorian ladies' corsets in patriotic colours, and the stage, if it did not purge thick amber and plum-tree gum, did its best with custard-pies and yards of sticky dough. The effect of all this was to divorce the characters from even the farce's pretence at veri-similitude, and to emphasise throughout that the whole thing was a " play within a play," performed for the benefit of Christopher Sly who—as in the original play *The Taming of a Shrew*—re-mained on the stage throughout. This effect was further stressed by the actors dressing and making up for their parts in full view of the audience : one saw, for instance, that the player of Gremio

(Robert Helpmann) was a young actor who added his wrinkles and assumed the mask and gait of decrepitude before our eyes.

Now there is a great deal (why not admit it ? There is *everything*) to be said for this last interpretation of the play. Sly's disappearance early in the action of the later Folio play—perhaps in order, as has been suggested, to suppress the overplaying of the comedian Will Kemp—has always been something of an anomaly, and Guthrie's was not the first modern production to restore the original Induction and Epilogue and retain Sly as an auditor throughout. The play gains immeasurably in homogeneity from such an addition, and the more so since Sly is the richest and most typically Shakespearean character in the play. His tavern experiences and wealth of rustic names and allusions foreshadow the Bullcalfs and Feebles of Gloucestershire and the Mistress Quicklys and Bardolphs of Eastcheap. The fact that his place in the narrative is restored, and the Petruchio-Katharine episodes given their true emphasis as " a play within a play ", does not, however, at all necessitate that the whole thing should be fantasticated beyond the limits of natural farcical comedy. Komisarjevsky, in a production of the same play at Stratford-on-Avon, produced the Induction as a Louis Quatorze ceremonial ballet to a background of Haydn's " Surprise " Symphony ; but the *Taming of the Shrew* play itself did not exceed the normal limits of farce and one's interest in Katharine and Petruchio as human characters was never completely submerged.

In the Guthrie production it was submerged and intentionally so. One's acceptance of the play, therefore, depended entirely on the nature of one's personal sense of humour, and it is here that I find my difficulty. The harlequinade had plenty of original invention that had nothing whatever to do with Shakespeare's play (if it was Shakespeare's), but it demanded in the audience a natural taste for a particular kind of slapstick fun and in this, alas, I appear to have been lacking. The burlesque appeared to me to have amusing moments—partly as a result of the acting—but as a whole evening's entertainment to become wearisome and forced. The general impression I had—and still have—was that the actors had a gala time and enjoyed themselves considerably more than the audience. This is perhaps natural frustration—breathes there a man with soul so dead that he wouldn't rather throw a custard-pie than watch one being thrown ?

It is only fair to add that my cautious expression of opinion in this review springs from the fact that I am informed by an actor who appeared in the production (and for whose views as a rule I have the highest respect) that in his opinion it was the most brilliant of all Guthrie's comedy productions, and one of the three best the producer ever directed. (With his selection of the other two— *A Midsummer Night's Dream* and the modern dress *Hamlet*—I find myself in entire agreement). I am told also that this view of *The Shrew* is shared by one of our finest Shakespearean actors, who was not in it and whose opinion, therefore, cannot have been affected by the personal happiness of throwing custard-pies and knitting himself into cardigans of dough. Whether this was the general professional reaction I cannot say, but actors' opinion is never, I think, to be despised.

There remains the acting, which can only be judged as deliberate burlesque and not by any normal standards of characterisation : except, perhaps, in the case of Sly himself, who had a rubicond interpreter in Edward Chapman, and the very young and good-looking Lord of Michael Benthall, now attracting some attention as a producer and ballet scenarist. Roger Livesey, battling with gusto against a rather unserviceable voice, gave indication of being an interesting and surprisingly subtle Petruchio in any other production, and in the meantime a highly acrobatic and uproarious one in this one. The same might be said of Ursula Jeans's spirited and spitfire Katharine. Esmé Percy appeared to have enormous fun with Baptista, Thomas Heathcote, of the St. Denis Studio, was a humorous and promising Tranio, and Peter Glenville, who had suffered early in his career from some precocious forcing in big rôles at Stratford-on-Avon, showed a new gift for burlesque as Lucentio.

The only other actor to emerge triumphantly from the holocaust was Robert Helpmann, who now supplemented his success as Oberon with a clever, decrepit and rather pathetic Gremio, and a virtuoso performance in the smaller part of the Tailor. This was a brilliantly mimed piece of outraged dandyism, with an affected accent, an excess of brilliantine and a quite revolting centre parting. This figure of effete fun listened to Petruchio's railing with indifference, until the insult " Thou remnant ! " pierced his professional heart and he departed in high dudgeon and in tears. For this entertaining reading of a normally irritating character we must, I believe, thank Guthrie, but like so many good producers' ideas it depended on the actor for its ultimate success. Helpmann also turned up among Petruchio's servants in the most exhilarating custard-pie scene ; upon which—not for the first time at a Shakespearean performance—one could only murmur deliriously " What, has this thing appeared *again* to-night ? "

The Taming of the Shrew was the last production of the season, and though we did not know it we should not enter the Old Vic again for almost a year. Even then it would be for two plays only —the last flash of glory before the old theatre fell a victim of the ' blitz.'

CHAPTER VI

PLAYS IN THE SUBURBS

ROMEO AND JULIET

S H O R T L Y before the end of this season before the War, it was officially announced that Tyrone Guthrie had been appointed Director of both theatres—the Old Vic and Sadler's Wells—in succession to Lilian Baylis. Because of duties of organisation he therefore relinquished, for the time being, his position as active producer of the Old Vic Drama company, and Murray MacDonald— a former director of the Old Vic students—was named as producer for the following season. This opened at Buxton as arranged during the summer, but the outbreak of War prevented the plays ever reaching the Old Vic itself. The management transferred to head-quarters at Burnley in Lancashire, and it was from here that subsequent activities of the Vic-Wells companies were directed.

The plays originally arranged for production at the Old Vic in the autumn of 1939 therefore only reached the London suburbs. The company played at Streatham Hill Theatre early in October and at Golder's Green in November, but otherwise remained on tour in the provinces. One of the Buxton productions—Goldsmith's *The Good Natur'd Man*—was played for, I think, only one performance at Streatham Hill. The later performances announced on the programme were cancelled, so having booked for one of these I was unable to see this play. Robert Donat appears to have made a brilliant success in it as Mr. Croaker, a character-comedy rôle quite outside his normal romantic range. Norman Ginsbury's *Viceroy Sarah*, also in the Buxton repertoire, never reached London.

Romeo and Juliet was the only Shakespearean play given in London, and it marked the first appearances of Robert Donat and Constance Cummings in an Old Vic company, as well as the return of Marie Ney in the part of the Nurse. The production of Murray MacDonald was less distinguished than the cast, although the difficulties of touring conditions may have been responsible for some defects of lighting. The general tone of the production seemed to me " routine," and an unadaptable setting caused the curtain to be lowered too often for smoothness of action, and the play itself to be unnecessarily " cut." The scenery of that fine theatre artist, Roger Furse, was disappointing ; its strawberry pink colouring had a cardboard effect, and one missed that sense of velvet Italian nights and burning Italian days, of white masquerade and flaring torchlight, that brought the Renaissance passion of the play to life in John Gielgud's production at the New Theatre. There was little suggestion of that ominous clash of Montague and Capulet that echoes through the tragedy like a doom, although the Prince who quelled the strife (Andrew Cruickshank) was better acted than in any production I have seen.[1] For once the man had true authority, and the most savage riot would have stilled at his word. Cruickshank also played the Chorus and Apothecary : an interesting triple feat in varied keys.

The heart-blood of this play is its poetry, and although it needs the actors to give it wing not the most prosaic rendering can quite subdue its music. Shakespeare in the young bounty of his genius spills his word-magic without stint, and often in flat contradiction of character. Even Capulet, that fussing, clucking, quick-tempered but convivial rooster, pipes into song as sweet as any nightingale. His " well-apparell'd April," and his line at Juliet's death—

> Death lies on her like an untimely frost
> Upon the sweetest flower of the field—

are as purely lyrical as the phrasing of a Sonnet. There is indeed much of the feeling of the Sonnets in the verse of *Romeo and Juliet :* it has the same chiselled style and melting melody, the same sense of delicate fingers plucking the strings of a harp. But already there are sounds of a richer harmony, a music striking deeper into passion and pain. Later Shakespeare was to give the words he allotted to his characters a sharper and more individual edge : he would not waste dramatic time in gilding a plain statement of fact as he gilds Benvolio's—

> Madam, an hour before the worshipp'd sun
> Peer'd forth the golden window of the east.

[1] This was written before I had seen Peter Brook's recent production at Stratford-on-Avon, in which Robert Harris gave a superb performance of the Prince of Verona, investing the man with a haggard authority and most subtly conveying his personal grief and anger at the death of his kinsman, Mercutio.

He would use far more prose and heighten his poetry by contrast. Yet even here, in the earliest of the tragedies, he is beginning to differentiate : there is true contrast of quality between Romeo's pretty allegories about his love for Rosaline—the self-dramatisation of a youth airing a first romance which has touched only the surface of grief—and the mature ecstacy of his passion for Juliet later. The first has the thin piercing sweetness of a flute, the second the depth and richness of a 'cello.

" Imagination is the great list of genius " wrote Leigh Hunt, and already in this play Shakespeare's imagination is lifting the mere verbal tunefulness to a new feyness and fire.   Romeo shaking " the yoke of inauspicious stars from this world-weary flesh," standing rapt with misgiving of some consequence hanging in the stars ;   Juliet's sudden fateful prevision of a love " too like the lightning, which does cease to be, Ere one can say, it lightens "— these strike a new note of darkened radiance, shadowing even the moonlit fantasy of Mercutio's " Queen Mab," and throwing into brighter relief Romeo's first flaming response to beauty—

> O, she doth teach the torches to burn bright !
> It seems she hangs upon the cheek of night
> Like a rich jewel in an Ethiop's ear.
> Beauty too rich for use, for earth too dear.

Imagination, then, as well as poetry is a necessity in the players. Who will forget Peggy Ashcroft's imagination as Juliet, that quality of iridescence and air and impulse that lent her love wings ?   Constance Cummings caught it only at moments, but she never made the mistake of subduing the poetry or binding the soaring spirit of the child-lover in the sophistication of a woman's passion. Juliet grows in passion of course, and in grief and responsibility too ; but she is as artless and free from coquetry as a wild bird. The candour of her " I have forgot why I did call thee back " shows that. She loves with the depth of a woman—

> My bounty is as boundless as the sea,
> My love as deep ; the more I give to thee
> The more I have, for both are infinite—

but at the same time with the freedom from inhibition, the limitless generosity, of a child.

We can, I think, follow Granville-Barker and dismiss the theory that no actress can play Juliet until she is too old to look the part : the essence of it is impetuosity, a lightness and innocence that make the verse sing and the hearts of the spectators young.   It is the bad Romeo and Juliet who oppress the Balcony Scene with the melancholy we feel rightly later in the bedroom scene, when the shadow of doom is indeed falling across their lives.   The Norma Shearer-Leslie Howard performance in the film was ruined by this self-conscious sense of tragedy, and the best comment on the error is still that of Leigh Hunt, writing of Fanny Kemble's Juliet : " We think she is not aware of the very foundation of it : which is a love so trusting and so joyous, that all its after melancholy is founded on its very hilarity—or the dancing buoyancy of the first flood of youthful passion and delight, suddenly frozen by calamity."

Constance Cummings caught this " dancing buoyancy " best of all in the scene in which Juliet waits for the Nurse, where she had a flashing yet child-like impatience.   She played always with feeling and ingenuous charm, and though fair as a northern lily did not lack the warm blood of the south.   Her speech was clear and tuneful and on the whole remarkably free from an American accent.

Robert Donat as Romeo made the mistake of early seriousness which Constance Cummings avoided.   He was at moments almost lugubrious, and the whole performance suffered from the lack of music in the actor's voice.   He spoke the part in a monotonous down-scale intonation and in spite of his clarity of diction it was obvious he was, vocally, miscast.   There is romantic fire in this actor but little lyricism, and Romeo's pulsing melody was not within his range.   On the other hand he worked on and developed his characterisation even in the brief interval between the performances at Streatham Hill and Golder's Green, and whatever of Romeo could be *acted*—in particular the challenge to Tybalt after Mercutio's death—he played with spirit and intelligence.   I should classify this as a gallant but incomplete performance by a first-rate actor playing against his natural style.

Marie Ney's Nurse was an excellent characterisation though perhaps a little derivative : I should describe it as Edith Evans's Nurse after a slimming course.   André Morell missed the poetry of the " Queen Mab " speech completely and indeed almost destroyed its intelligibility by hurry.   His death scene, taking a realistic view of the man's gasping agony and frustrated fury of revenge, was, however, harrowingly played, and he gave the character a robust and dangerous vitality that emphasised the Renaissance swagger of the portrait. The harsh, powerful head, flash of teeth and earring, tossing mane flecked with grey, gave this Mercutio an Italianate vigour ; there was the right bitter mockery and a certain concern for Romeo—trying to laugh him out of his romanticising—that emphasised the man's greater age and experience. Stewart Granger, a spitfire Tybalt, helped to make the duel between these two a clash of spirit as well as muscle.

If, as William Poel suggests, Benvolio was originally played by Shakespeare himself, we miss to-day the latent fun of this character. All the quips about the " hazel eyes " and head like an egg are lost on us ; and so to an extent are Mercutio's mocking references to his quarrelsomeness—an accusation that must have amused Elizabethans " in the know," for the few accounts that have come down to us all stress Shakespeare's mildness and peace-loving tact. Shakespeare, in fact, in this part was probably making fun at his own expense, and perhaps one day an actor will try the effect of fitting his make-up to the tradition. Manning Whiley, a young actor who had understudied for Roger Livesey as Petruchio at a matinee of *The Taming of the Shrew*, and had previously played Hamlet in German at Frankfurt, was a handsome and (in the physical sense) un-Shakespearean Benvolio. All his work for the Vic showed romantic quality, and his elocution was of a high order.

Hubert Harben was a gentle Friar Lawrence, but lacked the bustle and twinkle of humour George Howe quite rightly brought to the part in Gielgud's production. The Lady Capulet was Sonia Dresdel, then virtually unknown in London. She gave a new force and control to a character who is often played far too old—from the text she can hardly be thirty—and it was possible to recognise in her scenes with Juliet and her husband an actress of obvious intelligence and subtlety. No other actress I have seen in this tiny part has ever made any impression on me whatsoever, but when I read the play to-day it is still Sonia Dresdel's inflexions of voice and movement that spring to my mind. There are reserves of character in this actress the West End has still never tested.

THE DEVIL'S DISCIPLE

SHAW'S witty interpretation of the melodramatic formula was written in 1897 : the first of the " Three Plays for Puritans." It remains one of the liveliest and most compactly rounded of his plays, and it was successfully revived in the West End by Martin Harvey some eight years before the Old Vic production.

The appeal of the play to Harvey was obvious. Dick Dudgeon, with a Shavian twist, is in all externals the hero of romantic melodrama made popular by Harvey in such plays as *The Breed of the Treshams*. Here are the same scapegrace charm, the same suggestion of a heart of gold beneath the reprobate's banter, the same heroic self-sacrifice ; and the plot contains even the bland melodramatic trick of the last-minute rescue from the scaffold. Yet is is just that Shavian twist that gives the whole character and play its new spirit and ironic fun. It is melodrama brought without sentimentality into the cool light of reason, and transformed by a wit not the less dazzling for its underlying irony. As a result the play has twice the intellectual seriousness of the average melodrama as well as twice its fun ; and it survives to-day on that basis of humour and truth, while the romantic melodramas of the Harvey school have been whistled away by the wind.

Dick's scene with his outraged puritan family at the reading of the Will—that age-old comedy of disappointed expectations that has come down to us in various dramatic forms from *Volpone* and *Gianni Schicchi* to *The Shaughraun*—presents us with the typical romantic " black sheep " ; reckless, sardonic in repartee, but with a flash of real anger and kindness at the ill-usage of a child. It is after the man has given himself up to death in order to protect another that Shaw really takes the theme thoroughly in hand, and refuses to gild it with sentimentality. Dick's own analysis of his heroism is ruthless, though it doesn't lessen one's admiration of the man.

> All I can tell you is that when it came to the point whether
> I would take my head out of the noose and put another man's
> into it, I could not do it. I don't know why not : I see myself
> as a fool for my pains ; but I could not and I cannot.

He demolishes the woman Judith's hope that the sacrifice was for love of her with typical Shavian clear-headedness : but Shaw's refusal to play on the melodramatic string wins an added respect for his hero. Shaw and Dick too can jest in the face of death, and they shock the conventional heroine by doing so. But Shaw takes good care to show that he does not think hanging itself a laughing matter, and Dick's outburst on the scaffold, " with the horror of death on him," has a ring of urgent passion.

> Hark ye, General Burgoyne. If you think that I like being
> hanged, you're mistaken. I don't like it ; and I don't mean to
> pretend that I do. And if you think I'm obliged to you for
> hanging me in a gentlemanly way, you're wrong there too. I
> take the whole business in devilish bad part ; and the only
> satisfaction I have in it is that you'll feel a good deal meaner
> than I'll look when it's over.

Robert Donat spoke this speech with the right bitter wrath.
To all the rest he gave the dashing grace and quick cynical wit
of the Shavian romantic : his mockery was first-class, and his
charm had an edge to it. In any turn of humour he was quick in
the uptake, most notably in that scene with Judith in the prison
where, after a sudden flare of political passion, he drops his masculine idealism before the woman's blasting common sense.

> DICK : Well, let us cow them by showing that we can stand
> by one another to the death. That is the only force
> that can send Burgoyne back across the Atlantic and
> make America a nation.
> JUDITH : (*impatiently*) Oh, what does all that matter.
> DICK : (*laughing*) True, what does it matter ?

The collapse from rhetoric got its quick laugh ; but Shaw is shrewd
here in weighing the man's wider vision against the woman's single-
minded concentration on the danger to the man she loves, and Donat
did not make the mistake of missing the genuine note in the first
speech, although he pricked its heroism like a bubble in the second.
Altogether this was a performance of virility and humour, with the
right blend of anger and impudence.

On the surface General Burgoyne is a still better part for the actor
and certainly the wittiest character in the play. But the actor who
presumes on the wit at the expense of other characteristics will lose
the magnificent completeness of Shaw's portrait. The first guide
as usual is in Shaw's stage direction :

> *General Burgoyne is 55, and very well preserved. He is a*
> *man of fashion, gallant enough to have made a distinguished*
> *marriage by an elopement, witty enough to write successful*
> *comedies, aristocratically connected enough to have had oppor-*
> *tunities of high military distinction. His eyes, large, brilliant,*
> *apprehensive and intelligent, are his most remarkable feature . .*

We have in fact here a picture of debonnair distinction, with the
brain reflected in the eyes, and it was an advantage of André
Morell's performance that he brought the description to life, and
gave the character a bright surface quality of supercilious detach-

ment. One sensed force under the polished irony, a sting in the sarcasm, and in the heavy lines of the face the troubled authority of the expert surrounded by fools and bunglers.

Two later directions—though not a word of dialogue—show the man under the mask : one when the General studies the report " *with knitted brows and careworn looks, reflecting on his desperate situation and Swindon's uselessness* " ; the other when he is " *visibly shaken* " by Judith's outburst of pent-up indignation : " Is it nothing to you what wicked thing you do if only you do it like a gentleman ? Is it nothing to you whether you are a murderer or not, if only you murder in a red coat ? " Morell seized his opportunities here with imagination, and in his " Jobbery and snobbery, incompetence and red tape ! " the lava of anger cracked the suave surface of the man's sophistication. For the rest the mask held, and the acid witticisms flowed off the actor's tongue with a deceptive and honeyed urbanity.

Stewart Granger's Pastor Anderson was on the youthful side, lacking the weight of person and of years ; but it had vigour and alacrity of spirit, if hardly the man's ripe philosophy. Sonia Dresdel's Judith was ideal : " *pretty, proper and ladylike* " as Shaw suggests, but cracking quickly under nervous strain, and opposing a whitefaced, humourless earnestness to Dick's mocking realism. Her outburst to Burgoyne in the Trial had authentic anguish and scorn, and convinced us (and Burgoyne too) that right in this case was on Judith's side.

Mrs. Dudgeon's harsh and vindictive puritanism was strikingly painted by Esme Church, the play's producer, Recha Brodbar caught something of the wild crushed fear of the misused Essie, and Thomas Heathcote gave the lumpish Christy a lighter but disarming naïvety of his own. The sour family group at the reading of the Will was humorously produced and acted, and Max Adrian's Major Swindon, tight-lipped and waxen-faced under Burgoyne's lash of contempt, sketched the man's rigid stupidity with a chilling precision.

SAINT JOAN

SAINT JOAN, the third play in the suburban repertoire, was plainly but admirably produced by Esme Church, with scenery and costumes " arranged " by James Hoyle. This " arrangement " (presumably from the Old Vic wardrobe stock) was artistically done. Dark simple curtains threw the costumes into colourful and luminous relief, and one's attention was held by the characters and the play's thought. If this is the greatest and most dramatic of all Shaw's plays, it is also one of those in which the idealogical conflict is most marked and which makes the biggest demands on the mental concentration of the audience. The production and acting, therefore, which do not make lucid the drift of argument, as well as the drift of dramatic action, have failed to reveal the true values and spiritual greatness of the play ; they have given a picture of the burning of a saint for sorcery without its essential background and motive force, the clash of opposing interests and ethics which makes the burning possible. They have underrated Shaw as disastrously as C. E. Montague, who once came a spectacular cropper as a prophet by writing that " Mr. Shaw's serious thinking is just the ordinary staple quality of that of the best-educated modern people, but his wit is genius." We who have lived to see the great politicians, writers and artists of the world pay tribute to Shaw on his ninetieth birthday know that though his wit is, indeed, genius, it is the quality of thought behind the wit that has made Shaw unique in our time.

Modern history, touching the depths of human cruelty and degradation, has, since Shaw's play was written, given its political theme a contemporary application people were loath to admit before. Indeed, modern history compares unfavourably with that described by Shaw, for its tragic mistakes have been on a larger scale, and performed with a cynical disregard for ethical conviction that would have shocked Joan's judges. Warwick alone might, perhaps, have seen and appreciated them as political necessities, as his subtle and callous mind had condoned the burning of Joan. " The secular arm " of the mediaeval Nevilles was not so different in opportunism and outlook from the secular arm of modern fascism, and neither was above using the Church as the instrument of a purely political expurgation. Not that Shaw, I think, intended at all to emphasise any modern parallel when he wrote *Saint Joan*, and working on the records of the Trial he is careful to make clear the drama's place in its period, and the current thought, science and superstitions that gave rise to it.

LA TREMOUILLE : And who the deuce was Pythagoras ?

ARCHBISHOP :   A sage who held that the earth is round,
                   and that it goes round the sun.
LA TREMOUILLE : What an utter fool! Couldn't he use his
                   eyes ?

In such brief bald touches he builds up his story in time, and shows
the fashionable scientific ignorance of the minds that were to
condemn Saint Joan.

Joan's own spiritual vision is outside this narrow period material-
ism and dogmatism. Whatever she may have accepted of the
factual beliefs and superstitions of her time, she is ready to drop
them immediately on the credit of her own senses and at the prompting of her voices or imagination ;   and having dropped them,
she will support her new view with a peasant's logic as strong and
intractable as that of her accusers. It is an integrity that kills
her, but it is the essence of Joan, and the actress who stresses the
feminine spirituality at the expense of this masculine strength
of opinion will have distorted the character as drawn by Shaw.

I felt Constance Cummings's blonde prettiness against her here.
Joan should seem stained with the red clay of the common earth,
raw-boned and tanned like a peasant by the winds of the open
fields. The flaxen, beautifully waved short hair, the peaches and
cream of the cheeks, the feminine curves, belied every bit of this,
and it destroyed the sexual neutrality that, as Shaw himself has
pointed out, is historically recorded of Joan. " To the more
romantic spectators I must break the news that though Joan inspired strong likes and dislikes, and was not at all bad-looking,
she had no love affairs," he has written. " There is overwhelming
testimony that her complete neutrality in this respect was accepted
as evidence of her divine mission by her soldier comrades."

Apart from this lack of ruthlessness with regard to her appearance
Constance Cummings's Joan had fire and inspiration and did not
lack solidity of character. She caught the impetuosity on the
Loire and conveyed Joan's final passion with strength. André
Morell's Beauvais was superb : sheathed in sombre black and
purple, with a livid face and eyes like burning coals, this might
have been a portrait of the Dutch school. Beside this saturnine
fanatic Andrew Cruickshank's Warwick took on the poise and
slippery opportunism of the master diplomat. Stewart Granger
as Dunois, Ernest Hare as de Stogumber and Max Adrian as the
Dauphin gave good performances, and in the Trial scene Manning

Whiley's small sketch of Brother Martin stood out by reason of its sympathy and beauty of speech. The Grand Inquisitor's long speech was delivered with quiet distinction by Hubert Harben.

After the November visit to Golder's Green this company was not again seen in London, and when the Old Vic reopened in April, 1940, for the first time since the beginning of the War, the company was largely a new one.

CHAPTER VII

JOHN GIELGUD RETURNS

KING LEAR

T H E production of *King Lear* on 15 April, 1940, drew to the Old Vic a distinguished first-night audience. It was in several senses an historic and exciting occasion : it marked the reopening of a famous theatre after many months of enforced closure, the return of John Gielgud, the greatest Shakespearean actor of his generation, to the scene of his earliest triumphs, and Harley Granville-Barker's first personal supervision of a stage production of Shakespeare after many years devoted to scholarship and study.

The production was officially on the programme attributed to Lewis Casson, but the following note was added : " It is based upon Harley Granville-Barker's ' Preface to *King Lear* ' and his personal advice besides." Barker, in fact, was present at the theatre at a number of rehearsals, and the whole production and much of the acting owed a great deal to his direction and imaginative ideas. Casson must, however, have put in a good deal of loyal spadework in planning a highly-detailed production in the first place, and he was doubtless a lucid and sympathetic interpreter of the master's suggestions.

This was a Renaissance *King Lear*, but with enough of barbaric force to make the action seem authentically placed in time. In this it also followed William Poel, an earlier commentator than Barker, who had been the first to see in Edmund a typical offspring of the Italian Renaissance, with a flash of Machiavelli's Prince. Barker's stage blazed colour, but with darkness beyond. The glowing satins and jewelled earrings bespoke a Court decked in splendour, a living witness to the King's passion for pomp and power. Lear himself on his first entrance was no senile uncombed chieftain dressed in a nondescript nightgown (a not unusual stage presentation of the character), but a great King still proud in person and mind, robed in blue satin and rich furs and with white hair and curled beard carefully trimmed.   The emphasis, therefore, was on an active octogenarian rashly dividing his kingdom and divesting himself of cares of State before he was, in physique and temper, ready to relinquish authority :   an interpretation that threw the real nature of the scene, and the inevitability of the later tragedy, into sharp relief.

Gielgud himself, tall enough to convey royalty and putting on an additional weight of virile majesty, reinforced this first impression magnificently in his performance.   One felt the force of his presence almost before he appeared, and at his thumped sceptre the Court held its breath in fear.   The superb head, with its high-marked cheekbones and forcible nose, had the regal poise of one accustomed to rule without question, and the voice held possibilities of thunder. Yet there was nothing inflexible in this strength :   the hands were pliant and sensitive, and the voice melted to sweetness at the turn to Cordelia.   Amid the fret and storm of passion one felt the old King's hurt, although his exit was rock-like in its outraged dignity and wrath.

The next entrance at Goneril's Palace, booted for hunting, re-emphasised the man's unabated authority as well as his physical activity.   One could imagine this vigorous elderly tyrant on a horse—a picture at which, confronted by a nightgowned Lear, the mind usually boggles.   But here more than ever one felt the cracks in the man's spiritual armour :   the knight's tentative line about the Fool's having " much pined away " since Cordelia went into France was received with an obvious pang, and later, after the terrible scene with Goneril, the King's agony of mind, half-listening to the Fool's bitter prattle, was movingly expressed.   His " Let me not be mad, not mad, sweet heaven ! ", whispered with a hand suddenly pressed to the forehead and wide distracted eyes, had a blinding prevision and was the imaginative peak of the performance. The rage at Goneril was, nevertheless, a royal rage, and he spoke the curse, as Barker intended, standing stretched to his full height on a flight of steps, his voice calmed to a deadly quiet that pierced like cold steel through the passages of wrath.   The effect was stupendous, as quietness on the stage often is.

In the scene with Kent in the stocks the savage impatience returned.   " Tell the hot duke " reverberated thunder ;   but the break here, the forcing down of the " hysterica passio " with its sense of intolerable physical strain, was finely done.   There was

XLIV.—*Romeo and Juliet* (1939). Constance Cummings as Juliet,
Robert Donat as Romeo and Hubert Harben as Friar Lawrence.

XLV. — *Romeo and Juliet* (1939). The Death of Mercutio : Stewart Granger as Tybalt, Robert Donat as Romeo and André Morell as Mercutio.

Angus McBean.

XLVI. — *King Lear* (1940). "I think this lady to be my child Cordelia . . ." Jessica Tandy as Cordelia and John Gielgud as Lear.

XLVII.—*King Lear* (1940). Storm Scene : John Gielgud as Lear, Stephen Haggard as the Fool and Lewis Casson as Kent.

ngus McBean.

XLVIII.—*King Lear* (1940). John Gielgud as Lear.

XLIX.—*King Lear* (1940). Jack Hawkins as Edmund and Fay
Compton as Regan.

L.—*The Tempest* (1940)   Marius Goring as Ariel.

LI.—*The Tempest* (1940). "Thou shalt be as free as mountain winds . . ." John Gielgud as Prospero and Marius Goring as Ariel.

gentleness with Regan, the gentleness of misgiving as if the heart
feared to take another blow, and " Her eyes are fierce, but thine Do
comfort and not burn " had the pathos of a loneliness now longing
for affection.   The rage flung free again, and in the contest with the
elements—for the storm scene is nothing else—the actor's speech
rode the tempest with music and power.   I do not agree for one
moment with the critics who complained of lack of sufficient size
and sound here :   the voice, without degenerating to a shout,
blazed like beaten gold, and the tall slender figure—a tossing
cedar if not a storm-wracked oak—seemed by some effect of imaginative suggestion to become part of the drenching rain and the
tormented winds.

Beautifully Gielgud revealed the spiritual development of Lear ;
the new protective kindness with the Fool, and the illuminating
growth of pity for the oppressed at the prayer " Poor naked
wretches."   It is the true genius of Lear, this journey from passion
to sweetness, from pride to humility, from a king's tyranny to a
man's humane social feeling for poverty and suffering.

> Through tatter'd clothes small vices do appear,
> Robes and furr'd gowns hide all.

Mad, himself a victim of misused power, Lear learns the bitter
sociological truth that had escaped him when sane and a king.

There are moments of darkness and terror for him still, and to the
end the nameless gods shadow this play with a wanton malevolence.
But the gentleness that comes to him after the tumult of the storm
stays with him now as an integral part of his character, and the
anger at moments in the mad scene is an anger based on pity.   In
all these later passages of the play Gielgud was memorable.   No
actor I have seen has given such pathos to—

> The little dogs and all,
> Tray, Blanch, and Sweetheart, see, they bark at me.

His " we came crying hither " and " I am cut to the brains "
wrung the heart, and " Come, let's away to prison " had that form
of serenity won only after the deepest suffering.   The scene of the
recognition of Cordelia was exquisite, and Gielgud's—

> Do not laugh at me ;
> For, as I am a man, I think this lady
> To be my child, Cordelia—

was breathed in wonder, a music dying away in the air.   The
tenderness here was heart-breaking.

The Hardy-like gods had not yet finished their sport with Lear ; the terrifying " Howl, howl, howl, howl," a crescendo of sound off-stage until the King appeared with Cordelia's dead body in his arms, had a lost and echoing anguish, and Gielgud in all this last scene had a waxen immateriality, as if death had already touched him with a feathered wing. No actor can have better realised Bradley's description of " Lear's 5-times repeated ' Never ', in which the simplest and most unanswerable cry of anguish rises note by note till the heart bursts " ; and at " Look on her—look—her lips " this Lear died on a flare of hope more heart-rending than all the previous agony. This is, to my mind, still the greatest Lear, for it suggested a genius of spirit that lifted the passion to the highest plane of tragic imagination.

It is no exaggeration to say that the company as a whole was worthy of such a Lear. Jack Hawkins caught Edmund's " fierce quality " with a fine Renaissance vigour and a most valuable humour ; his slashing of his arm and childish forcing of his hurt on his father's attention raised, in fact, a laugh that almost destroyed the reality of the play. There was, perhaps, as in Olivier's Iago, just a fraction too much of that kind of humorous contact with the gallery that lifts the actor out of the play instead of the audience into it. But this actor's lusty relish in his villainy, his dashing adventurer's vanity, had value, and he showed he knew how to die.

Cathleen Nesbitt was a Goneril on the weak side—for this obviously most strong-willed of the sisters—but of a serpentine sensuality that held a certain languid fascination. Fay Compton's Regan had an icy venom backed by daemonic cruelty : a performance of astonishing power which left all traces of Mary Rose aeons behind in time, and transformed even the liquid silver of the voice into a cold, rock-hard crystal. Her " I am sick," ghastly pale, dramatically held the stage, and for a moment her terrible advancing death stilled the tumult of arms and passion.

Robert Harris, an actor who had played Hamlet at the Old Vic some years before, proved a magnificent Edgar, a part which in the wrong hands can easily go for very little. There is little any actor can do with the earlier scenes : the man is merely a pawn in the hands of his more vital and resourceful brother. Harris nevertheless conveyed even here a certain quiet integrity, and allowed himself to be led not altogether out of stupidity, but with the apparent intention of giving Edmund the benefit, laying low for the moment and keeping an open but watchful mind. The frenzy of his Mad Tom scenes was finely played, and with the right sympathetic drop back into his own character at the line—

> My tears begin to take his part so much,
> They'll mar my counterfeiting.

Too often this line is lost in the turmoil, but its significance is obvious : it was put in deliberately by Shakespeare to remind us of Mad Tom's true identity, which we are apt to forget in the course of the scene, especially if we haven't taken too much notice of Edgar's previous soliloquy which prepares us for his disguise.

Not that we were likely to have taken insufficient notice of it in this production, for Harris spoke it with the beauty of voice and lucidity of phrase that always marked his work at the Vic. There was " character " in this Edgar, and the development from taciturnity to strength and consequence was clearly marked. His dignity in the challenge carried for once due weight, and one understood why Albany coupled him with Kent as a possible ruler over the troubled kingdom. Harris is a good and reliable actor who in this part and his superb Orin in *Mourning Becomes Electra*, gave character performances of absolutely front-rank quality.

Lewis Casson, a lovely actor whom I have always considered underrated, was a Kent of sturdy loyalty and moving devotion, and he did not miss the cumulative virtuosity of the full-blooded diatribe directed at Oswald. Nicholas Hannen was an excellent Gloucester, Andrew Cruickshank a barbaric Cornwall and Julian Somers— who had played the same part in the Devlin production—a first-rate Oswald, characterised rightly as a fair-haired exquisite with the cowardice and insolence of the successful pander.

Jessica Tandy's Cordelia had a delicate and wistful grace : a performance full of sweetness if a little lacking in that strength of will she derives from her father. No Cordelia could have more tenderly complemented Gielgud's playing in the tent scene. Stephen Haggard's Fool was a strange, frail creature with restless eyes, a cracked wandering song, an odd grotesque mixture of " natural " and jester. I thought the performance queer and disconcerting at first, but found it " grew " on one the more one saw the play. This exquisite actor gave greater performances—his Falder in *Justice*, his Marchbanks in *Candida* and his performance in a Russian play, *The White Guard*, put him high among the best of our younger and more sensitive actors : but this curious little bundle of broken wit, Lear's Fool, was his last performance on the stage, and so must always have a special place in our memory.   Before he was killed on active service in 1943 he wrote a letter to his young sons which was published under the title " I'll Go to Bed At Noon."   The strange, sad last words of Lear's Fool, which were also Haggard's own last words on the stage, formed the actor's epitaph.   It is difficult to hear them now without thinking of him.

The scenery and costumes for this production were beautifully designed by Roger Furse, and over and over again during the performance one felt the unseen impact of Barker's dramatic vision in gesture, pose or inflexion.   Gielgud himself wrote at the time, with that humility and generosity that distinguish him as an artist : " Barker is the real hero of *King Lear*, and everything that is well-shaped and effective in my performance I owe to him."   The play continued until 25 May, 1940, and Gielgud's last performance on that date must be one of the greatest and most moving he himself has given or this generation has seen.

THE TEMPEST

T H E second production with John Gielgud, *The Tempest*, was produced at the Old Vic on 29 May, 1940, my birthday : a fact that has impressed itself on my memory since it is one of the very rare occasions on which the Old Vic management has celebrated this event in a fitting manner.   *The Tempest* had, however, greater and less personal claims to historical importance.   Coinciding with the fall of France and the disaster of Dunkirk, it bravely continued playing for five weeks to dwindling audiences.   People were not in the mood for the theatre, air-raids had not begun but the threat of them hung heavily in the air, many had lost sons and husbands at Dunkirk, and Shakespeare's magic must have seemed frail and inconsequential to a people never devoted to culture and now over-whelmed with national disaster.

The " other-worldliness " of the play that drove many people away kept a handful of us frequenting the theatre once or twice a week.   This was not entirely escapism.   Partly it was a feeling that if catastrophe came, especially in the form of bombing or invasion, we might more happily " take it " with the actors in this theatre we had loved than anywhere else.   Still more, I think, there was the loveliness of the play itself, with its sense of fadeless

beauty and of the enduring things—poetry, philosophy, life itself—
that survive generation after generation of wars, death and calamity.[1]

> The rarer action is
> In virtue than in vengeance.

This is the spiritual magnitude Prospero reaches at the last, though
not without a struggle with his all-consuming anger, his hatred of
the forces of evil he must vanquish. Is there a touch of Christ in
Prospero ? Was this, perhaps, Shakespeare's inner allegory ?
One feels it, momentarily, in his disquiet and distress at the intractable evil of Caliban, the primitive man, on whose redemption
he has lavished his care—

> A devil, a born devil, on whose nature
> Nurture can never stick : on whom my pains,
> Humanely taken, all, all lost, quite lost . . .

And at Miranda's " Brave new world " one feels the stab of his
ironic pang : " 'Tis new to thee."

There is more bitterness here than Christ ever knew, and nowhere
in his last plays does Shakespeare show signs of supporting any
orthodox religion. But as he grew older, his sense of the world's
evil seems first to have overwhelmed him, as in *King Lear*, and then
to have moved onwards to a new spiritual quiescence and even
hope. If Shakespeare himself was speaking through Prospero,
as many believe, and was referring to his own leavetaking of the
theatre at the words " I'll drown my book," we have, perhaps, in
Prospero's conflict with evil, despair and renewed spiritual victory
the history of Shakespeare's own psychological development.

The experience of some personal tragedy, precipitated by human
malignancy, seems implicit in these last plays. If this is true the
scar, though still visible, began to heal in *The Tempest*, and the
final picture is one of conquest and hope. Miranda and Ferdinand
represent the hope of humanity—the hope of the younger generation
healing the rifts of the past—and even Caliban sues for grace. If
Shakespeare in this, the last and most mystic in feeling of his plays,
does not suggest that the animal in man has been completely con-
quered and subdued, and the forces of evil will not recur, he at least
ends his play on a query.

Nearly all stage productions of *The Tempest* are unbearable
because they fail to suggest the beauty that leaps through the verse

---

[1] "The enchanted island seems far more real to me on certain evenings than
the whole war," wrote one of the actors to me at this time.

and the enchantment that is the very substance of Prospero's island. Taking as their cue some ironic comments of the courtiers on the barrenness of the island, the producers of the Old Vic production, Marius Goring and George Devine, and the designer, Oliver Messel, created a world of rock and sand that seemed to have been lifted from a painting by El Greco. It shimmered through gauze like a desert landscape in Mediterranean heat, and Prospero's shining transparent cloak seemed as if it might truly make him invisible, part of the world of fantasy. There was bareness here, aridity even, but the masque of Iris and Ceres carried a glow that matched the quality of the words :

> You sunburn'd sicklemen, of August weary,
> Come hither from the furrow . . .

The poetry of the masque has a harvest richness, the colour of ripe corn and poppies, and Messel's designs translated the vision into the same tawny hues of scarlet, cornflower blue and gold. The three speeches of the goddesses were musically spoken by Renée Ascherson, Vera Lindsay and Oriel Ross, and at Prospero's dismissal (and Gielgud beautifully played this sudden moment of disturbed recollection) the scene evaporated in air, brushed away like a cobweb in the morning dew.

A critical young Irish actor—the best of his generation—summed up Gielgud's Prospero to me some years later in the brief sentence : " It had magic." This indeed was the essence of it, although Gielgud drew a realistic enough portrait when the character was, so to speak, " off duty " as a magician. A younger Prospero than most, beardless and spectacled, he gave the character a certain wry humour and scholastic irony. In the very first speech one caught the note of serene persuasive power, and at " Thou art inclin'd to sleep " the lift of the wand and silken texture of the voice lulled like a spell. With the call to Ariel—

> Come away, servant, come ! I'm ready now.
> Approach, my Ariel ; come !

the actor suddenly transported us into the fairy world, and this atmosphere he maintained through all the great crescendos of this play's poetic imagery. I cannot imagine the " cloud-capp'd towers " speech more beautifully spoken, and—

> we are such stuff
> As dreams are made of, and our little life
> Is rounded with a sleep—

melted away like the sound of violins in the distance.

" Ye elves of hills . . ." was, however, the magical peak of the performance.   Tracing a sweeping circle on the ground with his wand, the actor seemed surrounded by the invisible walls of his own enchantment ;   unearthly, apart, an instrument of unseen forces and elvish destiny.   There are three distinct changes of mood in this great speech—

> Ye elves of hills, brooks, standing lakes and groves,
> And ye that on the sands with printless foot
> Do chase the ebbing Neptune . . .

And later—

> I have bedimm'd
> The noontide sun, call'd forth the mutinous winds,
> And 'twixt the green sea and the azured vault
> Set roaring war : to the dread rattling thunder
> Have I given fire . . .

Finally—

> But this rough magic
> I here abjure ; and, when I have required
> Some heavenly music,—which even now I do—
> To work mine end upon their senses, that
> This airy charm is for, I'll break my staff,
> Bury it certain fathoms in the earth,
> And deeper than did ever plummet sound
> I'll drown my book . . .

The first is faëry music ;   the second has the oceanic swell and volume of passion ;   the third is like subsiding waters after flood and storm, a calm stream leaving the mountain torrents for the sunlit plains below.   Gielgud's vocal and temperamental range covered all three moods with ease, and at the end seemed to gather together all the conflicting chords of the play in a serene harmony.   The relationship with Ariel—firm, yet tender—was exquisitely expressed throughout, and the rising pulse of anger dramatically " placed."

Jessica Tandy was a Miranda of ethereal enchantment : a delicate spring flower that seemed to have blossomed miraculously in this arid soil.   She was perfectly matched by her Ferdinand, to which part Alec Guinness gave a grave haunted music, as if bound by invisible threads in the island spell.

> Where should this music be ? i' the air, or the earth ?
> It sounds no more . . .

The magic vied with Prospero's own.   So, in its own sense, did that of Marius Goring as Ariel. This was a creature compounded equally of earth and air ; silvered, leaden-coloured almost, but with a quick quivering poise of the head that belonged neither to bird nor man, but to some weird immortal spirit imprisoned in mortal toils and painfully eager to be free. In all his contacts with humans one sensed the unfeeling curiosity of the sprite : not cruel, but cool and remote, as if the world of humans was as strange to him as his world to the mortals. At Prospero's recital of his sufferings under Sycorax he writhed in the dust, reliving his agony with a wild poetic terror. But his " Do you love me, master, no ? " had a strain of near-mortal wistfulness, dying upon the instant.

Beside these sensitive spirits, mortal and immortal, Jack Hawkins's Caliban, more ape than man, had a ferocious earthy savagery and superb gusto. His roaring-drunk " Freedom, hey-day ! hey-day ! freedom ! " put a preliminary strain upon the Old Vic walls and rafters that I have always suspected made Hitler's task easier the following year. On the other hand the beast was not unlovable. Shakespeare performed wonders with Caliban, and in his mistaken worship of Stephano and gradual disillusion, even in his rumbling resentment at domination and pain, there lurks a human pathos. Hawkins vividly suggested the slow groping towards humanity, the cringing self-pity, and the one moving response to beauty that for the moment places the brute on the spiritual plane of civilised mankind—

> Be not afeard : the isle is full of noises,
> Sounds, and sweet airs, that give delight and hurt not.
> Sometimes a thousand twangling instruments
> Will hum about mine ears ; and sometimes voices,
> ·That, if I then had waked after long sleep,
> Will make me sleep again ; and then, in dreaming,
> The clouds methought would open and show riches
> Ready to drop upon me : that, when I waked,
> I cried to dream again.

Owing to enlightened direction and playing the group of shipwrecked courtiers from Milan and Naples had a good deal more life and humour than normally appears. There was a remarkably subtle and saturnine performance of Antonio, the usurping Duke, by Marne Maitland, an actor whom for reasons unknown I had never seen before and have not heard of since.[1] André Morell as

[1] Since this was written he has reappeared as a striking Cornwall in *King Lear*, performed by the Bristol Old Vic Company at the Embassy Theatre in London during the summer of 1947.

the King of Naples and Andrew Cruickshank as the dubious Sebastian put the best face possible on poor material, and as kind old Gonzalo, offering ineffectual comfort to the King for the loss of his drowned son, Lewis Casson gave a dry gentleness to a part it must have been incredibly painful for him to play. (His own son was reported missing, during the run of *The Tempest*, in naval operations off Norway, and until his safety was confirmed this potential tragedy must have hung over the company like a cloud.)

W. G. Fay, with bits of the Abbey Theatre, Dublin, still clinging to his voice and person, gave Stephano an Irish brogue and Celtic temper. This transposition into Gaelic worked, on the whole, remarkably well, and the line " This is a very scurvy tune to sing at a man's funeral " fitted the brogue so well that one almost began to wonder if Shakespeare hadn't intended it. Frank Tickle was a droll Trinculo and Alfred Atkins as the Boatswain subdued his recalcitrant passengers with vigour.

During the last two weeks of the run Peggy Ashcroft played Miranda and gave the part a warm, glowing beauty that seemed strangely earthly after Jessica Tandy's fragile grace. It was a lovely and feminine performance, though in a quite different key.

The Old Vic Theatre never opened again. When the next season was due to begin, the following autumn, air-raids had commenced on London, and the company remained in the provinces. The Theatre was severely damaged in an air-raid on 19 May, 1941, and although in the future a new theatre may arise on the Waterloo Road site, the Old Vic as we and Lilian Baylis knew it passed away for ever. Perhaps no more fitting play than *The Tempest* could have been chosen for its swan song. By a happy chance also the two last productions—this play and *King Lear*—were worthy of its greatest traditions.

BIRTHDAY FESTIVALS

O N E tradition worth recalling here passed away when the Old Vic company migrated to the West End. This was the Annual Birthday Festival, held every year at the Old Vic on Shakespeare's birthday, 23 April, or the nearest practicable date. Instituted by Sir Philip Ben Greet in 1915, it continued annually until Monday, 22 April, 1940, and consisted of a full evening's programme of scenes from Shakespeare's plays, the reading of Sonnets and often a burlesque or " revel " written specially for the occasion on a Shakespearean theme. In addition to the current season's company many former Old Vic actors and actresses, if they were free to do so, were invited to appear : the Festival as a result took on the atmosphere of a " reunion," and enabled the always loyal Vic audience to welcome back its many favourites and see them once again act in Shakespeare on the Old Vic stage. The theatre was always filled on these occasions, and gallery stools began to appear in the New Cut before dawn on the morning of the Birthday Festival.

It was a warm, intimate, friendly custom : one which gave former Old Vic players a feeling that they were still a part of a living Old Vic tradition, not something relegated to the dustier and forgotten back shelves of its past history. Inevitably the performances suffered in some cases from under-rehearsal ; but some of them provided flashes of unexpected brilliance or beauty, and gave the newer members of the audience a glimpse of a great performance they would, perhaps, never see in full.

It was at a Birthday Festival in 1936 that Ben Greet spoke his last words on the stage. He appeared as Shylock in *The Merchant of Venice* Trial Scene, and after a moving speech of reminiscence he left the stage in tears. I think everyone realised the end must be near. A fortnight later he died in hospital, and the Vic lost the actor, producer and friend to whom it owed more, perhaps, than to anyone during its earliest days in the 1914-18 War.

It was at a Birthday Festival, too, that Sybil Thorndike, another regular visitor connected with the Old Vic's earliest history, broke tradition by reciting the first *Henry V* Chorus in a modern midnight blue picture gown, with a long necklace of great white beads. The stage effect was as striking as the fire-stamped and humorous delivery. " Modern-dress " extracts occurred occasionally of necessity—for instance when the players concerned snatched a moment before or after (or even during) their West End productions in order to appear, and could not allow themselves time to change. Curiously, they often provided the most illuminating interpretations in the Festival. I have never seen the Murder Scene in *Macbeth* played more excitingly, or with a more revealing psychological insight, than it was played by Marie Ney and Frank Vosper in front of the curtain at the Festival of 1936. She was in a modern black evening gown, he in the blonde wig and dressing gown he wore as the murderer in *Love from a Stranger*. In 1939 John Gielgud spoke Hamlet's " How all occasions " soliloquy in a plain suit, red tie and trilby hat—in tribute, his generous speech afterwards suggested, to the " modern-dress " Hamlet recently played at the Vic by Alec Guinness, a young actor who had begun in Gielgud's own company.   Here again the rendering was magnificent—its emotional sensibility heightened, perhaps, by the excessive " nerves" from which Gielgud obviously suffered on these occasions.

What else flashes to mind from this heap of odd yet often memorable performances ?   Wilfrid Walter giving the little-known Jack Cade speech from *Henry V I, Part I I*, and bringing that obstreperous democrat to life in a vital character-sketch ; Ion Swinley and George Hayes, leading actors of the 1923-24 season, joining forces once again as an Othello of anguish and power and a Iago of evil force ; Esmond Knight's dashing charm and fiery elocution as Hotspur ;   Donald Wolfit as Brutus and Robert Speaight as Cassius putting up a valiant Quarrel Scene in spite of the obvious fact that they should have been playing each other's parts ; Robert Harris reading Sonnets in a voice of spun gold, and Alec Guinness doing the same, in 1940, for Milton's " Sonnet on Shakespeare " ; Peggy Ashcroft's dew-drenched Viola and Godfrey Kenton's beautifully spoken Falconbridge ; Russell Thorndike, supported by a lugubrious and indifferent dog, as Launce in *Two Gentlemen of Verona ;* Jack Hawkins as a malevolent Richard III ;   Michael Redgrave singing folk songs in his *Beggar's Opera* costume ;   and Esmé Percy, the unlikeliest-looking Othello who ever took the stage in a turban too round and too large for him, " getting it over " by sheer beauty of speech and genuineness of passion.   In 1938 Shaw's *Dark Lady of the Sonnets* was performed in full with John Abbott as Shakespeare, Jessica Tandy as the Dark Lady and Marda Vanne as Queen Elizabeth.

The fun of the concluding " revels " was unequal in quality, and in later years it became more usual to replace them by longer extracts from one of the season's plays.   In 1930 the performance of Maurice Baring's *The Rehearsal*, with John Gielgud as the young actor cast for Lady Macbeth, appears to have been a riotous success. In the more *extempore* revels concocted by Frank Napier and Russell Thorndike, I remember with pleasure Maurice Evans boldly burlesquing his own Hamlet some days before he played the part for the first time, and Bruce Winston and Tyrone Guthrie (the Oliver Hardy and Grace Revnell, so to speak, of the Old Vic) tripping about in ballet skirts as Ariel and Puck in the frolic of 1938. The fastest and funniest Birthday finale I remember personally, however, was provided by a performance of the Pyramus and Thisbe interlude from *A Midsummer Night's Dream*, with Alec Clunes as the most deliriously comic Thisbe in—I should think—stage history. I can still see that grave actor, Ion Swinley, rocking speechless, tear-stained and helpless with laughter in his throne as Theseus.

The last item on the programme at the last Old Vic Birthday Festival in 1940 was the " Statue " scene from *The Winter's Tale*, with Veronica Turleigh as Hermione, Abraham Sofaer as Leontes and Jill Esmond as Paulina. A staid finish to a gay and nostalgic tradition.

On the front of all Shakespeare Birthday Festival programmes the following quotations appeared :—

> " Onely to keepe the memory of so worthy a Friend,
> and Fellow alive, as was our Shakespeare."
>
> *John Heminge* ; *Henrie Condell.*

> Born April 23rd, 1564.
> Died April 23rd, 1616.
> This day I breathed first : time is come round
> And where I did begin, there shall I end.
>
> *Julius Caesar*, v. 3.

I wonder how many people remember that other announcement which appeared regularly in every Old Vic programme for many years until the end of the 1939 season ?

> FREE SEATS—AT THE OLD VIC ONLY
>
> Owing to the generosity of the " Sunday Pictorial " twelve people will be admitted without charge to the Vic gallery, at all except special performances, or on Saturday, first or last nights.
>
> Please bring this kindness to the notice of those who could not otherwise afford to enjoy the performances.

This indeed—like the 7/6 stalls—is an attribute of the " people's theatre " which seems to belong now to a remote past.

CHAPTER VIII

WEST END INTERLUDE

KING JOHN

T H E loss of the Old Vic as a habitable theatre left the Vic Drama company for the first time in its history without a natural home. During the year following the production of *The Tempest*—the whole of the first period of air-raids—the company did not appear in London, although under the direction of Tyrone Guthrie the activities of all three Vic-Wells companies—drama, opera and ballet—continued without a break in the provinces. Of the number of Old Vic productions which went on tour, bringing a living drama to places which had never known it before as well as to recognised provincial centres, only a few during the next three years reached London. In all except four cases these were given hospitality for short seasons by Mr. Bronson Albery at the New Theatre, where the Sadler's Wells Opera and Ballet companies also played during the war years, gaining a new and enthusiastic West End public. These years at the New Theatre saw the beginning of the expansion of the Old Vic to the proportions and status of a national drama.

The first productions, beginning with *King John* on 7 July, 1941, were staged primarily for touring purposes and they appeared for short seasons at the New Theatre only as a crown, as it were, to their provincial itinerary. The production of *King John* by Tyrone Guthrie and Lewis Casson was adaptable and simple probably for this reason. It showed, on the other hand, all the stylised yet picturesque imagination that distinguishes Guthrie's productions of what one might call the " banner " class. The spare but suggestive scenery of Frederick Crooke, with its dark backgrounds luminous with the blaze of heraldry, had great atmosphere and beauty, and, as in *Henry V* some years before, subtle lighting and the use of dipping and uplifted standards gave an imaginative pageantry to English history.

147

The dramatic crests of the narrative were sharply marked, and reached a symbolic poetry when France and England, after a tenuous peace, broke asunder for war. Blanch, the princess of divided loyalties—English by race and French by marriage—became at this moment an abstract symbol of suffering disunity, torn almost literally by each side, a helpless centre-piece in a picture of rising frenzy. Her cry was the echo of that agony—

> Which is the side that I must go withal ?
> I am with both. Each army hath a hand
> And in their rage, I having hold of both,
> They whirl asunder and dismember me.

The effect of this expressionism was exciting and compelling, and it gave the play what a war-torn people were particularly able to appreciate at this time, the atmosphere of British historical greatness. Always in war Falconbridge's final words must work their stirring and moving spell :

> This England never did nor never shall,
> Lie at the proud foot of a conqueror,
> But when it first did help to wound itself.
> Now these her princes are come home again,
> Come the three corners of the world in arms
> And we shall shock them : nought shall make us rue,
> If England to itself do rest but true.

They were finely spoken at the New Theatre by George Hagan, an actor who had done some oddly quiet, subtle and distinctive work at Stratford-on-Avon (his Don John in *Much Ado About Nothing* had quite exceptional intelligence and style), but who here showed a new buoyancy, virility and elocutionary fire. His Bastard was vigorously imagined, compact of charm and rough spontaneous irony, getting both the humour of the back-chat and the basic loyalty and brave spirit under the cynical flash of the wit. One understood why such a man would choose to face the world as the bastard of Richard Coeur de Lion rather than take an estate and fortune as a supposed " legitimate ", and also why in his terse " It is a damn'd and a bloody work " he should express a true and deep abhorrence at the crime of Arthur's murder. Hagan showed in all this scene that he had not lost his natural instinct for taciturn feeling under his fire-new stamp of gusto and derision. It was his last stage performance before, like so many of his age, he disappeared for some years into the Royal Air Force.

As a character Shakespeare's King John tends to take third place to Falconbridge and Constance, although it has been played by a number of famous actors in the past, including Macready. There was a tendency to whitewash John in Elizabethan times, and certainly the significance of Magna Carta escaped recognition in that age of royal statesmanship and imperial expansion. Shakespeare, always interested in personalities rather than in historical trends and policies, shows the indifference of his period to the baronial secession (Magna Carta is, indeed, not mentioned in the play—a fact which would be inconceivable in a modern dramatist) ; but he does not follow current fashion by making John a sympathetic character, a kind of martyred deliverer of England from Papal domination. Perhaps the play would have been more coherent had he introduced the Papal theme more strongly ; as it is one has little sense of the clash of ecclesiastic and secular interests which trembles beneath the surface of events, and John's death by poison (casually attributed to an unknown and unseen monk) has a perfunctory air.

Yet the play holds as a martial drama, and the King's character, with its note of spiritual complexity, is not without interest. For John is both royal and weak, as quick as Richard II to clutch at the straw of the Divine Right of Kings, as subtle and ruthless as Richard III in his covert instigation to murder. He is altogether without the last King's boldness, and his passions are the passions of a weak character working himself up to violence and attaining only a transient fire. He is morose and uncertain in murder where Richard is brilliant and unscrupulous, and his guilt is fearful and ever ready to shift the blame. Shakespeare, however, is in many scenes far from uncertain in his touch, and the dialogue in which John suggests the murder of Arthur to Hubert has the born dramatist's sense of economy.

> JOHN. Death.
> HUBERT. My lord ?
> JOHN. A grave.
> HUBERT. He shall not live.

The exchange is pared to monosyllables, but the contact of the two minds is dramatic and unmistakable.

Ernest Milton, in a stylised red wig, suggested something of the " gloomy and timorous guilt " Macready is said to have brought to the part. He had the subtlety, the cowardice and the passing flash of royalty ; also the consuming and tearing rage that leaps up in the character like an ineffectual and quickly spent flame. The death scene, in which the waxen King flickered out of life like a dying taper, was superbly played, and one did not miss the faint glimmer of pathos under the man's treacherous insinuation. There is little poetry in *King John*, but this actor was peculiarly fitted to catch the macabre spirit of the lines about the " midnight bell " sounding " with his iron tongue and brazen mouth " on the drowsy ear of night. The voice here was like a wind soughing through the bare branches in a churchyard.

Constance is lioness to this nervous fox, and I suspect it is a mistake (at least until her last scenes) to treat her as wholly tragic. There is something comic in the nimble instinct of everyone on the stage to get out of the reach of her tongue, and one notes with amusement that Prince Arthur inherits something of her volubility (Hubert is naturally taciturn but it must be confessed that the little Prince, once he warms to his theme, gives him little chance to get a word in edgeways).

Mrs. Siddons was praised for making Constance seem more royal than a scold. Sybil Thorndike in the Old Vic production, as might be expected, did not let the possible touch of humour escape her, and she lashed about her with a vitriolic scorn. But this actress, with Greek tragedy in her bones, knows how to be regal too, and in her distraction there sounded that note of deep and heartshaking grief our stage rarely hears nowadays. The woman is naturally unbalanced in temperament, her maternal love and pride more frighten her miserable son than conciliate him, and John perhaps gives the key to the character with his early " Bedlam, have done ", which hints already at a mad strain. In this suggestion of distraught passion Sybil Thorndike was particularly successful.

In contrast Lewis Casson's Pandulph had the shrewd, sour reserve of the trained diplomat, and Ann Casson's Arthur had a boyish quality that was both attractive and simply moving. She was, though, " all the mother's, from the top to toe " (including the highly individual Thorndike voice), and therefore rather disconcertingly gave the lie to France's well-meaning effort to establish the Prince's legitimacy : " Look here upon thy brother Geffrey's face ". Since we were looking quite unmistakably upon Constance's face this took on an air of shocking expediency.

Esme Church's brief appearance as Queen Elinor established that elderly martinet's claim, " I am a soldier, and now bound for France ", and also the reason for her instinctive liking for Falconbridge. Abraham Sofaer was a dignified and sonorous French King, and Ernest Hare expressed a good deal of conscience and devotion under the grim and stolid mask of Hubert. Sonia Dresdel appeared in the unlikely rôle of Lady Falconbridge and Richard Wordsworth and Renée Ascherson made an attractive pair as the young lovers, Lewis the Dauphin and Blanch of Spain, although this young actress's promise at this period was marred by a tendency to scream at a climax. Later she was to be an enchanting Juliet to Basil C. Langton's Romeo, and an altogether bewitching Katharine of France in the Olivier film, *Henry V*.

THE CHERRY ORCHARD

T C H E H O V ' S *The Cherry Orchard*, in a translation by Hubert Butler, was produced shortly after *King John* at the New Theatre in the last week of August, 1941. The quality of the translation I frankly do not remember, and as I do not consider Constance Garnett's translation can be improved upon, and it is the only one I possess, I am using this in any quotations from the text. It is only fair to add that if the new translation did not heighten the beauty of the play it could not seriously have damaged it, for the atmosphere and poetic imagination of Tchehov's masterpiece were achingly present in this production.

" Atmosphere " is the key to all Tchehov's plays, and it pervades this one in the form of scattered cherry blossom, filling Madame Ranevsky's old Nursery with the sweet scent and whiteness of a Russian spring. Whether one glimpses the cherry trees or not through the stage window makes little difference : they are still actively present, a haunting link with the past that fills Madame Ranevsky and her brother with nostalgia and their minds with a fading enchantment.

The cherry orchard is the key to the play's action, a symbol of the transient things that are loved yet must pass away for ever, falling to the axe of those insentient to their beauty. Yet even the destroyer is not free from their subtle influence. Madame Ranevsky can only see the cherry orchard in the light of a serene past ; but to Trofimov it is a symbol of the suffering of the serfs who maintained it, and to Lopahin, the peasant turned speculator, its destruction is his crowning triumph over his beginnings. While Madame Ranevsky and her brother weep at the sound of the axe that destroys their childhood, he is already rapt with his own vision of a prosperous future, a future in which the cherry trees are replaced by summer villas, the orchard the centre of a new life which his grandsons and great-grandsons—descendants of a serf on the estate—will live to see springing up around them. For Lopahin, with his clumsy peasant's discomfort in a drawing-room and his shrewd financial mind, is in his own plodding, plebian way a poet too. " You have fine delicate fingers like an artist ", says Trofimov in the last scene, " you've a fine delicate soul ". And suddenly the whole man appears to us in a new and revealing light.

The first scene of *The Cherry Orchard* is filled with the bustle of arrival, the last with the bustle of departure. Life flows into the old house like a stream and away again, but the beginning and the end are quiet : Dunyasha and Lopahin waiting for the travellers in a frosty dawn, Firs, forgotten in the rush of departure, coming downstairs to die in the deserted house in which he had served from infancy. In between, the various lives interlink and mingle yet retain their odd lonely individuality : people soliloquise and chatter and no one listens, Anya yawns as Dunyasha flutters about her hundredth romance, Epihodov strums the guitar he calls a mandoline and boasts of his two-and-twenty misfortunes, the gauche German governess performs her conjuring tricks, Trofimov falls downstairs and searches for his lost goloshes, Varya, " like a nun ", waits despairingly for Lopahin's proposal that never comes. Over them all the white spectre of the cherry orchard broods like a mist of disaster, and nowhere more vividly than during that gay, unnecessary party that Madame Ranevsky holds with characteristic prodigality on the day of the sale.

Madame Ranevsky is the centre-piece of the play, for her love of the cherry orchard pervades her life with all the pain and sweetness of past association.

> Oh my childhood, my innocence ! It was in this nursery I used to sleep, from here I looked out into the orchard, happiness waked with me every morning and in those days the orchard was just the same, nothing has changed. (*Laughs with delight*). All, all white ! O my orchard ! After the dark glooming autumn, and the cold winter ; you are young again, and full of happiness, the heavenly angels have never left you . . . .

> If I could cast off the burden that weighs on my heart, if I
> could forget the past !

But the past breaks through even in this childhood paradise, she
cannot tear it out of her heart ; the drab atmosphere of her Paris
room, with its comfortlessness and smell of tobacco, creeps into
the world of cherry blossom, and in the party scene, when her
changing moods of gaiety and nervous despair give her a strange,
moving iridescence, the passion of her heart is suddenly revealed.

> I love him, that's clear. I love him ! I love him ! He's
> a millstone about my neck, I'm going to the bottom with him,
> but I love that stone and can't live without it.

In that moment we know that whether the cherry orchard is sold or
not Madame Ranevsky will return to her worthless lover. It is the
last link that might have held her, and it is breaking : the end is
inevitable.

Athene Seyler played Madame Ranevsky with the poise and
humour of a mistress of comedy ; but her grief was not surface grief,
it penetrated into the deep waters of an emotion all the greater
for the character's natural instinct for happiness. This was a
lovely performance by an actress who has style at her very finger-
tips, and can catch the radiance of a laughter shot with tears.

As Trofimov, the perpetual student—pompous, idealistic,
touchily independent and sensitive, a figure of fun with a strange
streak of pathos—Walter Hudd achieved perfection. This fine
character actor, too rarely seen in London, gave the part the sense
of dried-up emotions that might still warm at a touch, and at the
end of the first Act, when the sleeping Anya is led tenderly across
the stage by the devoted Varya, his sudden quiet outburst—" My
sunshine ! My spring !"—had a lingering sweetness. It is a
mistake to present Trofimov as a sententious clown ; his speech
on socialism—it is nothing less—is the nearest Tchehov came to
a serious analysis of social ills, and Hudd gave the character here
the eager mind of an idealist who really knows what he is talking
about.

James Dale gave a proletarian reality to Lopahin, but did not
miss the man's blundering sympathy and the visionary exultation
of his drunken triumph when he announces he has bought the
cherry orchard. Nicholas Hannen played the sentimental Gaev,
cannoning off the red and pouring out his soul to a bookcase, with
the right embarrassed and fussy charm, and Rosalind Atkinson was

ideally cast as the restless, busy and unhappy Varya. O. B. Clarence as Firs, James Donald as the flashy and disagreeable Yasha, Olive Layton as Anya, Lucy Griffiths as the Governess and Stanford Holme as Semyonov-Pistchik (that genial Russian Micawber whose " something " surprisingly does turn up) made a strong supporting cast.

Tyrone Guthrie's production had a quality of poetry that made the cherry orchard an intangible presence in the action. The teeming life of the play, its character and fluctuating moods, its arrivals and departures, was brilliantly suggested, and quite rightly Madame Ranevsky's emotional revelation in the party scene dissolved in gusts of laughter. The pathos was deepened by the contrasting comedy, and in the scene of the party the cross-currents of dancing and conversation, of nervous foreboding and joyous abandon, realised the perfect Tchehovian pattern. Frederick Crooke's setting here, with its glitter of light and rich wine-coloured curtains, was extremely beautiful, and the costumes of Sophia Harris were charmingly in period.

OTHELLO: THE MERRY WIVES OF WINDSOR

A LONG provincial tour preceded and followed the next New Theatre season, in which the Old Vic company presented *Othello* and *The Merry Wives of Windsor* with the co-operation of C.E.M.A. (the Council for the Encouragement of Music and the Arts, now known as the Arts Council). This was the first time an acknowledgment of C.E.M.A.'s assistance appeared on an Old Vic London programme, but this alliance had commenced early in the war and has continued with the coming of peace.

Othello, with the Czech actor Frederick Valk in the title rôle, was produced at the New Theatre on 22 July, 1942. It was succeeded by *The Merry Wives of Windsor* on 3 August, and revived for a further week on 22 August. *The Merchant of Venice*, with Valk as Shylock, had been announced for this final week, but the production was cancelled and not seen in London until the following February.

Generally speaking the foreign actor of Othello has one tremendous advantage over an English player—the advantage of temperament. William Poel described Salvini's Othello—perhaps the greatest the English stage has seen—as a " sleeping volcano ", and Bradley talks of the " fury of the elements " with which the character seems infused. English actors, as a rule, are neither volcanic nor elemental and this is where Valk, with his limitless reserves of passion and primitive power, undoubtedly scores. Emotion surges up in this actor like a tidal wave, submerging and uprooting every obstacle that lies in its path. He is monumental as an Epstein, a vast vessel of wrath in which suffering and rage contend stormily for dominion. And the fury is all the more terrible when it is deliberately under control. His—

> If I once stir,
> Or do but lift this arm, the best of you
> Shall sink in my rebuke—

has the menacing stillness that precedes an earthquake. In that appalling quiet the very skies seem about to pour down stinking pitch.

Yet Valk's physique aids him only in a sense : his bulk gives him power, but detracts from his royalty. He has nowhere the " leonine grace " of Kean, " whose little person ", writes Leigh Hunt, " absolutely becomes tall, and rises to the height of moral grandeur, in such characters as that of Othello ". In movement he tends to " bounce ", and only in repose does he attain true dignity and suggest the man " of royal siege ". In such moments he is superb—

> Let him do his spite ;
> My services which I have done the signiory
> Shall out-tongue his complaints . . .

The calm conviction of this suggests natural greatness, the greatness of one who knows his value and can appraise it impartially, without vanity. For this actor, who can give to animal instincts a cataclysmic frenzy of unleashed ferocity, is no mere thunderer without brain : he can direct the storm as well as yield to it, and calculate his oceanic calms as well as hurricanes. His puzzlement and slowly rising pain have the lumbering and massive pathos of the bear baited, and his one failure of calculation is in the scene of the murder of Desdemona.

> It is the cause, my soul, it is the cause . . .

There is a dreadful calm in this speech, an emptying of passion : the level beat of the metre is inexorable, murder has become a sacrifice and the bleak and barren wastes of justice seem to stretch in icy vistas over the Moor's flaming hell of revenge. The hell breaks through the ice before the end, but the flames lack their former heat, and die even with the blowing. There is nothing left then but a boundless agony and a passion which, washed in steep-down gulfs of liquid fire, turns on the Moor himself the scorching violence he had suppressed in the killing of his wife. But Valk's passion is a torrent which once let loose is not stemmed until the life has left Desdemona's body ; his climax of rage is too prolonged, and as a result his performance lacks, at the end, the drama and elasticity of contrast.

The other lack is of poetry. It is a disadvantage that must nearly always weigh against the foreign actor's advantages of temperament, and Valk when he played Othello for the Vic was, for long passages of the play, all but unintelligible. As a result the music of the language became discordant and incoherent, " all sound and fury, signifying nothing ". One could not begin to appreciate that quality in the character that made Granville-Barker speak of Othello as " the poet born " and Bradley write that " there is no love, not that of Romeo in his youth, more steeped in *imagination* than Othello's." The actor may have carried the imagination in his heart, but he was without the instrument through which to express it. In his later performances of Othello, with Donald Wolfit as Iago, he has acquired far greater clarity and one loses the sense only in moments of rushing excitement or emotional stress. I should, perhaps, make it clear that as I saw this performance with Wolfit very recently it is possible that this study of Valk's Othello—apart from the obvious improvement in the quality of the speaking—derives as much from that as from his performance for the Old Vic.

Unfortunately the Old Vic Iago, Bernard Miles, was equally pedestrian of speech and an unmistakable whiff of Cockney gave an unexpected aroma to his performance. At an Othello from Middle Europe and a Iago from Wapping the senses reel, although the plebeian quality of this Iago might be supported on the grounds of that vulgarity many commentators have read into the character. Iago, flatly states Granville-Barker, is a " nobody and has his way to make ", and it is possible that the taunt of " a great arithmetician ", flung at Cassio, springs from the envy of a man whose own lack of military education is the cause of his thwarted advancement. Othello, the greatest general in the State, is not likely to have made a mistake in choosing Cassio for his lieutenant, and Iago's greater experience in battle was no doubt counter-balanced by an inferior theoretical knowledge and ability.

This would explain the cankering jealousy both of Othello and Cassio, and that curious inferiority complex that seems to work its way like a serpent through the man's armour of vanity and genius. The suspicion that he has been supplanted—in his wife's affections as well as his career—gnaws his inwards, as he says, " like a poison-ous mineral " : it is by no means the only motive force behind Iago's gangrenous venom, but I suspect it is far from being mere self-deluding bluff. For in this tortuous and complex psychology evil has many hidden roots, even though the monstrous plant of malignity that grows from the soil is out of all proportion to the seed from which it generates. It is, I think, to deny Shakespeare's greatness as a creator of character to imply otherwise.

But there is imagination in Iago as well as proletarian coarseness. He is an artist in crime who exults in his creative malevolence, and is driven to overreach himself by the fatal and reckless spirit of the gambler. Little of this recklessness or imagination leavened Miles's performance : it lacked intoxication of spirit and conscious power. But within his limits this excellent character actor and comedian managed his Shakespearean metamorphosis with dex-terity, and his hatchet-faced craft and insinuation gave the ensign a certain foxy humour.

Freda Jackson was an outstanding Emilia : ribald and warm-hearted, and giving a fierce contempt to her repudiation of her husband—the fiercer for her obvious devotion to him until that moment. Her grief was for her misplaced passion as well as for Desdemona, and in the last scene she quietly held the stage even against this Othello. Her face, movingly expressive, suddenly became the centrifugal point of the drama, mirroring Othello's tragedy as well as her own. Hermione Hannen seemed unneces-sarily weak-willed as Desdemona but Laurence Payne proved a well-spoken, intelligent and more-than-promising Cassio. The production was by Julius Gellner and the scenery and costumes by the inevitable Mr. Crooke.

Falstaff is quite a different kind of mountain to Othello, although in his way as difficult to scale. In *The Merry Wives of Windsor* the actor's task is, in a sense, harder than in *Henry I V*, for the character's colossal reputation as a wit is built on the earlier plays and in *The Merry Wives*, written to order as a result of public (and it is hinted royal) demand, the whole fleshy edifice tends to be reduced by the demands of farce. Yet something of the spirit remains beneath the layers of fat and the new ludicrous entanglements of amorous disgrace, and that cheerful wit of Falstaff that battens on his own obesity flashes out still on occasion. At such moments it is seen that the coinage is still current.

The scenes with Mistress Ford have a certain ingenuity of fun, and Sir Hugh Evans is a " character " after the heart of the creator of Fluellen (Falstaff's line about the " Welsh fairy " is still apt to get the biggest response, whether the audience be in Stratford or St. Martin's Lane). But Shallow here is a dim shadow of the forked radish that pushes its way through the soil of the earlier play, and how dated now seems the Gallic volubility of Dr. Caius !

In the study the play is practically unreadable ; yet—strange anomaly—how difficult it often is to resist in performance ! The actors of the Old Vic company, under Esme Church's direction, played the farce for all it was worth and rightly left one too little time to carp or analyse. Frank Petley, the hero of many Melville melodramas at the Grand Theatre, Brighton, in my childhood, startled me by playing a Falstaff of rich gusto and charm. I have had a greater respect for the actors trained in *The Lights of London* and *The Two Little Vagabonds* ever since. Frederick Bennett played Sir Hugh Evans as well as he played Fluellen, Richard Wordsworth made an amusing flaxen spindle of Slender, Laurence Payne buried his identity as the deplorable Dr. Caius, and Ralph Fraser and Ernest Hare were the jealous and complacent husbands, Ford and Page. (Has any actor, I wonder, surpassed Donald Wolfit's Ford ? People now remember only his Falstaff, but like his Gratiano in *The Merchant* his Ford must take its place among the forgotten masterpieces of the minor Shakespearean gallery.)

Renée Ascherson was a pretty Ann Page, and Freda Jackson and Rosalind Atkinson made effective Merry Wives. But I suspect these parts to be actress-proof, like so many that derive their being from farcical situation and not from character.

THE MERCHANT OF VENICE

T H E Old Vic Drama company, again with Valk as its leading player, did not reappear in London until 16 February, 1943, when *The Merchant of Venice* was produced at the New Theatre.

LII.—*King John* (1941). Death of the King : Ernest Milton as
King John.

LIII.—*The Cherry Orchard* (1941). Walter Hudd as Trofimov and
Athene Seyler as Madame Ranevsky.

LIV.—*The Cherry Orchard* (1941). James Dale, Olive Layton,
Athene Seyler, Rosalind Atkinson, O. B. Clarence, Nicholas Hannen
and Walter Hudd.

LV.—*Othello* (1942).   Frederick Valk as Othello and Bernard Miles
as Iago.

LVI.—*The Russians* (1943). Michael Golden as Safonov and
Freda Jackson as Valya.

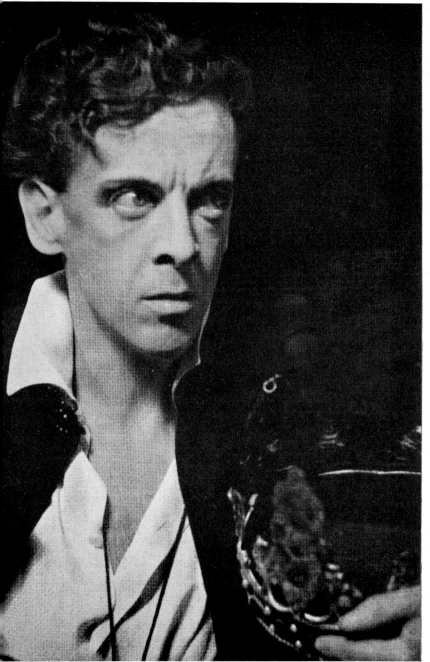

ony.

LVII. — *Hamlet* (1944). "The play's the thing . . ." Robert
Helpmann as Hamlet.

LVIII. — *Hamlet* (1944). "The King's rouse": Production by Tyrone Guthrie and M i c h a e l Benthall.

Mandinian

LIX. — *Hamlet* (1944). "'Tis true, 'tis pity . . .". Basil Sydney as Claudius, Lawrence Hanray as Polonius and Margot Graham as Gertrude.

LX. — *Hamlet* (1944). Robert Helpmann as Hamlet and Pamela Brown as Ophelia.

Mandinian

The key to *The Merchant of Venice* is Shylock, and critical controversy will rage as to the sympathetic or unsympathetic interpretation of the rôle as long as there are actors capable of bringing it to life.   But for long passages of the play the Jew does not appear and these passages, like the " pound of flesh " theme itself, can only charm the interest if they are regarded in the light of a fairy tale.   Portia, the beautiful heroine who can only be wooed and won by a choice of caskets, is as much the fabulous princess of a fairy tale as the legendary Turandot, whose suitors must solve her riddle or answer their failure with their lives.   And Venice itself, with its masques and young gallantry and picturesque exoticism, must have had for the Elizabethans the same quality of unreal enchantment.   The best productions of the play have always stressed this element of fancy, and in 1938 at the Queen's Theatre John Gielgud achieved, with the help of a fine cast and settings which had the spacious beauty of a Canaletto, a quintessence of colourful romance.

This does not mean that the characters themselves are unreal ; but their humanity and warmth are gilded with fantasy.   Portia's natural wit and gaiety of heart glow like those sunny locks which " hang on her temples like a golden fleece ".   She is both a great lady and an impulsive romantic girl, with a prodigality in love that lifts her far above the object of it.

> You see me, Lord Bassanio, where I stand
> Such as I am : though for myself alone
> I would not be ambitious in my wish
> To wish myself much better ; yet for you
> I would be trebled twenty times myself ;
> A thousand times more fair, ten thousand times
> More rich . . . .

There is an echo here of Juliet's love which is " as boundless as the sea " :   the same generosity and the same candid humility. The true enchantment of Portia is here and not in the far less personal plea for mercy.

Bassanio has nothing of this magic.   His moralising on the caskets does not escape sententiousness, and the figure he cuts as a spendthrift and borrower is at best a poor one.   Nor do his attempts to save Antonio strike one as more than perfunctory.   Yet I doubt if Shakespeare intended this impression, although he never seems truly to have warmed to his material, and it is significant that William Poel and Granville-Barker, practical men of the theatre, have both rejected Arthur Quiller-Couch's description of the character as " fortune-hunter, hypocrite and worse ". Such a reading would in fact set an impossible task for the actor : the story demands a romantic figure here, a hero and successful wooer, and provided the actor has the charm and grace to suggest this the audience is not likely to look too closely into motives and actions.

Nevertheless as a living character Bassanio, like the musical-tongued Lorenzo, never comes completely to life, and the various " Sallies "—Salarino, Solanio and Salerio— are about as distinguishable as three dried herrings. Antonio himself, who admits his wearying propensities only too candidly in his first speech, has merely negative virtues, and his melancholy is as pathological as Hamlet's but without a spark of Hamlet's poignancy and intellectual interest. The good actor—as Leon Quartermaine in the Gielgud production proved—may make something of his suppressed anxiety, tension and subsequent relief in the Trial, but he must compose his bricks without verbal straw.

Only Gratiano of these Venetian gallants flickers spasmodically to life.

> Let me play the fool :
> With mirth and laughter let old wrinkles come . . .

For a moment or two he sweeps across the scene like summer lightning : merry and wise, lightly stressing the jest of his own volubility, even for an instant holding us with a note of bitter-tasting philosophy :

> who riseth from a feast
> With that keen appetite that he sits down ?

> All things that are,
> Are with more spirit chased than enjoy'd.

The note passes, and he just misses becoming one of the memorable Shakespearean minor characters ; but his witty foolery " lifts " the play in a manner none of his companions succeeds in doing, and his wooing of Nerissa provides the quick-witted actor with one or two opportunities of invention.

What of the comic and oriental elements ? Launcelot Gobbo, with his harrying conscience, is one of Shakespeare's less inspired but nevertheless endearing clowns (with Shakespeare the poor man and the apprentice are never completely lay figures), and an

Andrew Leigh may make much of him.   Tubal is a piece of shapeless
clay from which the actor may mould a " character " or nothing,
Jessica a dark Eastern beauty who may be striking visually and
even suggest a certain warmth and resourcefulness of spirit.
(" She plans her elopement with the same fixedness of purpose as
the father pursues his revenge " notes William Poel).   Morocco,
splendid in " the shadow'd livery of the burnish'd sun ", is the
basic material for an Othello, and Arragon a " fantastic " whose
one scene may crakle merrily if the actor knows how to set a
match to it.   The best Arragon I have seen, that of Donald Layne-
Smith, raised the one big laugh of the play with a sly double-meaning
hesitation and emphasis at—

never in my life
To woo a maid—*in way of marriage.*

Over them all towers Shylock : devil incarnate, persecuted Jew,
wronged father—which ?   A little, I suggest, of all three, and the
great actor will stress the vindictive savagery without losing the
touches of humanity which Shakespeare—just because he *was*
Shakespeare—could not keep out of his creation. . For Shylock
has dignity as well as ferocity, huge pride of race, a contempt of
Christian masques and fopperies, even a dry humour that gives a
tang to his curt, business-like replies.   He shrewdly witholds his
decision while Antonio and Bassanio press their necessity, and to
Bassanio's " Be assured you may " (i.e. take Antonio's bond)
he has ready an ironic " I will be *assured* I may ".   Even in the
Trial scene, when murderous wolvishness, lashed by his daughter's
betrayal, has gained complete power over his senses and will,
he retains the wit to answer Gratiano's " Can no prayers pierce
thee ?" with a sardonic " No : none that thou hast wit enough
to make ".   And in the midst of his half-comic raging at the loss
of his daughter and his ducats (which incidentally gives the nebulous
Solanio his one opportunity to shine as a mimic), the imagination
of Shakespeare has produced that poignant and revealing mark
of human feeling ; the pang at the loss of the ring he had of Leah,
his dead wife.   " I would not have given it for a wilderness of
monkeys ".

To us to-day Shylock's rebuke of Christian anti-semitism has
a claim to our respect, and even Shakespeare—who did not, I
am certain, think of Shylock as a " sympathetic " character—
could not have been unaware of the moral force behind his " Hath

not a Jew eyes ? Hath not a Jew hands, organs, dimensions, senses, affections, passions ?" The whole speech has an inescapable ring of sincerity and as spoken by Frederick Valk, a Shylock of titanic dimensions, it became, appropriately enough at that time, the thunder of Jewry against Nazidom. The actor here was extraordinarily moving, but without for a moment descending to sentimentality. The performance had leonine royalty and the cruelty of the jungle, but something besides that swept the hackneyed play into magnificence.

The rest of the company, in comparison, seemed merely competent. Kay Bannerman's Portia suffered from a modern manner, but it had a sunlit humour and charm that caught more than a gleam of the fairy princess. Andrew Leigh proved himself once again the most disarming and amusing of contemporary Launcelots, Angela Wyndham-Lewis, who had done some neat work earlier in the War at the Oxford Repertory theatre, was Jessica and Lee Fox Bassanio. The production was by Esme Church, and although (probably for touring reasons) the decoration of Roger Ramsdell was not elaborate, it did convey something of the silken texture and colour of an Italianate romance.

THE RUSSIANS : GUILTY

F O U R plays during the war period were presented by the Old Vic company in London at theatres other than the New Theatre. The first of these was a revival of *Abraham Lincoln* at the Playhouse Theatre on 13 April, 1943, with Herbert Lomas in the title rôle. Of the others, Peter Ustinov's *Blow Your Own Trumpet*, produced at the Playhouse Theatre on 11 August, 1943, ran for only ten days and I was unable to see it. The production was by Michael Redgrave, the setting (of a Soho café) by Feliks Topolski and the cast included Esmé Percy, André Malandrinos, Lilly Kann, Ernest Urbach, Arnold Marlé, Michael Warre, Marione Everall and Elwyn Brook-Jones. The author wrote the play when he was twenty, and although it did not repeat the success of his *House of Regrets* mention was made of its " flashes of brilliance."

The Russians, produced also at the Playhouse on 10 June the same year, was a remarkably fine play by the young Soviet dramatist Konstantin Simonov. The play was based on the author's experiences as a reporter on the Russian front during the war, and the action takes place in a town partly occupied by the Germans and partly by Russian guerilla troops beseiged, and waiting almost without hope for reinforcements, on the other side of the river.

In part this play had the quality of a documentary, but it was far more than that. It was the work of a born dramatist who, with terse yet moving veracity, could draw living people reacting under the stimulus of a war more immediate and horrible than we in this country were forced to face. Valya, the guerilla girl scout, and Safonov, her commanding officer, holding their love at arm's length, as it were, because of the need for service and the danger of death, could yet move us with the flicker of feeling that penetrated their reserve, and their one love scene, as the girl is about to go on an exploit that may cost her her life, was passionate in its restraint. In these strong, gallant people of the Soviet, facing death by firing squad or torture, feeling the horror of it but casting off their fear with a careless phrase, one could still recognise that peculiar " Russianness ", that inner spiritual sensitivity, that one knows in the—on the surface—far different and purposeless characters of Tchehov. " You're a dreamer, Safonov ", says Vasin, the veteran soldier. " Of course I am " is the reply. " We Russians are all dreamers. We fight the better for it ". The first two sentences might apply to a character of Tchehov : it is the last that points the difference in spirit, the quality that brought the Russian people, for all their dreaming, through the bitterness of invasion and war.

They seem hard, these people, at first, hidden in a shell of curtness and responsibility. It is at the end of the first scene that the shell first breaks, and that ending is the work of a natural dramatist. A wounded man, one of the Russian guerillas, has fallen across the threshold and died at the feet of his comrades. The following dialogue occurs :

> MOROZOV : (*He unexpectedly wipes away a tear with his sleeve*).
> I thought I was used to it, but I feel sorry for people.
> (*Looking at Valya*) Why aren't you crying, driver ?
> VALYA : I can't, Sergei Ivanik. I've already seen everything
> I never thought I should see. I can't cry. I can't cry
> any more.

And suddenly these strange, grim people, fighting with the enemy at their very doors, are real people, not people without feeling but people on whom horror has piled so high that their feelings, locked within them, can no longer be easily expressed.

The picture of life behind the Russian lines, so short of water that men shave in vodka, is shown with atmosphere and humour. Always one feels death at the very door. But there are no mock heroics. It is of the village cottage, with its little river and two birch trees, that Valya thinks when she thinks of the country for which she is fighting, not some great abstraction of communism, not even of " Russia " as a whole. But the effect of the play was such on our own war-scarred people that when Vasin raised his death cry on the banks of the river to which he had, in a deliberate feint, brought outnumbering German troops—" Glory to the Russian arms!"—the Playhouse audience thundered its applause. We could feel for these people and their heroism for all their taciturnity.

The play became true melodrama only, perhaps, in the scene with the sadistic Freudian German officer in the house of the Quisling Mayor : that figure was a little outsize, but the impact of the scene was tremendous. It was superbly acted by Russell Thorndike as the terrified and cringing Mayor, and by Olga Lindo as his wife who, tortured by her husband's cowardice and by the shock of the death of her son, drags them both to the scaffold by a deliberate act of murder. Frederick Horrey as the German was also excellent, and Rosalind Atkinson, as an elderly Russian woman sentenced to be hanged, touched a note of true emotional power in her virulent denunciation of her oppressors.

As Valya and Safonov, Freda Jackson and Michael Golden played finely throughout, and the first, in the scene after her torture, vividly showed the intolerable strain of pain and sleeplessness that was almost, though not quite, cracking the nerve beneath. Her collapse in tears at the joy of relief was movingly done. Franklin Dyall as Vasin, David Carr as a young journalist turned soldier and Arthur Hambling as a guerilla who pretends to have gone over to the Germans also gave outstanding performances in an excellent cast. The play was excitingly produced by Tyrone Guthrie with settings by Frederick Crooke, and it ran for nine weeks.

The fourth play, *Guilty*, translated by Kathleen Boutall from Zola's *Thérèse Raquin*, marked the reopening of the Lyric Theatre, Hammersmith, by C.E.M.A. on 18 April, 1944. It also marked the return of Flora Robson to the London stage after several years' absence in America. The play had previously been on tour with the Old Vic company, and its production meant a welding of some important forces in the serious theatre.

Zola's story is strong meat for the stage and its turbulent and sordid passion provides magnificent opportunities for the actors. These were magnificently seized. Inevitably the psychological development in the novel cannot be as fully and subtly explored in the play ; but the havoc wrought by guilt in the characters and minds of the lovers is, perhaps, more dramatic for its suddenness. The violent recrimination and searing mental torment of the last scene comes, in the play, with a shock of genuine horror. Throughout this scene the figure of Madame Raquin, who knows the secret of her son's murder but, stricken by a paralytic stroke, cannot denounce his murderers, looms like a terrible and avenging ghost. No murder play has a scene of more petrifying tension and Violet Farebrother, concentrating into her eyes alone the whole pent-up lava of the old woman's sardonic balefulness and frustration, here bestrode the play like a Colossus.

Flora Robson also achieved in this scene a dreadful intensity. This was emotional acting of rare power in which face, voice and gesture mirrored the sickening agony and fear of a character not strong enough to face the consequences of murder. Obliged to play against her physical type, she nevertheless painted a nervously vital portrait of the sensuous and passion-fevered Thérèse. Personality and appearance were basically wrong, yet the actress forced belief. Michael Golden's Laurent was too pleasant in the early scene to make his murderous intent credible, but he also suggested much of the weakness and strain of the squalid final scene. O. B. Clarence, Roy Malcom, Frank Petley and the charming Kay Bannerman comprised an admirable supporting cast.

The production by Guthrie, with period *décor* and costumes by Reece Pemberton, caught the drama and squalor, but the scene was underlit and some of Flora Robson's finest expression was reduced in power as a result.

HAMLET

T H E Old Vic production of *Hamlet* at the New Theatre on 11 February, 1944, had no preliminary tour and was staged only for the duration of the London run. It opened in a blitz to the sound of gunfire and falling shrapnel, and police regulations forced the cutting of the play to ensure that the performance ended at 9.30. After the first night this meant that even the opening battlement scene had to be omitted, and at the first performance the disappearance of electricians to do Air Raid Warden work intensified the gloom of a production which was planned along lines of Rembrandt chiaroscuro, but never intended to go to the extremes of darkness of which many critics complained. The Hamlet, Robert Helpmann, also opened under the handicap of influenza and a bad throat, and although quite rightly the first night critics, unaware of this, judged the performance on its merits, there is no reason why the fact should not be noted at this distance of time. It does in some measure—though not I think in totality—explain the great advance in suppleness and strength made by the actor vocally as the run of the play continued.

The production was planned by Michael Benthall in collaboration with Helpmann, but owing to the fact that Benthall, then serving in the Forces, could not get leave to take rehearsals, all active work on the production was undertaken by Tyrone Guthrie. As a result, Guthrie's mentality to an obvious extent coloured a great deal of the action, and the design of certain scenes, echoing some of his former productions, was recognisably his.

It was a rich and exciting production. The emphasis was entirely dramatic, and the producers managed to suggest both the pace of events and the treacherous labyrinth of Danish Court politics. Occasionally probability was sacrificed to effect, and the sudden lowering of stalactites from the ' flies ' in Hamlet's second scene with the Ghost—presumably to give the illusion that the two had descended from the battlements to a cave by the sea—seemed an elaborate and artificial device which was quite unnecessary with the adaptable permanent set already available. The thrusting of Hamlet's first scene with the Ghost into the confined space of a small parapet at the extreme side of the stage also gave a cramped effect to the scene, and destroyed the illusion of the Ghost's elusiveness and intangibility. The spirit was too close to the characters, and Hamlet with the lift of a finger could have touched it.

Yet as always with Guthrie there were magnificent touches : the Players rich in vagabondage, heaping the stage with baskets and glowing velvets and that " property " crown which was to inspire Hamlet with his notion to catch the conscience of the King ; the game of chess that provided Hamlet with a mimic King to toy with and dash to pieces ; the King's growing fear of the lurking danger of assassination ; Hamlet hunted through the darkened Palace by the

King's satellites and finally trapped in a ring of steel. Leslie Hurry's monumental setting echoed the note of the production ; terror stalked this castle's corridors, and the stage pictures and opulent costumes emerged from the background with a luminous Renaissance beauty, though the chiaroscuro tended sometimes to mask the actors' play of expression.

The opening scene at the Court, with the King and Queen at the peak of a glowing group of carousing courtiers, and Hamlet sitting dwarfed, white-faced and reticent at the foot of a massive column, finely evoked the atmosphere of Danish profligacy at which the Prince burned in smothered resentment. There was the same sense of dramatic contrast in the " How all occasions " scene later, when the virile and capable figure of Fortinbras, a high immobile Napoleon on the side parapet, was balanced against a cloaked and seated Hamlet, with scholar's forehead and slender physique, far below. Helpmann, lucid and grave in thought, played this scene beautifully, and, as he moved slowly below Fortinbras after his speech, his pause and glance at the figure above, and drawing together of his cloak, subtly pointed the contrast of thinker and man of action.

The danger of Guthrie's method of production is that it tends to suggest a tragedy by Tourneur rather than by Shakespeare, and it throws on Hamlet the whole burden of the play's philosophy and poetry. This Helpmann over-lightly but bravely carried. It was six years since he had played Oberon so brilliantly, and hardly less since his appearances in *The Taming of the Shrew ;* but in spite of his inexperience in sustaining so long and important a speaking rôle, his Hamlet was one of the most interesting and moving of recent years.

Of the three qualities which George Henry Lewes named as essential to a great actor, and which he called " conceptual intelligence ", " representative intelligence " and " physical advantages," Helpmann possessed the first two in an unusual degree, and the third with one drawback born of this inexperience. His intellectual grasp of Hamlet's character was obvious throughout ; his power of representation, called by Lewes " mimetic power ", had long been proved in ballet, particularly in such parts as Satan in *Job*, the Rake in *The Rake's Progress* and Hamlet in his own ballet, where he has attained a remarkable degree of plastic force and imagination ; his physical assets included a body which was slight in build but a perfectly-trained instrument of expression, and a face elfin, mobile and easily changed by make-up. His voice was musical and clear, but especially in the Ghost scene tended to take too weak and hysterical a pitch. There was too much of self-pity in this Hamlet at first to lift the emotion on to the higher plane of tragedy, and a certain measured and inelastic rhythm of diction detracted from the vocal variety, and made Horatio's reference to Hamlet's " wild and whirling words " strangely irrelevant to the facts. This was Purcell music rather than Beethoven ; both a 'cello note and flash of power needed to be added for the actor's range to include passion as well as pathos.

As the run proceeded a great deal of this strength and flexibility of voice began to appear. This actor will never produce an organ bellow, but his natural vocal range is sufficient for all emotional purposes outside the heroic, and suppleness and depth came to him more easily as the habit of dialogue overcame his early nervous restriction. The melody is sweet on the ear, and in his more recent performance in *The White Devil*, as well as in his later performances as Hamlet, one could hear the richened play of harmony.

The dominating note of this performance was intellectual ; the very emotion sprang from the brain, as it should do, for Hamlet suffers always with the head rather than the heart. His is a mental agony drawn to a fine degree of frustration and pain, and in Helpmann's eyes and high, clear brow—a white screen on which the thoughts were thrown up like moving pictures in a cinema— the torturing doubts passed like shadows. He was delicate, super-sensitive, but always with a certain suggestion of force beneath. The soliloquies were spoken with crystal cogency, and nerve and brain were taut-strung as a violin. Neither the madness nor glint of menace was shirked ; but the contacts with Horatio and the Players had an ingenuous sweetness, there was irony, grief, a beautifully played death scene (glancing at the venomed sword with a fascinated incredulity, wondering at death as the life drained out of him), and never any doubt that here was a mind, though poisoned, of natural sensitivity and charm.

Not that this was for one moment a " sentimentalised " Hamlet. There was gall behind the sweetness, and the taunting of Polonius (the " fishmonger " or " pander ") had an acid contempt. (The composition of Hurry's setting, with its passages of approach receding into the gloom, had made Hamlet's overhearing of the plot to " loose " Ophelia to him very clear). Ophelia herself fared no better, and it was, perhaps, a criticism of the performance that this Hamlet made one believe not only that he did not love Ophelia now, but that he had not loved her in the past and never could have loved her. One momentary melting into pity, sitting beside her and touching her shoulder as she collapsed in tears, did not alter this impression. " It was not an absorbing passion " wrote Bradley of the Hamlet-Ophelia relationship and one agrees, but Helpmann's cold wrath did not even suggest the passing of a spring-time idyll.

The Play Scene was pure Renaissance drama, Hamlet moving down the stage with a cat-like velvet malignity and, kneeling suddenly behind the Queen, startling her with a " Madam, how like you this play ?" like the snap of a pistol-shot. His mimicry of Osric had a mocking wit, and he played with Rosencranz and Guildenstern as easily as with the red king he had picked up from the chessboard and dallied in his hand. The subtle touches were innumerable : one remembers the first scene when his face at the King's reference to his marriage mirrored his silent pain, and the stubborn line of his shoulders which, as he backed the audience at the Queen's entreaty, underlined his brief " I shall in all my best obey *you*, madam." Emotionally the " rogue and peasant slave " soliloquy was the peak of Helpmann's performance, and at " O vengeance " he swept the chessmen off the board in a torrential frenzy. The recovery here was finely marked, and the gesture at—

> Why, what an ass am I !
> This is most brave

—literally pushing back the tears—was extremely moving. A nervous tattoo of the fingers on the " property " drum stressed the deadly rumination of " The play's the thing ", and the inflexion on " flesh ", more sad than bitter, in the taunt to the King— " Man and wife is one flesh "—was a touch of peculiar imaginative insight. The sadness of this Hamlet's drawn, transparent mask gave his " Alas, poor Yorick " the same mordant quality of sorrow : the horror at mortality was dimly suggested, at a long way off as it were and softened by a wry yet not unfeeling twist of humour.

The humanity of Helpmann's Hamlet—perhaps its most outstanding characteristic—was particularly marked in this scene. It was equally apparent in the far more restless and anguished scene in the Queen's closet, where his flow of real tears after the appearance

of the Ghost gave a sudden strangely touching quality to the relationship of mother and son. His glance at his sword at the Queen's
" Thou wilt not murder me "—bewildered, frightened, half-real-
ising how dangerously near he might have been to this—I found
illuminating. Nor have I ever heard the " heart's core " speech,
the advice to the Players and the fey " Thou wouldst not think
how ill all's here about my heart " better spoken. The realisation
of treachery in the duel, and subsequent cold fury, were finely
done, and the way the actor stretched his failing hand towards the
Queen at " Wretched Queen, adieu ", and dropped his arm as the
weakness of death flowed over him, lingers in the memory.

Margot Graham's flame-haired, voluptuous Queen, blindly
groping to help this too-much-changèd son, was exactly the right
foil to Helpmann's interpretation. The performance stressed the
lazy well-meaning sensuality of a beautiful woman, but did not
miss the new heart-heaviness of—

> To my sick soul, as sin's true nature is,
> Each toy seems prologue to some great amiss.

Leaning against a pillar, the radiant creature in emerald seemed
suddenly drained of happiness, and she shrank from meeting the
mad Ophelia as from a further blow. The queenliness and poise,
however, remained to the end, and the speech describing Ophelia's
death was to my mind beautifully delivered. Pamela Brown
brought to Ophelia's madness a frantic pain, and a cry that turned
hell to harshness rather than to prettiness ; it was a grim but vivid
performance, though in the first scenes too intelligent and assured
to suggest Ophelia's fatal inadequacy.

Basil Sydney's ruthless and crime-haunted King, Charles Deane's
Fortinbras and Lawrence Hanray's Polonius, a diplomat whom
age had toppled over into sententiousness, were also notable, and
Charles Hickman in a striking character sketch brilliantly showed
Osric's complicity in the juggling with the foils. Dennis Price
was a self-effacing but warmly-spoken Horatio, and Gus McNaugh-
ton a refreshingly natural and quietly pointed Gravedigger. Some
of the rest were barely adequate, but the gathering together of so
good an all-round team was a notable achievement at such a time.
The music composed by Constant Lambert seemed reduced in
performance—probably owing to the police regulations about
timing—to a fanfare of trumpets.

In spite of air-raids this production played to increasingly large audiences until 8 April—a long run for *Hamlet* at the best of times. With the public Helpmann's Hamlet proved popular, and his human qualities, pathos and clarity of intellect rapidly outweighed some initial prejudice against a dancer attempting the part. The notices in the daily press were critical, though on the whole fair, but the longer literary reviews showed in several cases a far deeper appreciation. Two critics—James Redfern of " The Spectator " and the anonymous critic of " John O' London's Weekly "—named Helpmann's Hamlet without compromise as the best they had seen.

The Old Vic experiment, though a bold one, might therefore be said to have been justified, and Helpmann's later performance as Flamineo in Webster's *The White Devil* has shown new force and fluency of expression and something of the potential vividness of his dramatic range. Both his daemonic intensity and rich vein of clowning have been fully exploited in ballet, and though Helpmann's unique genius is as a mime—partly because in that field he has no serious rivals—there is no reason why the dramatic theatre also should not draw on his talent and versatility. Hamlet was, apart from Oberon, the first important step and by no means an ineffectual one. If he plays the part again—which is to be hoped, for he is a natural Hamlet—the performance should be an outstanding one.[1]

[1] Since this chapter was written it has been announced that Helpmann is to play Hamlet in the Stratford-on-Avon Shakespeare Festival in 1948, alternating in the part with Paul Scofield.

CHAPTER IX

THE NEW TRIUMVIRATE

PEER GYNT

T H E productions of *Hamlet* and *Guilty* in 1944 marked the end of Tyrone Guthrie's long and successful personal directorship of the Old Vic drama. He had carried out the arduous duties of this directorship throughout the War in addition to his work as administrator of all three Old Vic-Sadler's Wells companies (Opera, Ballet and Drama), in which he had latterly been assisted by Bronson Albery as Joint Administrator. It is impossible in a book of this nature to measure the extent of this work, but it had involved the institution of the Old Vic wartime régime at the Liverpool Playhouse in addition to the supervision of many provincial tours and London seasons at the New Theatre.

Under Guthrie's administration and directorship the Old Vic drama company had enormously increased its national scope and achieved new standards of production and execution. Now he felt the need to return to more active work as a producer, for which his commitments as a director and organiser had lately left him little time. He therefore relinquished his position of control with regard to the drama, but remained, for one further season at the New Theatre, administrator of all the Old Vic companies. This was in order to see the three companies " on their feet " as separate entities, with complete autonomy under their individual directors. When he left, the Old Vic Board of Governors remained the only official link between the three companies. The Arts Council continued its association, and as in the past Messrs. Howard Wyndham and Bronson Albery continued to offer the drama company the hospitality of the New Theatre for its London seasons.

John Burrell, Laurence Olivier and Ralph Richardson succeeded Guthrie jointly as directors of the Old Vic Theatre Company, and they undertook the succeeding seasons at the New Theatre on the understanding that the plays would in future be presented on a repertory basis. This meant that several different plays would appear in each weekly programme and would continue in the repertoire, if possible, throughout the season. This is the procedure followed by all national theatres abroad and it will remain the basis of future Old Vic developments.

The first play to be presented under the new triumvirate was *Peer Gynt*, produced at the New Theatre on 31 August, 1944. It was a " cut " version in a new text by Norman Ginsbury, whose translation, though it had the advantage of naturalness and collo- quialism, tended to give a pedestrian quality to the language. One missed the soar and glitter of poetry, especially in the first scenes where Peer's mind should seem to skim through the clouds, as if on the surface of a rainbow. His fancy is multi-coloured, and the aerial excitement of the description of the ride on the reindeer needs the rhythm and imagery of verse to sustain it. Here it flopped like a moth with dampened wings, and Ralph Richardson's energy could not give magic or music to the words.

As the young Peer Richardson lacked imagination and the requisite youth. He is not an actor of fantasy, and the rich soil of the earth clings to his personality. Where he scored was in the uncouth, shy, sly ruffianism of the peasant, a kind of gauche alertness that, though it could not be lit by poetry, could still be subdued to tenderness by Solveig, softened and shamed by the death of Ase. He could move easily in the bizarre if not in the lyrical, and in the Troll scenes and scenes with the Green Woman (brilliantly played by Margaret Leighton) his rapscallion vigour was of immense service. As the eastern potentate the bland Richardson brand of comedy was successfully used, but he was finest of all in the last scenes, where his personality merged completely with that of the elderly Peer, and he suggested the gnarled and knotty hardihood of an oak swept by the sea wind. The train of thought in the " onion " soliloquy was remarkably sustained and in many ways the climax of the performance.

The character of Peer demands exceptional virtuosity in the actor : Richardson bounded through the fjords and over the lower mountain slopes of the part with ease ; only the ice-clad poetic peaks escaped his ravishing stride.

On a level with this performance was Sybil Thorndike's Ase ; a peasant whose spirit seemed lined, seared and toughened by adversity just as her face was lined, seared and toughened by the sharp winds of the north. There was a lashing, corded loyalty about this performance, and when the overworn fibre frayed the old woman's stillness and distress were deeply moving. Joyce Redman's Solveig was bright and clear with a child-like radiance, and in graphic contrast Nicholas Hannen's Troll King had a grotesque and paunchy viciousness, like a maggot that had crawled out of a green slime. Harcourt Williams as Begriffenfeldt was as mad as the maddest Hatter, and Laurence Olivier, in an exquisite small performance, gave the Button Moulder a strange, stern benignity that filled the scenes in which he appeared with a sense of quiet power. " Quality " is the best word to describe this performance, and it revealed in the actor a new and shining beauty of control.

Peer Gynt is, however, a challenge to producer as well as to actors, and it requires the utmost imagination to harness Ibsen's imagery and transform it into visual terms. Tyrone Guthrie's production lacked the national colour of the earlier one by Henry Cass, and the settings and costumes by Reece Pemberton had, in the Norwegian scenes, an arid harshness of hue and outline. In its way this was not without effect, for it gave the producer elbow-room with his lighting and enabled him to achieve sculptured, three-dimensional effects with his figures and choreographic groupings.

A programme acknowledgment was made of certain arrangements of grouping and movement by Robert Helpmann. Helpmann, in actual fact, collaborated with Guthrie in the production of the Troll scene and the scene of Peer's abduction of the bride, and also in the episode with the Green Woman. He also arranged the basic grouping of the Lunatic Scene, which echoed the fantastic terror of the Bedlam scene in Ninette de Valois's ballet *The Rake's Progress*. His work here, however, was confined to grouping and Guthrie produced the scene in the orthodox sense of directing acting and dialogue. Helpmann in the elopement scene used the movements and pattern of his watching crowd to convey a mental picture to the audience of Peer's climbing of the peaks with the stolen Ingrid. He visualised his trolls as a writhing mass of grey hairless bodies, a living dung-heap of festering maggots upon which the Troll King perched giddily, an obscene cartoon of corrupt royalty. This collaboration of dramatic producer and choreographer showed how the influence of ballet may, by giving flexibility and force to the grouping of characters, loosen and free the imagination in plays of this type.

R I C H A R D   I I I

P E E R   G Y N T was Ralph Richardson's big opportunity. Laurence Olivier's came with *Richard I I I*, produced by John Burrell at the New Theatre on 26 September, 1944.

This was a highly-coloured and exciting production of a highly-coloured and exciting play : brilliantly served by its leading actor, but by no means relying on this one performance for its dramatic impetus and cohesion. Morris Kestelman had designed scenery which had the expressionistic quality of a mediæval painting : a tumble of picturesque toy buildings in streets diminishing in perspective, yet always planned and framed to suggest coherence and not confusion. The brightness was ringed in darkness, and with careful lighting Doris Zinkeison's costumes emerged luminously from the background and were not submerged by it.

There were several original touches in the production. Jane Shore moved seductively across the first scene, a laughing and sensuous ghost from whose embrace Lord Hastings tore himself at his first appearance. There was nothing against this light-footed and suggestive apparition except the fact that those of the audience unacquainted with the play were unlikely to have understood the allusion, at least in the opening scene. A more effective interpolation was the appearance of Anne, a wan and sleepless spectre, sitting immobile at the side of the stage throughout the coronation scene. Already on this silent and suffering figure one remarked the pale cold finger of sickness and death. Richard's—

> Come hither, Catesby : rumour it abroad
> That Anne, my wife, is very grievous sick—

had in these circumstances a dreadful relevance which his auditor, with a sickened glance, was quick to appreciate. Joyce Redman, eloquent and passionate before, played Anne in this scene with an unobtrusive but moving sense of fatality.

The blaze of heraldry in this production emphasised the play's significance as history, and the figure of Richmond, a golden deliverer with the light of royalty about him, further clarified the political issue. For once a production of this play realised the spirit of civil war behind the action, and in Richmond's last speech one felt the triumphant clarion of peace, the true significance for the English of the merging of the white rose and the red. The glorious vista (as it must have seemed to the Elizabethans) of the

Tudor age opened in panoply before the future Henry VII. For Shakespeare's contemporaries this was history very near to their own times—almost within living memory. Richmond was grandfather to their reigning queen. It is impossible for a modern audience to be stirred in the same way and for the same reason, but I think this production did get nearer to the spirit of these last scenes than any I have seen.

Ralph Richardson played Richmond with a kind of humane splendour, representing both English majesty and solid yeoman English worth. His personality, always very individual and difficult to subdue completely, fitted the part, and it was too much to expect the new and film-conscious West End audience not to recognise the actor before the character. The rippling murmur that greeted his entrance had as its audible basis " Oh look ! There's Ralph Richardson !" Richmond, through no fault of the actor, came in a very bad second in this establishment of identity.

As in Guthrie's production of *Richard I I I* for the Old Vic some years before, some interpolations from Gloucester's *Henry V I* soliloquy appeared in Richard's opening speech, but Olivier emphasised the hint of loneliness and isolation less than Emlyn Williams. Olivier's was a Richard of jesting impudence : jocund, intrepid, vivid in craft and dangerous in humour. Lank of hair and glittering of eye, he had a lean sinuous buoyancy of movement ; subtle as a serpent, he sounded Buckingham on the murder of the princes with a honeyed astuteness which veiled a hidden fang and lurking venom. His rage was royal, and his—

> Cold friends to me—what do they in the north,
> When they should serve their sovereign in the west ?—

was like the howl of a wolf who sees the trap opening before him. He died with a dreadful and inhuman reluctance, returning blow for blow and gash for gash until he seemed literally torn from life, a resisting fury, by an invisible and relentless hand. He was a Richard, as Bradley described, with " the glory of power about him ".

Sybil Thorndike played Margaret with an agued intensity ; her hands, quivering with age and nervous passion, gave the half-mad queen an added terror, and she delivered the curse as if the woman's wandering mind had become transfixed, for a moment or two only, with a poisonous and prophetic hatred. Margaret Leighton as Elizabeth—that " pale shadow of the House of Lancaster "—moved like a dim wraith of grief among the " cursing women ", and Harcourt Williams played the dying Edward as if he were, indeed, sinking distractedly out of life.   George Relph was a Clarence whose level-metred intonation missed the poetry of the undersea dream of death, but his intelligence and sensitive hands gave interest to the character.   A young actor, Michael Warre, played Hastings with noticeable assurance and clear diction, and Nicholas Hannen was a bluff and vigorous Buckingham. The final fight was excellently arranged by Peter Copley and the incidental music was by Herbert Menges.

ARMS AND THE MAN

I N the two further plays produced this season—*Arms and the Man*, produced on 5 September, 1944, and *Uncle Vanya*, on 16 January, 1945—the acting honours were fairly evenly divided, not merely between Olivier and Richardson but between the other leading members of the company.   Both plays require first-rate acting of several leading parts, and their sensitive grasp of the widely divergent moods of Shaw's " extravaganza " and Tchehov's " tragic farce " showed the Old Vic players' excellence both individually and as a team.

> After fifty years this early satire of Shaw's remains as fresh and piquant as ever. Its cavalry charges are as out of date as the bustles of the ladies : but though tactics and fashions may change, human psychology does not, and behind the brutality and stupidity of war we must still find the same Vansittartism, suicidal courage, hero worship and sham. Shaw was the first to make a hero of the soldier who has the common sense to know the right moment to run away ; and Captain Bluntschli, who not only runs away but prefers chocolate creams to ammunition, remains a perennial joy.

In wartime *Arms and the Man* has a flash of topicality which is not without effect on the receptivity of the audience : one's reaction to it at such a time is particularly acute, and for this reason I have quoted the above extract from a short review I wrote in " The Tribune " of an earlier production of the play, given by the Oxford Repertory company in 1942. The impression of the play then was red-hot, and perhaps it is true that it needs war or experience of war to give its full sharpness to the political and psychological truth underlying Shaw's debunking and buffoonery. Shaw's own dictum—" Seriousness is only a small man's affectation of business "—should warn us against mistaking his flippancy for lack of purpose.

> . . . he makes his characters turn their moral garments inside out and go about with the linings displayed, flaunting the seams and raw edges and stiffenings and paddings. Now this simply does not occur in real life, or only to a very limited extent ;   and the artist who makes it his main method of character-presentation, at once converts his comedy into extravaganza.

This is William Archer on the first production of this play : graphically analytic, but tight-lipped, one feels, and a little disapproving. But Shaw never has aimed and never will aim at purely realistic characterisation :   he gives his creatures always the benefit of his own loquacity and his own keen exposing intellect, and like a jester sets the revelations spinning with a volley of acidity and sugared wit.   This does not mean that the people themselves are not real :   the moral garments are turned inside out, but the lining is authentic.   It is only the frankness of the display that is abnormal.

In this truth game of *Arms and the Man* Bluntschli represents, I should say, a perfectly normal type ;   blunt, shrewd, practical and humorous, without illusions but without cynicism either. It is his amused candour that evokes Raina's surrender and self-revelation, just as it is Louka's bold peasant's common sense— the outspokenness of a class that has nothing to gain, either in the way of caste or social refinement, by sham—that evokes that of Sergius.   Neither Raina nor Sergius has ever suffered from self-delusion, and Raina is not even consistently deluded by Sergius. (" I wondered whether all his heroic qualities and his soldiership might not prove mere imagination when he went into a real battle " expresses her inward doubt before she has been two minutes on the stage.)   When they turn their psychological garments they merely reveal to others the stiffenings and paddings they had long been aware of themselves.

Sergius comes nearer to caricature, and it is difficult, perhaps impossible, for an actor to treat him seriously without losing half the fun.   Laurence Olivier's performance in the Old Vic production was flamboyant burlesque, with all the flourish of the " operatic tenor " in clicking heels, twirl-provoking moustache

and rakish pill-box. It missed " *the half-tragic, half-ironic air,
the mysterious moodiness, the suggestion of a strange and terrible
history that has left nothing but undying remorse, by which Childe
Harold fascinated the grandmothers of his English contemporaries* ".
But this more neurotic aspect of Byronism is all my eye and Shaw's
stage direction : the rapier flash of the dialogue gives the actor
little chance to exploit it. Olivier showed enough solid plaster
and loam under the baroque façade to keep in touch with humanity ;
it was a long-distance call, but the contact was there, and we got
the fun of the pricked bubble of romance no less than the inflated
heroism. Within this gorgeous temple there burnt a small candle
of disarming charm, and the tiny flame gave a certain warmth
to the whole portrait that was not entirely belonging to caricature.

The story of Raina and her chocolate-cream soldier has itself
a touch of tender charm the average Shaw play lacks. The satire
is good-humoured : there is mockery but little sting. This is
probably one reason for the play's popularity—the reason it could
even be turned into a musical comedy with success. The other
reason is Captain Bluntschli, a part in which only the third-rate
actor could completely fail. At Oxford during the war it was
brilliantly played by Cyril Cusack, the best modern interpreter
of Synge's *Playboy of the Western World* and an actor with the
Irishman's ability to express a volume with a lifted eyebrow.
His mischievous ironic detachment was exactly right, and his
swaying drowsiness in the first scene had the drug-like sensory
influence of bees droning on a summer afternoon. Ralph Richardson gave a less absorbed and more individualistic characterisation ;
full of personality and charm as well as the man's natural capability
and twinkling astuteness. The susceptible Raina was obviously
doomed from the moment this baby-faced, button-nosed giant,
with the sleepy forehead and eyelids but alert eyes, stepped into
her room.

Margaret Leighton, tall, slender and fair as an arum lily, was
an enchanting Raina, with a shy humour lurking behind the romantic
dignity. Joyce Redman's Louka—insolent, amusedly and slyly
observant, but with a vein of clear-headed passionate integrity—
showed both skill and versatility. This bold sketch was in remarkable contrast to her grave, sweet Solveig and rapt, doomed child
Bridget in Paul Vincent Carroll's *Shadow and Substance*. Sybil
Thorndike and Nicholas Hannen made the older Petkoffs vigorous

and good-hearted people obviously only a generation removed from the soil, and Sydney Tafler quietly hit off Nicholas's shrewd servant's eye to advantage. The comedy was excellently produced by Burrell and the scenery and costumes of Doris Zinkeison had the colour and gaiety of a Balkan festival.

UNCLE VANYA

T H E Old Vic production of Tchehov's *Uncle Vanya*, in the translation of Constance Garnett, was a distinguished addition to the repertoire. John Burrell, the producer, did for this play what Michael St. Denis did for *The Three Sisters* ; he gave it poetry and life and heightened its atmosphere with many touches of domestic realism and sensitive observation. *Uncle Vanya* is not the easiest of Tchehov's plays to produce, for here, as in life, tragedy is for ever on the verge of toppling over into farce ; Tchehov's characters are not big enough, and he knew they were not big enough, to carry their heartache heavily, and the producers and actors who have the courage to recognise this, to present their human weakness and idiosyncrasies with amusement as well as tenderness, as Tchehov has done, will make of this play the delicately observed cross-section of real life that it is and not, as so often, an uncomfortable masterpiece steeped in Slavonic gloom.

The Old Vic production and performance excellently achieved this balance ; the laughter sprang naturally from the text alongside the pathos, and the lethargic stream of Russian country life of last century, with its idle currents of philosophy and frustration and sudden ripples of temper and desire, was admirably depicted. The atmosphere was considerably helped by Tanya Moiseiwitsch's settings, charmingly designed and completely in period. One felt these rooms had been *lived* in, their doors led not, as is the impression in so many stage sets, directly backstage but to passages and other rooms with windows looking out on to the trees and cornfields of Southern Russia. This artist gave to her landscapes the fine texture and grace of a Corot, and her clothes, like her rooms, had character and utility in addition to revealing an artist's eye for line and colour. Margaret Leighton's tall, fair, indolent beauty as Yelena in particular she dressed superbly.

Nevertheless production and design will never save a play by Tchehov if the quality of the acting is not of the highest. His plays live by character, and the very atmosphere hinges on the purely human factor. As we watch that first scene character after character unfolds itself like the pages of a book : Uncle Vanya, rumpled and still drowsy from his nap, weakly protesting his disillusion and dreaming aloud of Yelena's loveliness ; the Professor, " who has been lecturing and writing about art for twenty-five years, though he knows absolutely nothing about art "; his young bored beautiful wife lazily crossing the scene—indifferent, miserable almost without realising it, creating a strange, negative yet destructive disturbance in the minds of the men who watch her ; Astrov, the handsome, gone-to-seed doctor, musing aloud on his blunted emotions and passion for forestry, tugging at his " stupid " moustache ; the quiet Sonya, whose absorbed love for him blazes suddenly to life, a pure fierce flame beside Yelena's lazy, sensual feeling of attraction. And in their wake move other characters, less important but no less clear : the Nurse Marina, old now and outside life's passions, a listener and not an actor ; Vanya's mother, to whom age has brought no philosophy, only a more rigid absorption in political pamphlets and her adored son-in-law, the Professor ; the mild Telyegin, whom they call " Waffles ", strumming his guitar and telling his unassuming tale of self-sacrifice for the wife who left him years ago . . . .

They open their hearts like petals to the sun, lulled and brooding in the haze of the garden heat. Only in the next scene, with the storm raging outside the closed windows, and the Professor complaining querulously in his chair, do nerves begin to snap. The atmosphere is charged with these frayed and sensitive nerves, with the fatigue of watching by a sick-bed long into the night. " When one has no real life one has to live on illusions ": and both Vanya and the Doctor find their illusions in drink. Yet it is Sonya, without this burning solace for unhappiness, who suddenly radiates a queer, inexplicable joy in the midst of her frustrated love. " He has said nothing to me . . . His soul and his heart are still shut away from me, but why do I feel so happy ?" This strange, fleeting happiness, piercing through grief like a shaft of sunlight, is more moving than all Vanya's self-pity and Astrov's caged bitterness and regret. Nothing shows more clearly Tchehov's insight into the vagaries of misery and the human heart ; Sonya's cry rings with truth.

The crackling explosives of the next scene are the combustible residue of the night's storm ; tragedy brushes shoulders with absurdity, and Uncle Vanya's entrance with the autumn roses— " exquisite, mournful roses "—to find Yelena in the Doctor's arms is a moment like the still centre of a maelstrom. Then in the midst of the riot Marina's voice is heard above Sonya's choking sobs : " Never mind, child. The ganders will cackle and leave off . . . They will cackle and leave off . . . "; and the philosophy of age, which has seen so many crises break and pass like a summer tempest, carries us over quietly to the placid domesticity of the following scene.

The rage and murderous revolt are spent ; Waffles holds wool or chatters with the Nurse or strums his guitar by the fire ; the Professor and his disturbing wife take their departure ; the ringing sleigh-bells of the Doctor recede faintly into the distance ; Sonya fills the inkstand and she and Uncle Vanya begin to work once again at the accounts, work which only for them can dull the pain of living.

> We shall live again in the old way, as we used to. We shall have breakfast at eight, dinner at one, and sit down to supper in the evening ; everything as it should be, like other people . . . like Christians !

The old Nurse's complacent conservatism brings a murmured contentment into the scene ; everything settles down to normal, Sonya breathes her longing and her faith, only Vanya's involuntary stab of agony—" My child, how my heart aches ! Oh, if only you knew how my heart aches !"—breaks through the new calm and clings dimly to the past.

It is impossible to praise too highly the performances of the Old Vic company in this play. Sybil Thorndike's old Nurse, gnarled and luminous as a picture by Rembrandt ; Harcourt Williams's portentous, tetchy, yet at moments pathetic Professor ; Margaret Leighton's languid Yelena ; Joyce Redman's firm and deeply touching Sonya ; George Relph's drab, flat-chested, good-hearted Waffles—all were finely contrasted characters drawn from life. Ralph Richardson, playing with a perfect balance of sensitive-ness and humour, brilliantly delineated the seediness, ridiculousness, suffering and rebellion of Uncle Vanya. His scene with the autumn roses was most moving. As Astrov Laurence Olivier was also admirable, conceiving an eccentric character with quiet restraint and without flamboyance. This is the character through whom, as in so many of his plays, Tchehov expresses his peculiar nostalgia, not for the past, but for the future, and Olivier caught both the vision and the man's inherent and passionate urge for living.

The Old Vic Company continued to play this repertoire at the New Theatre until 14 April, 1945. They then toured the English provinces for four weeks and for six further weeks, under the auspices of E.N.S.A., played on the continent, where they visited Antwerp, Ghent, Hamburg and Paris. In Paris they played to the Forces for one week at the Marigny Theatre, under E.N.S.A., and then moved to the Comédie Française, where their performances were seen by the critics and general public in a special fortnight's season. The repertoire on this continental tour comprised *Peer Gynt, Richard III* and *Arms and the Man*. Both productions and acting evoked high critical praise and helped greatly to increase the Old Vic's reputation abroad as the highest representative of English classical performance.

HENRY IV, PARTS I AND II

THE company returned to London for their first post-war season on 26 September, 1945, with a new repertoire consisting of *Henry IV, Parts I and II*, Sophocles' *Oedipus Rex* in the translation of W. B. Yeats and Sheridan's *The Critic*. The last two plays appeared in the same bill, and *Uncle Vanya* was revived on 13 November.

Henry IV, Part I was the opening play and *Part II* followed on 3 October. There was a special interest in this concurrent production of the two parts of *Henry IV*, for it is rare to have the Shakespearean histories played in such a way that the audience may follow the historical events and get thoroughly to know the characters in all their facets. In the case of *Henry IV* the method is particularly relevant, for the two parts, as Dover Wilson has rightly insisted, constitute one whole play rather than two separate ones, and only the fact that each part is as long as the average full-length play necessitates the division in stage performance. It is only in juxtaposition that one can fully appreciate the richness of Falstaff and the development of the relationship of the King and Prince Hal.

One of the values of the Old Vic performances was in their establishment of this royal relationship, and this was greatly assisted by Nicholas Hannen's sympathetic and very human interpretation of the King. So often a regal cipher, Henry IV became in the actor's hands something much more : a king anxious indeed to preserve peace in his kingdom, but also a father saddened by the dissolute fecklessness of his heir and eldest son, trying with patience and an almost wistful disappointment to bridge the rift. The reconciliation at the King's death-bed in *Part I I* could be doubly appreciated with these earlier contacts fresh in our minds.

Another scene in *Part I I* that, small though it is, gained immensely in poignancy by this juxtaposition of the two plays, was that in which we see the sad little trio of Northumberland, his wife and daughter-in-law heavy with the news of Hotspur's death. Instinctively our minds were carried back to the charming badinage of Lady Percy and her husband in *Part I*, to Hotspur's own radiant vitality and eager, fire-consumed impatience. Margaret Leighton as the bereaved young wife and Miles Malleson—a superb " comic " with a wider range than many had suspected—as Northumberland played this little scene with simple pathos.

John Burrell's production, and the acting generally, gave the historical tapestry of these plays a living animation that was unusually refreshing. Roger Furse's costumes had the right Froissart quality, though Gower Parks's scenery gave a rather darkening and sometimes clashing note to the picture. *Part I I*, on the whole, seemed to me better produced than *Part I*, where there was overmuch delay through shifting scenery and where the company tended to lack " voice " for the copper-plated cadenzas of Shakespeare's verse. The notable exception to this criticism was Laurence Olivier, who as Hotspur revealed less a voice than a full instrumentation of vibrancy and colour. The rhetoric poured out like molten silver, and that anomaly that caused Shakespeare to give to this fire-eater and ballad-derider the brightest poetry in the play was drowned by the actor in a raging music.

Yet the man lived too : pricking that airy bubble, Glendower, with his wit and scepticism, " drunk with choler ", braving the " perilous gash " of Northumberland's sickness with his indomitable and resilient temper—

> I rather of his absence make this use—
> It lends a lustre and more great opinion,
> A larger dare to our great enterprise.
> Than if the Earl were here.

Olivier's warm, quick-blooded, exceptionally human performance gave the character a new charm, and the slight stammer of a man whose eager spirit chafes against the chains of mere words. Lady Percy's—

> And speaking thick, which nature made his blemish,
> Became the accents of the valiant—

was apparently his clue to this slight tussle with a recalcitrant " w " that characterised this Hotspur's speech. Most movingly he died in such a tussle.

> No Percy, thou art dust
> And food for—

" For worms, brave Percy " supplies the watching Prince, looking at the limp young body at his feet.

Esmé Percy was a Hotspur as bell-toned as this, but no actor other than Olivier can have given a more bitter and dying frustration to the words " O Harry, thou hast robbed me of my youth ". This was a fine performance because one was throughout totally unconscious of the actor. The mannerisms and appearance were those of a born soldier and a mediæval soldier at that ; square of shoulder and jowl, rough of cheek, the movements springy, firm, vibrant with nervous energy. This sinking of identity was the more remarkable since it was achieved with the minimum of make-up.

Ralph Richardson's Falstaff, a grand buffoon and rapscallion in *Part I*, proceeded in *Part I I* to a still richer understanding which could catch the sombre illumination of " Do not bid me remember mine end " and suggest, as Falstaffs do rarely, the attraction of the man for the Prince as well as the considerable brain behind the wit. This was a metamorphosis assisted by make-up but by no means entirely dependent on it : for Richardson's greatness—and I think the word is justifiable—in the part was a greatness of spirit that transcended the mere hulk of flesh. The portrait had a glow on it, matching the glow of Shakespeare's metaphor, and illuminating the outrageous charm of the man that bursts through the rolls of fat and reprobacy as his rotund paunch threatens to burst through his belt and doublet.

> Poor Jack, farewell !
> I could have better spared a better man—

is the Prince's brief but telling epitaph over the knight's supposed corpse at Shrewsbury, and Mistress Quickly and the ragamuffin Doll succumb to his magic like butter before a fire.

There is a huge *enjoyment* in the man that is, at moments, irresistible, and Richardson magnificently caught this relish of life, this bursting youthfulness of spirit that gives a boyish mischief to Falstaff's subterfuges and glib explanations, and puts a ring of truth into his " You that are old consider not the capacities of us that are young ". For in spite of his ripe corruption of senses and physique, his overflowing wit and agile mind, Falstaff has never completely grown up. He attacks life like a greedy child confronted with a rich plum pie, and his huge digestion assimilates both fruit and stones and never ceases to crave for a second helping. His fear of death is a child's fear, touched for the first time with the shadow of the inevitable but putting the thought behind him as something remote yet strangely disturbing. His feeling of attraction for the Prince is, I think, genuine : " yet I am bewitched with the rogue's company ". The shock of Hal's rejection has a spiritual as well as a material basis. All this Richardson beautifully realised : the man crumbled in spirit, though his " Master Shallow, I owe you a thousand pounds " was not without dignity. The performance in these last moments looked forward to the death of Falstaff in *Henry V*, and one could really believe in that death as the death of a broken heart.

Michael Warre was a light-weight Prince Hal ; one missed the royal dazzle and the " mad wag " of Falstaff's description. The actor was intelligent and sympathetic with the King, but inclined to superciliousness with his raffish companions, and although he played the battle scenes with all the nervous energy his slight physique allowed one simply did not believe in his defeat of this Hotspur. Harcourt Williams, bristling with daemonic eloquence, was the best Owen Glendower since Lewis Casson's lyric-intoxicated Prophet and Welsh Bard, and the taverners, headed by Sybil Thorndike as Mistress Quickly and Joyce Redman as an unglamorized Doll Tearsheet from the gutters of Southern Ireland, were abundantly alive. The rural accents suggested, however, any *locale* but Eastcheap.

As Shallow Laurence Olivier, magically transformed from the valiant Hotspur to this rustic " cheese-paring ", acted with a quiet and cheerful senility, and Miles Malleson as Silence flowered into song with riotous drollery. George Relph was an excellent Worcester, though he lacked the voice for Pistol, and Nicolette Bernard—

a young actress of great promise—brought a sly and vivid impudence to the Chorus of Rumour.

OEDIPUS : THE CRITIC

T H E double bill of Sophocles' *Oedipus Rex* and Sheridan's *The Critic*, produced respectively by Michel St. Denis and Miles Malleson, was presented at the New Theatre on 18 October, 1945. It proved one of the most brilliant and exciting first nights in Old Vic history, and a triumph for Laurence Olivier both in the capacity of tragedian and comedian.

In Oedipus Olivier tackled a part of heroic dimensions, a part which tests to the uttermost the actor's tragic resource and power to suggest a noble character driven and consumed by the dark fires of his own destiny. This figure marked down by fate for its own inscrutable purposes is one of the great imaginative creations of dramatic literature, and as an acting part belongs to the same mould as Lear, Othello and Macbeth. Yet in the twenty-three centuries since the play was written the number of actors of whom we have record in the part is astonishingly low. The earliest was Polus, who played Oedipus within fifty years of the author's death and whose stamina was such that history tells us he was able, at the age of seventy, to act a leading part in eight tragedies within the space of four days. The American actor Herman Vezin played the less exacting sequel, *Oedipus Coloneus*, in 1876, and the French actor Mounet-Sully, inspired by a famous production at Harvard in 1881, acted Oedipus Rex later the same year.

The only previous English actor in the part, outside amateur productions, appears to have been Sir John Martin-Harvey, who played in the production by Max Reinhardt at Covent Garden in 1912 and again at the same theatre in 1936. Those who remembered Sully seem to have accepted Harvey's without question as the greater performance. He played, wrote H. W. Massingham in " The Nation " of 20 January, 1912, " with a beauty and depth of feeling, and with a power to make his face and body and voice express the most shattering experiences of the heart, for many years unsurpassed on the English stage. His representation places him in the line of the great actors of the past, and in the first rank of his living contemporaries. His " Oedipus " is studied, but not over-studied. He has chosen its great moments with fine thought and selection. I do not believe that the modern stage yields a more thrilling effect than the freezing of Mr. Harvey's face into the likeness of the Greek tragic mask as there creeps upon it his first vision of the sin which God may have meant to lay upon him . . ."

This was before I was born, but the performance I saw the actor give twenty-five years later, when he must have been approaching Polus's hale seventy, did not seem to me appreciably less fine in its pathos and its power than this earlier description suggested. Certainly, from the receding elipse of the Covent Garden Grand Tier, it retained its beauty of mask and matchless melody of voice.

But *Oedipus* is more than a receptacle for great acting : it is also a great play. Its dramatic construction is unequalled in Greek tragedy, and anticipates Ibsen in its power to pile revelation on revelation until the whole tragic fabric of the past is laid bare and rended by a new anguish. Modern dramatic criticism, which over-emphasises Oedipus's lack of volition in a sin to which he is foredoomed by fate, seems to me to miss the fact that the characters are still vividly drawn and bear a certain moral responsibility and guilt. Jocasta's dark sacrifice of her child—an act of fear for which, in her shame, she bitterly attacks all priesthood and superstition—Oedipus's passionate temper which roused him to murder if not to intentional parricide, and to condemn the loyal Creon without a hearing, are paid in blood. It is not for nothing that Aristotle named Oedipus as the ideal tragic hero, since with greatness and nobility of character he combined defects of temper and justice that helped to precipitate his own doom.

This human aspect of the tragedy was dramatically realised in the Old Vic production ; partly owing to some very fine acting which presented the characters as living people of real variety and suffering, and partly to W. B. Yeats's prose dialogue, which brought a quickened realism to the clash of personality. Yeats's condensed version lacks the rhythmic pulsation of the Gilbert Murray translation used by Harvey ; but its spare firm contours have the beauty of sculptured bronze. It matches the Sophoclean starkness, which is very different from Euripides' supple lyricism, and the " placing " of words is strong and serene.

> Children, descendants of old Cadmus, why do you come
> before me, why do you carry the branches of suppliants, while
> the city smokes with incense and murmurs with prayer and
> lamentation ? . .

Oedipus's opening speech sets the measure and pattern, and beautifully Olivier spoke it.

The production as well as the acting heightened the drama of the story, and divided the emphasis clearly between the Olympian and the humane. The suppliants in the first scene, in loop'd and window'd raggedness, were the living poor, and the old man who led them, movingly spoken by Harcourt Williams, had something of the protective tenderness of an East End pastor. By setting the play back in time to the more primitive Greece of which Sophocles wrote, Michel St. Denis, aided by a setting of extraordinary beauty and fatality by John Piper, at the same time achieved a sense of darkening and malignant destiny which was lost in Reinhardt's more austerely classical production. Antony Hopkins's music, used sparely but with haunting effect, intensified the fate-charged atmosphere. I cannot imagine the Chorus of Priests, in which Yeats soars into beating verse, more effectively yet simply produced or finely spoken. It was right, I am sure, to stylise the costumes here and reduce the choreographic movement to a bare minimum. The voices, very rarely punctuated by music, provided all the effect necessary, and one was spared the embarrassments of Reinhardt's Dalcroze Eurythmics. There were no impressive crowd scenes, as at Covent Garden, but the drama broke through clean, and Marie-Hélène Dasté's costumes, striking against Piper's chalk-white pillars and lowering sky, provided all the needful colour.

" Mr. Olivier's Oedipus is one of those performances in which blood and electricity are somehow mixed. It pulls down lightning from the sky ". Thus wrote the American critic, John Mason Brown, of Olivier's later performance in New York, and no power on earth is going to get me to compete with this, especially in the sagging inspiration at the end of a long book. Suffice it merely to record that Olivier's noble and flashing performance placed him on the highest pinnacle among modern tragic actors, that he magnificently marked (not with Harvey's frozen Greek mask but with a fey terror of his own) Oedipus's first prevision of his doom, and that the cry that was torn from him when he finally realised the truth will echo for ever in the ears of all who heard it. Such a cry must have mounted heaven and seared the heart of Apollo.

In the final scenes only, perhaps, he lacked Harvey's pathos : anguish runs through this actor's veins like fire, but he just missed the exquisite tenderness and sensitivity with which Harvey as the blinded Oedipus illumined the meeting and parting with his children. Murray's translation was here, however, more helpful to the actor than that of Yeats.

> Children ! Where are ye ? Hither ; come to these
> Arms of your .... brother—

Of the poignant significance of that tiny pause and hesitation Harvey made full and moving use.

As Jocasta Sybil Thorndike was hampered by a heavily jewelled mauve costume which was Mlle. Dasté's one error in taste as a designer. There was more mother than wife in this Jocasta, but Sophocles himself has suggested with remarkable insight the maternal protectiveness in the Queen's love for Oepidus, and her intensely feminine logic which puts far greater importance on his happiness than on the satisfaction of his urge for truth. Sybil Thorndike finely showed the agony behind Jocasta's desperate last attempts to save Oedipus from the revelation which she realises is about to break on him. Her own mute realisation a few moments earlier had been horrifically mimed, and in the scene in which she brought wreaths to placate the angry gods—" for now we are all afraid, seeing him afraid "—her foreboding ran like a cold current of fear through her trembling hands into the hearts of those who watched.

This actress is a great tragedian in Greek drama because she has the courage which these plays need from the actor—the courage to let out the emotional stops. According to the debased standards of West-End acting this is not " done " and it makes some people uncomfortable. But there is only need for discomfort if the feeling let loose is not genuine. The grief that wells up in Sybil Thorndike at such moments is real, not simulated, grief, and her Jocasta— small though the part is beside the towering figure of Oedipus— gave us full measure of it.

Ralph Richardson's Tiresias, the blind Seer, Blake-like in dimensions and imaginative conception, had a commanding dignity and a biting wrath. His clash with the King " lifted " the play to a new level of tension, and the quivering control of his denunciation awed even this Oedipus. In perfection of quality if not in scale, Richardson has never surpassed this performance : his personality was completely submerged in the part. Nicholas Hannen as the Chorus Leader had both humanity and vigour, and Miles Malleson (in a welcome touch of not-too-light relief) and

LXI.—*Peer Gynt* (1944).   Ralph Richardson as Peer and Sybil
Thorndike as Åse.

LXII.—*Peer Gynt* (1944). Scene of Peer and the Green Woman :
Ralph Richardson and Margaret Leighton.

LXIII.—*Uncle Vanya* (1945). Setting for Act I by Tanya Moiseiwitsch.

LXIV.—*Henry IV Part I* (1945). Laurence Olivier as Hotspur and
Margaret Leighton as Lady Percy.

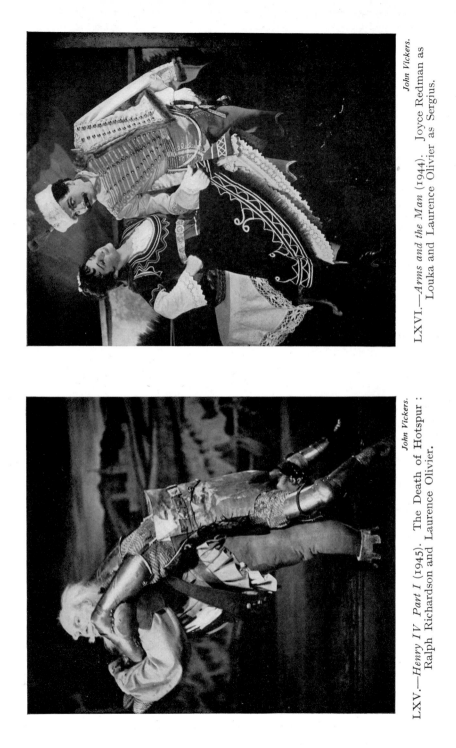

LXVI.—*Arms and the Man* (1944). Joyce Redman as Louka and Laurence Olivier as Sergius.

LXV.—*Henry IV Part I* (1945). The Death of Hotspur : Ralph Richardson and Laurence Olivier.

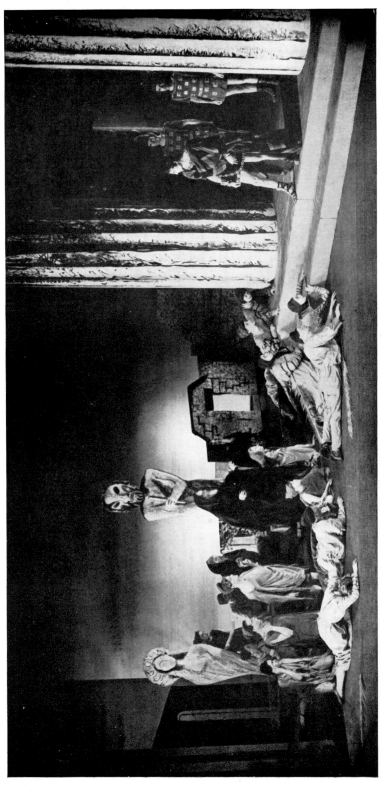

John Vickers.

LXVII.—*Oedipus* (1945). Scene with the Suppliants. *Décor* by John Piper.

John Vickers

LXVIII.—*Cyrano de Bergerac* (1946). Balcony Scene : Margaret
Leighton as Roxane, Michael Warre as Christian and Ralph Richardson
as Cyrano.

LXIX.—*King Lear* (1946). The Death of Cordelia : Laurence
Olivier as Lear and Joyce Redman as Cordelia.

LXX.—*Richard III* (1944). Joyce Redman as Anne and Laurence
Olivier as Richard.

LXXI.—*The Alchemist* (1947). Joyce Redman as Doll Common and
Nicholas Hannen as Sir Epicure Mammon.

George Relph gave beautifully marked character sketches as the Messenger from Corinth and the old Herdsman who reluctantly reveals to Oedipus the full horror of his doom. Michael Warre delivered the description of Jocasta's death with sympathetic restraint, and George Curzon caught Creon's phlegmatic and rationalistic temper although he needed, I think, more heat in the quarrel.

Sheridan's long-drawn-out theatrical joke, *The Critic*, seemed an odd choice to follow *Oedipus*, for it could not fail in some sense to quench the flame of the preceding tragedy. For the actors, however, and for those of the audience for whom the emotional strain of *Oedipus* was too intolerable to bear without relief, it provided a welcome foil. Miles Malleson's production was in its own class as brilliant as that of St. Denis ; a puff-pastry frothy with the cream of invention, and ending in a riotous sea-battle during which the former King of Thebes (now Mr. Puff) hurtled on a ground-row, with an expression more of astonishment than alarm, into the " flies." Tanya Moiseiwitch, always a superb decorator, yielded here to the intoxicating possibilities of her subject, and her Spanish Armada tossed corkily on the waves in a delirious conjunction of art and mechanism.

Not all Malleson's ingenuity with " business " and scissors could, however, quite mask the fact that Sheridan's play, beginning as stylish high comedy and tumbling half-way into farce, never " jells " into a complete whole. The joke of theatrical burlesque (of a style of drama no longer current) becomes dangerously strained at moments, though with the company brilliantly led by Ralph Richardson as the most profound of thoughtful Burleighs, Nicolette Bernard as Tilburina " stark mad in white satin," and Joyce Redman as a hilariously bedraggled and flirtatious Confidante, the thin patches were very smoothly darned over if not invisibly mended.

The wit of the first scenes in Dangle's house is of altogether a finer cut, and its edge remains as keen to-day as when it was written. " The number of those who undergo the fatigue of judging for themselves " is still " very small indeed ", and Puff to-day would find his natural métier in the world of the film " blurb ". One speech only has lost for ever its original savour and impudence :

N

> Mr. Dodd was astonishingly great in the character of
> Sir Harry. That universal and judicious actor, Mr. Palmer,
> perhaps never appeared to more advantage than in the colonel ;
> —but it is not in the power of language to do justice to Mr.
> King !

Not even an Olivier can hope to recapture the roar that must have greeted this speech at the first performance—when the hearers, Dangle and Sneer, were played by the actors Dodd and Palmer, and the speaker, Puff (living here dazzlingly up to his name !) was the redoubtable Mr. King himself !

Olivier was a bustling Mr. Puff of tip-tilted nose and appealing charm : a harassed bubble of ingenuousness and distress that bobbed about on the play's surface like a buoy in a troubled sea. His rattling volubility, and his trick of throwing snuff into the air and catching it in his nostrils, kept the comedy spinning. Altogether this performance, coupled with that of Oedipus, showed the actor to have a nice versatility in temperament and false noses, as well as the stamina of Hercules (on certain days the two plays were presented both at the matinée and evening performance— and apart from the emotional strain of *Oedipus* Olivier was on his feet in both plays almost throughout).

Miles Malleson himself, always an entrancing droll, made Plagiary a fretful porcupine of tetchy irritability, George Relph was an endearing Dangle and George Curzon a polished Sneer. One performance only in these first scenes lacked maturity of style and was difficult to hear, but Tanya Moiseiwitsch's setting and costumes had a spacious eighteenth-century air.

Oedipus and *The Critic* were performed on the last night of the London season on 29 April, 1946, and with *Uncle Vanya* and both parts of *Henry I V* formed the repertoire of the first Old Vic season in New York, which opened with *Henry I V Part I* on 6 May. Neither Sybil Thorndike nor Harcourt Williams appeared in New York, where Ena Burrill played all Dame Sybil's parts ; Harcourt Williams's parts of the Professor in *Uncle Vanya* and Glendower in *Henry I V* were played respectively by Nicholas Hannen and Harry Andrews. The company played at the Century Theatre for a period of six weeks, and once again foreign critical opinion set the seal on the Old Vic's growing reputation as an outstanding force in the English theatre. In addition to the repertoire presented at the Century Theatre the company also presented, by special request, broadcast versions of *Peer Gynt* and *Richard III*. These were coast-to-coast broadcasts sponsored by the Columbia Broadcasting System, and each continued without interruption for an hour and a half, an unusually long period for an individual programme to last under America's broadcasting system. The company were fortunately able to retain the services of their own producer, John Burrell (who had had considerable previous experience of broadcast production) and also their director of music, Herbert Menges, in these programmes, which as a result preserved an authentic Old Vic style of presentation. These broadcasts enabled the company's work to reach an infinitely wider American public than was possible through their New York performances and they aroused, in fact, nation-wide interest and enthusiasm.

KING LEAR

T H E third Old Vic season at the New Theatre under the direction of Burrell, Olivier and Richardson commenced on 24 September, 1946. *King Lear* was the chosen play, with Laurence Olivier as producer and leading actor. The advance booking for this production was phenomenal and several hundred playgoers failed in their application for First Night seats.

Olivier's production of this play was not of the same quality as his acting, and perhaps this was inevitable ; the interpretation of the part of Lear puts an almost Herculean strain on the actor's intellectual and emotional resources, and it is hardly possible that the actor labouring under such a strain, even in the stages of preliminary study, could spare an equally high degree of dramatic intuition on the staging of the play as a whole. Olivier's production was better than that of Donald Wolfit, with its rather shabby Stonehenge and dummy courtiers, but nowhere did it match the pictorial effect of Komisarjevsky's production at Stratford-on-Avon or the beauty, intellectual power and variety of pace and character of the unforgettable Granville-Barker staging at the Old Vic in 1940.

Roger Furse's piecemeal scenery against stormy skies was effective in the middle scenes, but the crazy coloured roofs and architecture of the opening scene cramped one's imagination, and there was too much masking of important figures by lesser ones.

This was particularly noticeable in the first scene, where one had no visual suggestion of Lear's arrogant and lonely isolation— an effect superbly achieved by Komisarjevsky, with his golden throne on a pile of steps etched against a vast open sky. In spite of the expressionistic scenery—the design was planned a little along the lines of that created by Furse for *The Skin of Our Teeth* and the ballet *Adam Zero*—there were long waits while scenery was noisily shifted, and the possibilities of what might, in some scenes, have become a good semi-permanent setting were not explored. The Saxon-Norman costumes somehow failed to achieve barbaric splendour or the living effect of the Bayeux tapestry ; the characters seemed confined rather than released by them, although the colour scheme was attractive—perhaps too pastel and " pretty " for this play's dark sublimities—and the use of amber paint on certain portions of scenery was effectively reminiscent of the romantic pigmentation of John Piper.

There was, however, one outstanding gain : the emphasis even before Lear's entrance on a Court well-used to the old King's sudden whims and passion for authority, and ready, not without amusement, to humour him—an impression fully corroborated by the actor when he appeared, and cast a critical and fussy eye over the dress and position of his guards. It is an interpretation that lightens the first scene but at the same time gives it a new and revealing plausibility ; and it added an endearing reality to Olivier's portrait which in imagination and pathos I would place close to that of Gielgud.

Like Gielgud, and unlike Wolfit, Olivier did not stress the senility of the character, but presented a royal octogenarian who had retained considerable elasticity and vigour of body and passion. The voice in rages and tempest had an awe-inspiring volume ; the thunder and lightning were in the King himself as well as in the stage effects, but Olivier also sensitively conveyed the spiritual regeneration of Lear's progress from tyranny to humane pity, and his scenes with Gloucester at Dover and the Fool in the storm, hugging them to his breast like battered children, had extraordinary pathos. So, too, had his surprisingly gentle " No more of that, I have noted it well " at the Courtier's comment on the Fool's pining since Cordelia went into France : one remembered at that moment Lear's blank, uncomprehending face at Cordelia's " Nothing ", when the tenderness that had come into the old tyrant's expression and voice as he turned to his most-loved child seemed stunned into insensibility before the pain of the blow penetrated to his brain and heart. Later one caught the same strain again—it had a " dying fall "—as Lear listened to the Fool's bitter, half-timid hints of this same dark folly of the banishment of Cordelia. They were no more than pale flashes across the rough volcanic surface of the King's authority and temper, but they showed the long-suppressed capacity for affection and sweetness that was to flower later in suffering and adversity.

It was in these moments, predestinate of pain to come, that one read Lear's real age : the bastions of virility crumbled, and the face was the face of an old man, tired and wistful for support. Behind the wall of pomp and imperious will one glimpsed the agony and humility of the Lear to come : the Lear who, with bare feet dangling, breathed his mad sad philosophy to the blinded Gloucester, succoured the shivering Tom with a fatherly care, held in his arms the dead Cordelia and raised that limp body like a sawdust doll, in anguish, to the sky.

Neither in the Tent scene with Cordelia nor in the final scene did Olivier quite equal Gielgud's tender pathos, although his thumping of Cordelia's heart with his hand at " She's dead as earth " had a terrible imagination. Nor—perhaps because of the humorous touch with its different dramatic values—did he always attain the same majesty and storm-battered spiritual grandeur. His greatest moment was in Lear's distraction before the storm, when, baited to a fury in which Heaven and Hell were inextricably mixed, his mind rocked and cracked under the strain of giving utterance to his grief—

> I will have such revenges on you both
> That all the world shall—I will do such things,—
> What they are yet I know not ; but they shall be
> The terrors of the earth.

Olivier's " terrors of the earth " was Aeschylean ; the sheer torrential sound of it swept across the senses like Niagara, but in all this raving music one could still hear the tortured cry of a drowning man. The sudden drop of the voice at " O Fool, I shall go mad ", the clutching at the jester for support and wild, broken flight from the scene wrung the heart as no other Lear at this moment has succeeded in doing. Olivier made his chief note of coming madness here, just as Gielgud selected the earlier " O let me not be mad, not mad, sweet heaven ". Olivier's kneeling in prayer at this line was less moving than Gielgud's simple gesture of lifting his hand to his temple.

In the whole scene with Regan that culminated in this flight into the storm the variety of mood was virtuistic. One felt the blinding echo of that rage with which Lear in the first scene had flung the coronet to the floor for Cornwall and Albany to part between them. His groping towards Regan had, in contrast, a melting beauty, and there was real effort, here, to subdue his rash impatience, to make concessions, to try and understand. But always the rage could be lashed at a touch ; Lear's temperance in adversity was still to come, and his cry at the renewed sight of Kent in the stocks—

> Death on my state ! Wherefore should he sit here !—

was like unleashed thunder. A great and moving performance, and companion-piece to the actor's Oedipus and Coriolanus.

Next to Olivier's Lear I would place Margaret Leighton's Regan and Alec Guinness's Fool. The languorous pure Saxon beauty of this Regan, a model for Rossetti, made the cruelty and sensuality the more horrifying : it was like honey turned rancid. After the blinding of Gloucester, when in her panting triumph one sensed a sadistic satisfaction, and in the choking agony of her death, the actress was terrifying. Guinness's Fool, with a clown's white face and wistful eyes, is the best I have ever seen. His dejection at a joke anticipated—" Yes, indeed : thou wouldst make a good Fool "—was a perfect professional touch : the drop of the droll, alert little creature's face aroused that kind of laugh that proceeds from a lump in the throat. Our last glimpse of him, his patter stilled, patiently holding out a tattered sleeve in response to Lear's ' draw the curtains ", was one of fey and touching devotion.

Pamela Brown's Goneril was as bold in evil as her sister was soft and indolent. There is iron and fire in this daughter of Lear, and Oswald's " Thy sister is the better soldier " had its justification at this Goneril's flashing—

> Where's thy drum ?
> France spreads his banners in our noiseless land.

Only once did the actress show fear : Lear's curse visibly shook her, but at the end she faced Albany's accusation with a white-hot courage. She had a different kind of sensuality to her sister's, but not the less marked, and her smile at the news of Gloucester's blinding and at her sister's death was the smile, slant-eyed, of a Javanese fiend.

Joyce Redman's Cordelia had that sunlit, golden joyousness one feels behind all this actress's work—even behind the mist of her tears. For me it had great charm, and her littleness made the effect of Lear's carrying her dead body deeply pathetic. Rightly, she gave the character a touch of her father's ingenuous pride but in doing so she allowed Cordelia's voice, in the first scene particularly, to become too strident, and Lear's—

> Her voice was ever soft,
> Gentle and low,—an excellent thing in woman—

could not touch us as it should.

Nicholas Hannen's gruff, loyal Kent had a touch of empurpled anger that in his rebuke of Lear clashed against the old King's own. It was anger based on love, and admirably pointed Kent's deep admiration of the King which cannot brook an action so unworthy of his idol. Michael Warre was more successful as Mad Tom than as Edgar, but Peter Copley, though he obviously understood the humour and attack the part required, was temperamentally miscast as Edmund, whose bastard's " fierce quality " needs more Renaissance flash and vigour than he could give it. George Relph's Gloucester also had intelligence but seemed hardly the man to get " sport " out of Edmund's making, let alone boast about it afterwards. The difference shown by these two performances was the age-old acting one between the ability to understand a part and the temperamental and physical assets required to translate that understanding into action. Harry Andrews in the smaller and less exacting part of Cornwall, on the other hand, had both the right quality and façade for the part. The music of Alan Rawsthorne had drama and quality, and was of great assistance to the atmosphere of the production.

The company was invited to represent the British Theatre at the UNESCO Conference in Paris, and *King Lear* was played at the Théâtre des Champs-Élysées during the last week in November. The New Theatre was occupied during this period by a production of Hardy's *Tess of the D' Urbervilles* by the Bristol Old Vic company, with Wendy Hiller and William Devlin in the leading parts. The normal Old Vic London repertory was resumed the following week.

AN INSPECTOR CALLS

J. B. PRIESTLEY'S *An Inspector Calls*, added to the repertory on 1 October, 1946, was the first new play to be produced by the Old Vic in London for a number of years. The play had had its first production in Moscow, and the New Theatre performances followed an initial week's run at Manchester before the London season opened.

I find some difficulty in writing of this play since it made a far greater impression on me the second time I saw it than the first. This was, I think, a question of technique. It is the kind of play of which primary elements, one feels, should be suspense and surprise ; but Priestley, in his story of a strange " inspector " who, in his enquiries, reveals the damning influence of a whole family in an unfortunate girl's suicide, lays his cards too quickly and too obviously on the table. Technically the device is transparent almost from the beginning, and even the trick double dénouement could be anticipated by those who remembered their Pirandello and Mr. Priestley's own earlier experiments in time.

This does not mean that the constructional idea was not clever ; but the over-forcing of certain points by repetition, and the too bare-faced coincidence by which every one of the same family, one could see, was to be implicated in the suicide, detracted from the play's reality and dramatic " bite ". The material for a one-Act play was, in fact, dragged out to three-Act dimensions, and neither the technique nor characterisation was of the quality one remembers in the author's *Time and the Conways, I Have Been Here Before* and *Eden End*.

The play was set in the year 1912 : an old trick of this author's who knows well the moving effect that references to the unsinkability of the " Titanic " and the remoteness of war, the characters' confidence in a long full life of peace and prosperity, may have for us with our greater and more bitter knowledge. On seeing the play a second time, when one already knew what was coming and was no longer perturbed by one's ability to anticipate it, one was able to appreciate more fully the play's social, moral and moving central idea, as well as certain astute touches of acting. This selfish rich trading-class family of the Midlands may be overdrawn, but it represents clearly enough a certain trend of social blindness —that lack of imagination and communal feeling, rather than actual wickedness—that makes tragedies like the death of the girl in this play possible.

The production as well as the acting finely reinforced this truth : these were real, respectable, self-satisfied people, embarrassed by revelations that brutally break through their social " taboos ", stirred momentarily in conscience or self-deceptively clinging to their own moral complacency, according to their inward nature. The group during the prospective son-in-law's confession of an indiscretion—the older couple with bowed heads, withdrawn, disapproving, not daring to look up—was natural and true. So was the way, the danger past, they reverted to their egoistic pursuit of big business and social respectability—though perhaps this was a little too instantaneous to be natural. The instincts were, however, too deeply ingrained to be moved by the force of a shock or outward impression. Younger minds are more impressionable, and Priestley was right to show the younger generation, the brother and sister with an inherent decency still unhardened by time, yielding to the call on their sympathy while their parents revert to their moral blind alley of snobbery and self-interest.

All of the performances in this play were good and two of them were to my mind of quite exceptional quality. Marion Spencer as the mother brought to her part a poise and distinction not seen on our stage since the death of Marie Tempest. Every movement of those complacently folded hands, every quick glance of awareness or hidden fear, was superbly timed. The woman was real in her selfish refusal to face the truth about herself, and real, too, in her genuine love for her son. The breaking down of her control— from icy dignity to a slow, troubled anxiety and finally near-hysteria—was brilliantly shown. Two moments of the performance stand out vividly : the disturbed recognition in her face at the sight of a photograph shown her, and her cry " I don't believe it !", stabbing in its sudden anguish, at the revelation of her son's guilt.

Alec Guinness as the weak son had a nervous restlessness which was in dramatic contrast to this aristocratic calm. There was fecklessness in the pose and movements, dissoluteness in the mouth, irresolution in the fingers plucking at a tablecloth or drumming on a glass ; but still in the fine lines of this thin, drawn face there lurked sensitivity, dry humour, possible charm, and the eyes were wide and intelligent. This is an actor who can be expressive with his back to the audience, and at moments he made the boy's

remorse and helplessness moving. Both he and Margaret Leighton
as his sister emphasised in their make-up a blonde family likeness,
and their joining of hands at the last blow that destroys their
hopes was spontaneous and touching. Margaret Leighton portrayed
cleverly a frivolous and rather silly girl shocked into real feeling
and a sense of responsibility, and as the father Julien Mitchell
characterised " big business " ruthlessly but without exaggeration,
and without forgetting that such a man may have genuine feeling
where his own family are concerned.

Ralph Richardson played the Inspector with quiet authority,
a glint of irony and a flash of anger where it was needed. The
part does not, perhaps, make exorbitant demands on the actor but
it does need that quality of mind and personality that can command
the action and hint at something more than human integrity. It
was admirably played at the second performance I saw by an
understudy, Ewan Roberts, who acted with a reserved understanding, and an undercurrent of watchful anger, that I do not think
were bettered by Richardson himself. His voice was pleasant
and clear and his manner throughout—a rare quality in an understudy—polished, easy and dignified.

Basil Dean was the producer of this play and Kathleen Ankers's
period dining-room setting gave variety to the scene by showing
an extra portion of the room—adding a fireplace or bookcase—
at the beginning of each Act. The play never achieved great
popularity and it was withdrawn from the Old Vic repertoire
on 22 March, 1947.

CYRANO DE BERGERAC

T H E third play of the season, Rostand's *Cyrano de Bergerac*,
was produced on 24 October, 1946, and seemed to fit more naturally
into the Old Vic repertoire. Although a comparatively modern
play (it was first produced at the Théâtre de la Porte Sainte-
Martin in Paris on 28 December, 1897) it had the " ring " of a
theatre classic, and that form of imaginative stimulus that is
life-blood to the actor. Strip the play of Rostand's Alexandrine
couplets and Gallic music, and it still lives as romantic drama with
a vision behind it, and a play for a great actor to enkindle both
with his bodily expression and his beating mind.

Is Ralph Richardson a great actor ? I had never thought so until I saw his Falstaff, though I placed him high among the finest of our day. If anything, even more than Falstaff, were to convince me it would be his playing of the death scene in *Cyrano de Bergerac.* This had the pale flame of absolute genius ; the light was penetrating and unmistakable. The man was like a white blasted tree torn up by the roots, yet still miraculously upright, magnificent even in dissolution. In his slow entrance and descent down the steps one felt the figure of death beside him, guiding and sustaining him in a last mockery of life. His recital of the letter, without looking at it, had an immortal tenderness, and the death fall, back into the arms of his waiting friends, was like the sudden quenching of a lamp. I remember no such death scene in all my years of theatre-going.

But there is, of course, far more to Cyrano than a death. Until the end he abounds with life, a life not the less physically energetic because it is half of the intellect and the spirit. For Cyrano has that genius for living in which the composition of a poem and the craftsmanship of a duel are one in intensity and enjoyment : even his physical misfortune, about which this avaricious lover of beauty has an abnormal sensitivity, cannot blunt the edge of his wit : indeed it whets it. Montague refers to Coquelin's " passion of joy in the thought of the character acted " and this passion of joy was what must have made his Cyrano memorable. It was a quality in which Richardson's performance was, in the first scenes, lacking. He tended to underplay and to underspeak the man's tingling robust vitality, and one missed the sweep and glory with which, for instance, Fred Terry, blazing charm and sunlight and a ringing vocal music, would leap on to a table and flash a romantic blade. Our modern actors have, perhaps, lost the knack of flamboyance. Terry and Martin Harvey in the theatre, and the elder Fairbanks in the cinema, were the last to possess it instinctively, but it is a quality that Cyrano, who is at least half D'Artagnan and " Rat " Reresby and Henry of Navarre, requires in the highest degree. It must not merely be possessed by the actor, it must be brandished like a sword, and Richardson's sword in this metaphorical sense never seemed to me more than half way out of its scabbard.

Where he scored was in the pathos that looms always behind the mask of the crack-brain duellist and the clown. All the moments of tenderness and nostalgia were exquisitely played,

and with an absolute understanding of the effect of physical stillness broken only by the simplest gesture, a fractional turn of the
head or flick of the finger. His intolerable suspense and incredulous
hope when Roxane first talks of the unnamed man she loves was
conveyed almost without motion ; the face revealed all. His
fading expression— " All gone "—when he heard of Christian's
death, and knew he could never now tell Roxane the truth, was
unutterably moving. From that round disfigured countenance
with the questioning witty eyebrow one saw the humour and eager
passion slowly drain right out, leaving it blank, sad-eyed and
desolate, like the face of a deserted child. The actor has not
the voice for the great scene below Roxane's balcony but he had
the feeling for it, and the magic flowed in spirit if not in actual
beauty of sound. One never doubted Cyrano's brain, his wit,
or his strange, lonely, magniloquent and love-tortured soul.

It is as impossible to convey Rostand's quality as a poet on the
English stage as it is to convey that of Shakespeare through a
foreign translation. This does not, to my mind, mean that the
great classics of each nation must not be translated and played
abroad ; the drama of every nation would be less rich without
this free interchange of material and ideas, and the theatre audience
infinitely more narrow in outlook. I do not therefore agree with
those critics who damned this revival on the grounds that it did
not and could not reproduce the full flavour and metre of Rostand's
verse ; nor do I agree that Brian Hooker's translation, originally
made for an American production of the play by Walter Hampden
in 1923, was totally unsatisfactory. It has clarity and lyrical fire,
and is excellently adapted to the stage, although a certain amount
of the lyricism was lost through " cutting " in Tyrone Guthrie's
production.

The point is that a play's heart beats not only through the
sound of the words but through the *sense*, and although we may
lose the intricate craftsmanship and music of the poet in translation
we need not lose either his intellectual force or his power of imaginative imagery. Only the bilingual can afford to resent a good
translation : and a vast proportion of playgoers (and even actors)
are not bilingual.

Except for this question of cutting Tyrone Guthrie's production
must rank among his finest achievements. No producer can so
vividly animate his stage pictures and breathe individual life

into his crowds, and the first scene of this play at the theatre in the Hôtel de Bourgogne reeked of period and the living atmosphere of the stage. If anything there was too much chatter and din, and the speeches of the principals tended to be drowned : but every character on the stage was alive, a real identity not sunk but stimulated in the flowing mass of the audience. Similarly in the scene of the seige of Arras these soldiers, sunk in sleep and hunger, had a raging individuality, and the smoke and noise and suffocating confusion of battle were at the end superbly realised. Guthrie has a quick eye for detail and the playing of two pages with a gun—at which they were silently and very quickly stopped by the alert Christian—was only one example of the way in which, by a piece of natural by-play quite outside the text, this producer can give humanity and freshness to the action.

Guthrie was helped throughout enormously by the designer, Tanya Moiseiwitsch, whose settings were a triumph of period atmosphere and theatrical skill. Her carved oak and darkening candlelight of the theatre scene, her windmill with battered wings against a leaden sky, and her beautiful last scene of falling leaves and opaque autumnal fog and melancholy, were among the highest creative achievements of recent stage design.

A remarkable small study of de Guiche once again established Alec Guinness as an actor of outstanding quality. Looking like a portrait by Van Dyck, he brought to the man an aristocrat's distinction, impeccable style, and the suave, lean-cheeked and subtle craft of a nephew of Richelieu. In the last scene the grey bitter lines of his face bespoke the ashen regretfulness of a man who feels, as he says, " a thousand small displeaures with himself ".

Margaret Leighton's Roxane was all moonlight and silver ; beautiful as Cyrano's dream but with a certain rippling amusement that softened the character's tendency to romantic vapidity. In a very long and accomplished cast Nicholas Hannen's Ragueneau, the poetic pastrycook, stood out in vigour and rich, almost Dickensian, geniality. Michael Warre, an actor of rather too much intelligence for that beautiful toy, Christian, achieved unexpected pathos when, silently and with hung head, he listened to Roxane's confession that it is Cyrano's soul that she loves. Cecil Winter as Le Bret and Harry Andrews as Carbon did sympathetic work as Cyrano's friends, and an actress named Sandra Jennings delivered

beautifully Sister Marthe's quiet line when the dying Cyrano says
she may pray for him—

> I did not wait
> For you to say I might.

The tiny part of the orange girl who offers Cyrano food was sensitively played by Pamela Brown at the beginning of the run and
by Joyce Redman—who gave it a winning brightness—later.

THE ALCHEMIST

I T had been arranged at the beginning of the season that *King
Lear* should finish at Christmas. Its last performance was given
on 4 January, 1947, at the height of its success, and Laurence
Olivier then temporarily left the company to work on his film of
Hamlet. The success with the public of *The Alchemist*, produced on
14 January, 1947, was therefore doubly welcome to the company,
since it encouraged the directors to feel that the Old Vic Theatre
Company might still draw in its new large audience without the
aid of Olivier's name and immense personal popularity.

The success of *The Alchemist* was in itself a surprise, for Ben
Jonson's satire of charlatanism is written in a period mixture
of slang, alchemist's clap-trap and classical allusion difficult for
modern ears to comprehend. The play lacks the universal brilliance
of *Volpone* and as character-comedy is inferior to *Every Man
in His Humour*, delightfully produced and acted at Stratford-on-
Avon for the Jonson tercentenary before the War. It has, however,
gusto and a toppling edifice of situation, and can capture laughs
enough if it is given the right pace in production and acting. In
this the Vic presentation might be accounted a success.

A composite setting by Morris Kestelman, more useful than
decorative, allowed one to see at once the street outside the Alchemist's house, the garden gate, the " privy " in which Dapper
was imprisoned, and (by the mere removal of the façade of the
house) a staircase, hall, study and a glimpse of the Alchemist's
laboratory (with stuffed crocodile and retorts) within. This
allowed ideal freedom of action, and the opening quarrel between
the rogues Face, Subtle and Doll Common was able to proceed
vigorously from garden to study by the mere disappearance of
the fourth wall as they battled their way indoors. The costumes,
deliberately placing the play a century later than Jonson intended,

were less successful. A programme note stated that this was
done because it was believed that the play's "comment on life
can apply to any period not excluding our own, so prone to gambling,
black-marketing, astrology, spiritualism, psycho-analysis and other
fields where charlatans practise cunningly, illegally, prosperously
and often amusingly". In theory, perhaps : but in practice
Jonson is more particular, and it is difficult to see the typically
Jacobean necromancies and superstitions of which he deals in any
period but his own. In any case, why leave in the widow Pliant's
objection to Spaniards—

> Never since eighty-eight could I abide them
> And that was some three years afore I was born, in truth ?

Even the average schoolgirl will place that "eighty-eight" as
1588, the year of the Spanish Armada, and the widow's age, in the
present costumes, as therefore something over a century !

Admittedly this is a minor harm : what matters is speed and
atmosphere, characterisation and high spirits, and these things
John Burrell's production had in good measure. All the sly
chicanery, the shabbiness of dress and mien, of the born charlatan
were in George Relph's Subtle, all the quick wit and bustling ingenuity of the professional decoy in Ralph Richardson's rapid metamor-
phoses as Face. The throat and ear-splitting words of the Alchemist's jargon rolled off their tongues with a practised duplicity,
and Richardson's butler turned knave twisted the plot neatly
into its final convolution.

Joyce Redman's Doll Common, first cousin to Shakespeare's
Doll Tearsheet but without her magic and transforming touch of
human feeling, was a slut and a termagant worthy such companions.
But could her bedraggled and raddled prettiness quite meet the
inspiration of Mammon's vision of her ?

> . . . . . but come forth
> And taste the air of palaces ; eat, drink
> The toils of empirics and their boasted practice ;
> Tincture of pearl, and coral, and gold and amber ;
> Be seen at feasts and triumphs ; have it ask'd
> What miracle is she ? set all the eyes
> Of court a-fire, like a burning glass,
> And work them into cinders, when the jewels
> Of twenty states adorn thee, and the light
> Strikes out the stars !

This bespeaks a royal and wanton beauty this brilliant little actress cannot encompass, but which I imagine Eileen Herlie in the Old Vic Liverpool production magnificently suggested. Nevertheless this Doll had a guttersnipe life and humour, and picked Mammon's pocket with a studious perseverance that was irresistibly funny.

Nicholas Hannen's Sir Epicure Mammon was the surprise of the performance, although perhaps his pastrycook in *Cyrano de Bergerac* should have prepared us for it. As a character actor Hannen has in the last few years made inconceivable progress. Previously I have always found him intelligent, subtle but entirely recognisable. He is now the one Old Vic actor who sends me scurrying in the first interval to the Box Office to ask if they're sure Mr. Hannen is playing and hasn't been replaced at the last moment by an understudy! His Mammon was immense in every sense of the word; only the voice was lacking for that poetry of the voluptuary that, like the poetry of *Volpone*, suddenly fires Jonson's scholarly verse to a sensuous beauty. The man's dreams of wealth are steeped in greed and sensuality, but the images blaze in jewelled splendour—

> My meat shall all come in, in Indian shells,
> Dishes of agat set in gold, and studded
> With emeralds, sapphires, hyacinths, and rubies.
> The tongues of carps, dormice, and camel's heels,
> Boiled in the spirit of sol, and dissolv'd pearl.

> My shirts
> I'll have of taffeta-sarsnet, soft and light
> As cobwebs; and for all my other raiment,
> It shall be such as might provoke the Persian
> Were he to teach the world riot anew.

This lack of voice for poetry seems likely to remain the one serious defect in the Old Vic company. The art of characterisation in the classics has never been more pronounced, but the art of lyric declamation is unmistakably waning. Only Olivier and Alec Guinness in recent seasons have shown that quality of music that can match poetry of phrase with equal richness of sound and rhythm.

Guinness's Abel Drugger in this play had a Cockney shyness, a kind of gauche and scruffy stupidity, that was both comic and touching. The tiny sketch was a complete character, and with the minimum of make-up transformed the actor's appearance and personality. The puzzling question as to why Garrick chose to play this very minor part, and how he managed to become famous in it, was presumably answered in a correspondence quoted at the time of this production by James Agate in " The Sunday Times ". From this it seems clear that Garrick appeared not in Jonson's original play but in a free transcription of it—perhaps the farce *The Tobacconist*, based on the Jonson play by Francis Gentleman— which was largely re-written in order to increase Drugger's opportunities.

Peter Copley's fanatical Ananias was undoubtedly the best of the other performances : the thin, lank-haired spindle of a man flickered and burned with an hysterical zeal. Margaret Leighton's silly, buxom and apple-cheeked widow was also a surprising transformation. The rest fitted well into the production but lacked this distinctive portraiture.

RICHARD II

F R O M 4 January, the date on which *King Lear* was withdrawn, until 23 April, the first night of *Richard I I*, there was no play by Shakespeare in the Old Vic repertoire. Appropriately Shakespeare's birthday, the occasion of Old Vic Birthday Festivals in the past, was chosen as the date of this revival : it was the first production of this play by the Old Vic Company for twelve years, and a testing piece for Alec Guinness in the minds of those who remembered that it was in this play that John Gielgud and Maurice Evans achieved perhaps their most brilliant Old Vic triumphs. The production also marked the début of Sir Ralph Richardson (who had been knighted in the New Year's Honours) as Old Vic producer.

The facts which, to my mind, most obviously emerged from this performance were (a) that C. E. Montague, in his essay on Richard as an artist in words, opened up a yawning trap for future actors of the part, and (b) that Alec Guinness, a superb character player and comedian, and an artist in everything he does, neverthe-less lacks the tragic and romantic qualities that can give a part such as this its necessary touch of virtuosity. Guinness's was a highly skilful and intelligent performance, subtle in detail, full of conscious craft ; but its very skill and sobriety wrecked it. One admired, but was almost totally unmoved. There was melody and sometimes anger, but never did one feel the lift and surge of

music that gave Gielgud's performance its peculiar grace and
magic, nor the mercurial rhetoric, the variety of mood and suffering,
that made that of Maurice Evans both exciting and heartrending.

Yet both these actors followed Montague to an extent : they
caught the spirit of the artist for whom poetic expression is both
a fulfilment and a release, whose vivid sensitivity to suffering
sets a spur to the imagination and crystallises into words that
probe the wound with beauty.   Richard's imaginative apprehension
of pain springs from the fact that he feels, as well as thinks, more
acutely than other men : he has the poet's vulnerability, and his
genius is the flashing reflection of his grief.   That depth and
genuineness of grief the actor of Richard must convey if his poetic
imagery is to move us and the historical drama is to be lifted on the
plane of tragedy.   Richard is one of the earliest of Shakespeare's
tragic heroes, far more than Brutus a shadow of the future Hamlet,
and the fact that Shakespeare does not spare us his early inade-
quacies should not destroy his later capacity to pierce our emotions
and command our sympathy.   It was their realisation of this—
that behind Richard's virtuosity of phrase there is equal virtuosity
of emotion, that the very intensity of his suffering forces itself into
verbal utterance—that gave Gielgud and Evans, and one assumes
Benson also, their special poignancy and fire as Richard.   They
acted from the heart as well as the head, and they moved us because
they were themselves deeply moved.

Guinness's acting was almost entirely of the head ; the withdrawn
and sensitive pathos of the parting with the Queen, his pain locked
up behind the pale mask of his face, was the nearest he came to
tragic emotion.   He made surprisingly little of the " little grave ",
and—

> For God's sake, let us sit upon the ground,
> And tell sad stories of the death of kings—

was played, incredibly, as a kind of poetic " showing off " to his
hearers.   One missed in the whole of this scene Richard's brilliant
instability of mood, his alternate rocketing into hope and plunging
into despair, and he gave up the crown as if he enjoyed the gesture
too much to feel its implications.   There was a fine and delicate
reluctance, caressing the metal, at Bolingbroke's " Are you contented
to resign the crown ?", and a flash of genuine intuition at " I
find myself a traitor with the rest "; but the sum total here as
elsewhere was of a surface melancholy unlit by the flame and agony

of tragedy. Nor was Richard's pride of kingship very marked, and the opening scene (perhaps owing to production) was far too " off dignity " and casual. There was a splendid cold anger in some of the rebukes to Bolingbroke and his attendant lords, but one felt the lack of royal heat, " Glistering Phaeton " is outside this actor's compass, he never suggested Gaunt's " rash fierce blaze of riot ", and his quiet humour, though telling on occasion, was not a complete substitute for Richard's gift of stinging irony.

Why, then, is it so difficult to dismiss this performance as a failure ? In all the criticisms one felt the critic torn between admiration and an inexplicable sense that the performance was not of the first flight, that something—one couldn't always be sure what—was missing. Several critics noted a lack of music, and it is true the speaking of the verse lacked the flexibility, range and orchestral colour of poetry at its most dramatic and lyrical. The tone, nevertheless, was sweet and tuneful, the elocution rhythmic and clear. Perhaps one might call it abstract rather than programme music—as in the acting itself one missed the stir and impulse of deep emotion. Yet the intelligence behind the performance was unmistakable : it was perceptible in every phrase, in every flicker of the face or the sensitive hands. Whatever was lacking in this performance was not brain ; the actor had patently—perhaps too patently ?—thought out the character in detail, had searched for the meaning of every word. He had painstakingly built up a character study of a man weak of temperament but quick of brain, secret of expression, feline of movement, and with a sharp and slightly contemptuous insight into the futile strife and ambitions of the stronger men around him. In a hand suddenly stilled in the act of stroking his chin, in the line of a shoulder or a back eloquent with displeasure, he put the man pictorially before us. It was recognisably Richard, if not the whole of Richard, and—with memories of Lear's Fool and Bob Acres and Herbert Pocket and de Guiche clamouring in the background—one acknowledged a character actor and an artist of considerable quality. The quality, though, was not that of a first tragedian ; personality, romanticism, emotional feeling, power—these are gifts this actor was not born with, and in the large degree has still to acquire. He is not, as the Old Vic audience had perhaps tentatively hoped, " another Olivier "; but he had the talent to carry Richard at least half-way to success, and in his own line of parts will most certainly prove one of the most brilliant actors the Old Vic has yet possessed.

Richard's " glory, like a shooting star ", should be the blazing centre-piece of this play's tapestry of characters, none of whom attains anything like his psychological interest although several have what is theatrically known as " their moments ". In this production Richard's failure to blaze meant that the other characters seemed to take on a corresponding importance, and a beautiful study of the dying John of Gaunt by Ralph Richardson proved, in fact, the dramatic highlight for the connoisseur of acting. For once the character was not built around the " big speech " but grew out of the play from the beginning : an aged man in whom one sensed former authority, mellowed by time, and whose glittering eyes as he stepped forward to greet his son showed love, pride and mental alertness. There was heartache and burning impatience in the speech on England, and the wrath was the failing wrath of a man dying before our eyes.

The tiny part of the Duchess of Gloucester, played by the fine actress Rosalind Atkinson, also touched genuine grief, and Sir Lewis Casson made a real character, not too over-laden with fussiness, as the unhappily neutral Duke of York (and incidentally set up a new Old Vic record of two actor-knights in one production !) Harry Andrews, an actor whom I had always considered in the past as possessing a fine voice and striking physiognomy, but with acting ability and intelligence yet to be proved, made a tall and commanding Bolingbroke and settled the acting query with credit. This actor's watchful, leashed impatience—distrustful of Richard's mood yet willing to placate him within reason—gave a solid ballast to the Renunciation scene and his quiet authority was ruthless yet not unlikeable. The opening quarrel scene was a little dulled by Richard's casualness and the fact that the Mowbray, though excellently spoken by Peter Copley, was too light in physique to complete the picture of warring feudal brawn pitched in contrast against the King's fine-cut elegance. This company has some fine character actors for secondary parts but there is a slight lack of weight and experience among the minor players that prevents the feudal uproar of such a play as this from acquiring its full masculinity. With Olivier's Hotspur in the later play still fresh in mind it was an unfortunate stroke of casting to present young Percy here as an eager but delicate-looking blond stripling with a sunny smile, and Michael Warre would be my last choice for Richard's murderer-in-chief. Nicholas Hannen gave, however, an accomplished account of the unscrupulous Northumberland, and George Rose—who, if my programme does not lie, was also the totally unrecognisable " angry boy " of *The Alchemist*—managed to stand out in speech and presence as Surrey, the Lord Marshall. Margaret Leighton was the Queen, a part not quite as bad as it here appeared owing to the cutting of one of her scenes.

Michael Warre's stylised setting of slender wooden pillars against a spacious coloured sky was criticised in some quarters. Actually it provided a useful framework into which curtains, a throne, transparent standards or a Gothic window could be quickly slipped to suggest a change of scene, and with the splashing Prussian blue and heraldic red of the costumes the scene attained at times a simple beauty. The illusion was imaginatively complete, if pared down to its physical essentials. I wonder if those who frown on expressionistic permanent settings have ever counted the number of lines of the play that had to be cut in Irving's archæologically exact productions, with their long pauses while the stage was being set for the next elaborate scene ? In Irving's *Hamlet* the omissions amounted to 1,191 lines, including many which we would now consider vital to the play and character.

Ralph Richardson's production achieved swiftness of pace and his omissions one felt were made from choice not necessity. Wisely he excluded all the side-tracking with regard to Aumerle's treachery, and the Duchess of York's comic importunity, which interrupts the dramatic narrative of Richard's downfall at the crucial point of the tragedy. He would have been still more wise if he had omitted the scene of the throwing down of the gages, which has never been known to excite an audience to anything but laughter. Otherwise he kept his narrative and groupings firmly in hand, and showed that as an experienced actor he possesses what many young and more heralded producers lack : the power to control acting as well as to compose pictures, and to direct his climaxes with a sense of both drama and character. The posing of Aumerle, drooping in despair, against a pillar at Richard's " little grave " speech was a touch one remembers, and the straggling line of attendants, one shouldering the luggage, that followed Richard across the skyline at Barkloughly like flotsam from the sea.

This was the last production of the 1946-47 season at the New Theatre and it remained in the repertoire, with *Cyrano de Bergerac* and *The Alchemist,* until the last night of the season on 31 May. It was also performed by the Old Vic Theatre Company in Edinburgh at the International Festival of Music and Drama in September, prior to the company's return to the New Theatre for their autumn season.

This book opened with *Richard II* and it ends with it : the wheel has come full circle, as must continually happen with the Old Vic Shakespearean repertoire. The comparison of productions and performances is always excitingly possible within this company, and the fact that the plays themselves are open to so wide a range of interpretation is a tribute to their vitality. English acting has something of the same vitality and variety, even within a generation, and the record of performances and productions in this book, if it has no other value, will I hope serve to emphasise this, and the importance of the Old Vic achievement.

POSTSCRIPT

O F necessity this book has dealt only with the Old Vic's London activities, but during and since the war period the organisation has achieved national scope and no Old Vic record would be complete without some reference to its further activities.

Most of the productions mentioned in Chapter VIII toured the provinces before and sometimes after their London presentation, and they represent only a proportion of the plays which were, throughout the war, taken by Old Vic companies both to the large provincial cities and the smallest villages. The presiding genius of these tours was Tyrone Guthrie, and it was his resourcefulness that adapted both drama and opera to the conditions under which the companies had to work. He cut *Macbeth* and linked it to a form of Greek Chorus, in an attempt to make the play more understandable to people to whom Shakespeare was but a name and who had never before seen a living stage performance. *Twelfth Night*, *Trilby*, *Thunder Rock* and *Candida* were among the plays produced on tour during this wartime period, but not seen with an Old Vic company in London. Saroyan's *Time of Your Life* was produced for the first time in England, and Laurence Housman's *Jacob's Ladder* for the first time on any stage. A special programme for younger children on the lines of the Chauve-Souris was also devised : it was the first forerunner of the present children's theatre company known as the Young Vic.

In 1942 the directors of the Liverpool Repertory Theatre, the Playhouse, which had suspended its activities owing to war conditions, let the theatre to the Old Vic for a period to extend until one year after the end of hostilities. Liverpool, therefore, for the next four years became the Old Vic's first permanent provincial centre.

The list of plays produced is an astonishing one, and shows considerable courage in the selection of a fine variety of plays representing both classic and modern drama. The plays included O'Casey's *Purple Dust* ; Eugene O'Neill's *Ah Wilderness* and *Anna Christie* (with Eileen Herlie as Anna) ; Pirandello's *Six Characters in Search of an Author* ; Ibsen's *A Doll's House, The*

Master Builder and *John Gabriel Borkman* (the last with an outstanding cast consisting of Eileen Herlie, Nancy Price, Frederick Valk and Mary Ellis) ; Jean Jacques Bernard's *The Sulky Fire* ; Obey's *Noah* ; Tchehov's *Uncle Vanya* and *The Seagull* (with Freda Jackson as Madame Arkadina and Nova Pilbeam as Nina) ; Sheridan's *The School for Scandal*, Farquhar's *Recruiting Officer* and Vanbrugh's rarely performed *The City Wives' Confederacy* ; Marlowe's *Dr. Faustus* ; Andreyev's *He Who Gets Slapped*, produced by Guthrie under the title of *Uneasy Laughter* ; Pinero's *The Second Mrs. Tanqueray* (with Eileen Herlie in the Mrs. Pat Campbell rôle) ; Beaumont and Fletcher's *Knight of the Burning Pestle* ; and *The Alchemist*, produced in modern dress by Guthrie in 1945 with settings by Tanya Moiseiwitsch.

The outstanding Shakespearean productions were *Hamlet* (produced by Peter Ashmore in 1945 with settings by Tanya Moiseiwitsch and with Peter Glenville, Eileen Herlie and Audrey Fildes in the rôles of Hamlet, Gertrude and Ophelia) and *Romeo and Juliet*, produced two years earlier by John Moody with Laurence Payne and Nova Pilbeam as the lovers. Eric Crozier, Peter Glenville, Noel Willman, Eric Capon, Robert Atkins and Esme Church were other producers not mentioned above. Apart from the established players, Eileen Herlie, then quite unknown in London, obtained her first extensive experience in leading rôles with the Old Vic at Liverpool. Audrey Fildes has since revealed her quality in London as Sonia in *Crime and Punishment* and Consuela in *He Who Gets Slapped*, and Laurence Payne has repeated his performance as Romeo at Stratford this year (1947). The Old Vic vacated the theatre according to their agreement in 1946, and the direction reverted to the Liverpool Repertory.

On 11 May, 1943, the historic Theatre Royal at Bristol, an exquisite little building which dates from the eighteenth-century, was reopened by the Arts Council after a certain amount of restoration. An Old Vic Company, headed by Sybil Thorndike, Stanford and Thea Holme and Kay Bannerman, appeared on this occasion in *She Stoops To Conquer*, but the Old Vic did not become permanently associated with the theatre until February, 1946, when a repertory company was formed on a permanent basis.

Already the list of productions is an interesting and varied one. It includes Farquhar's *The Beaux Stratagem* (with William Devlin and Pamela Brown) ; Wilde's *Importance of Being Earnest* ;

J. B. Priestley's *Jenny Villiers*; *Macbeth* (with William Devlin as Macbeth and Pamela Brown as Lady Macbeth); Denis Johnstone's play about Swift, *Weep For the Cyclops*; Tchehov's *The Seagull*; Shaw's *The Apple Cart*; *King Lear* (with a notable cast headed by William Devlin as Lear, Leon Quartermaine as Kent, Robert Eddison as Edmund and Rosalie Crutchley as Goneril); and Synge's *Playboy of the Western World* (with Cyril Cusack, the brilliant young Irish actor, as Christy Mahon and Wendy Hiller as Pegeen Mike).

Jane Henderson, who did some fine work with the Oxford Repertory company during the War and played Lady Bracknell for the Bristol Old Vic, has since created a remarkable impression in London as Mrs. Solness in *The Master Builder* at the Arts Theatre. The director and principal producer is Hugh Hunt. A Bristol Old Vic Theatre Club has been formed, with a membership of over 1,000, and a school of acting attached to the theatre was opened in October, 1946.

Something of the quality of the work of the Bristol Old Vic, which gives every indication of becoming the first provincial centre of national drama, could be gathered by Londoners from the production of Hardy's *Tess of the D' Urbervilles*, which was played by the Bristol Old Vic company at the New Theatre during the week beginning 26 November, 1946. The adaptation of this tragedy by Ronald Gow showed a dramatic appreciation both of Hardy's characters and of the fatality that broods over Tess's life like the dark shadow of unseen gods. The power of the novel was, moreover, finely translated in Wendy Hiller's performance of Tess, perhaps the most moving piece of acting this actress has yet given us. Her face with its windswept beauty and fine strong peasant's bones—a face that makes one think of flowering heather, sun on cornfields and the clean wind of the hills—was the perfect mask for Hardy's heroine, and her acting throughout was touching in its ardent and elemental candour. She was beautifully supported by William Devlin in the abnormally difficult part of Angel, and in the scene of the house in the forest, and final parting at Stonehenge, both artists caught the restrained and tender beauty of a great love brushed by the wings of coming death.

There was a remarkable character performance by Everley Gregg as Tess's mother and a sensitive one of her small sister by Hilda Schroder, a young actress who showed unusual quality and depth of emotion. She later played Cordelia in the Bristol *Lear*. The Mrs. Crumb of Jane Henderson and the Mrs. Brooks of Nora Nicholson also showed the strong character basis of the company's teamwork. The production of Hugh Hunt was excellent and Guy Sheppard's atmospheric settings—including an impressive Stonehenge scene of silhouette and copper-clouded sky—showed the standard of décor at Bristol to be high.

What of Old Vic activities in the future? A children's theatre, known as the " Young Vic," commenced its activities on Boxing Day, 1946, with a production of an Italian comedy, *The King Stag*, which after a season at the Lyric, Hammersmith, subsequently toured the provinces. Gradually a repertory, both of classic plays and plays written specially for children, will be built up and performed by adult professional actors. The aim is to make the Young Vic a children's theatre company along the lines of those in Soviet Russia, in which theatre values will not be sacrificed to those of pure education, but the minds of the child audience will be stimulated by an entertainment of the highest artistic standard. It is hoped in this way to build up an alert and intelligent potential audience of the future, an audience in whom a love of the theatre has been instilled from childhood. George Devine, assisted by Suria Magito, is the director of this theatre for children, which may eventually alternate tours with London seasons and produce branch companies.

The Young Vic is only one branch of the Old Vic Theatre Centre, which will, when its development is complete, comprise also a Theatre School and a Centre Theatre at which a junior Old Vic Company—like the junior ballet company already functioning at Sadler's Wells—will perform in London. The Old Vic Theatre School, under the direction of Glen Byam Shaw, opened in January, 1947. There are three separate courses in Acting, Technical Production and Stage Design, and the numbers of students are limited in order that individual talent may not be neglected and personal contact between instructor and pupil not hampered by over-large classes. Michael MacOwan and Christopher Hassall have lectured on the staff to the acting students, and Suria Magito is in charge of movement and physical training, on which the school places great importance. Instruction in fencing is included, and apart from voice production and acting rehearsals there are lectures on the history of literature and the theatre and on the stage's allied arts.

The courses in Production and Design are similarly practical and comprehensive. The full course of training is for two years (with a further intake of pupils each year), and at the end of the course a production will be staged by senior students of all three courses in their various capacities as actors, producers, lighting experts and designers. Under the guidance of true men of the theatre, whose professional work has proved their fitness to teach others, the Vic School should provide a valuable training, with an emphasis on practical craftsmanship as well as artistic theory.

The Old Vic Centre's Theatre, which will be under the direction of Michel St. Denis, cannot be created until the Old Vic, where it is hoped to establish it, is fully rehabilitated. Since the bomb damage sustained in May, 1941, is extensive it is doubtful if this can be done before 1949. When the theatre is built it will form the permanent residence of the junior Vic Company, which will draw a large proportion of its talent from the Old Vic School. St. Denis is in the meantime in charge of all the preliminary planning in connection with this development. The construction of the new theatre has been planned so that it may be adaptable to the production of plays of the past in the manner of their own period, as well as to the newest and most modern methods of staging. Modern British dramatists will be encouraged to write for the theatre, and it is hoped it will become a thriving centre for the development of talent in all the varied arts of the theatre.

A tour of Australia, with a newly-formed company headed by Laurence Olivier, is planned as a first step towards bringing the Old Vic's work in contact with the Empire and countries abroad. A second company of this kind may eventually achieve the same permanency and status as the present resident London company, and the companies may then alternate in London seasons and foreign and provincial tours.

The main Old Vic company will remain in the West End until the National Theatre is built on the site proposed on the south bank of the Thames. This alliance of the Old Vic with the Shakespeare Memorial National Theatre Committee was first made public on 28 January, 1946, and it marks by far the most important development in the Old Vic's recent history. It means in effect that the standard of the company's work during the last few years has been such that the National Theatre Committee has recognised the claims of the Old Vic as our nearest approach to an English National Drama company. An invitation has therefore been extended to the Old Vic Governors for the company to become the resident theatre company at the National Theatre when it is built. This invitation has been accepted, an agreement signed and a Joint Council set up consisting of representatives both of the Old Vic and the National Theatre Committee. The completion of the fund necessary to build, equip and endow the National Theatre is being accelerated, and it is hoped that a Royal Charter providing for the future government of the Theatre will be granted. The site provided by the London County Council has space available for a theatre with two stages, one large and one small. This will make possible the effective production of many different types of play, and it is planned to equip the theatre with every modern device for lighting and production.

The record of the Old Vic's achievements during the twelve years covered in this book shows that the ground has been magnificently prepared. The Old Vic, by a normal progression, now takes on quite naturally the status of the English National Theatre, and it will plan its future activities in full awareness of its future position. The story of the Old Vic is still unfinished, and the productions and performances described in this book represent only a section—though I think an important section—of its dramatic history. The progress from suburban repertory to National Theatre is almost complete, but the future is still to be written.

London.
1946-7.

POSTSCRIPT TO SECOND EDITION

S I N C E the Postscript of this book was written some of the plans foreshadowed have proved, at least temporarily, impracticable. The National Theatre on the South Bank still remains to be built. Both the Young Vic and, more important and disastrous, the Old Vic Dramatic School have been disbanded; and in November, 1950, the company left the West End and re-established itself, under the direction of Hugh Hunt from the Bristol Old Vic, at the rehabilitated Old Vic in the Waterloo Road. Here some attempt has been made to carry out the principle of two companies alternating in London and the provinces or abroad. The chequered history of failures and successes during these last few years, which have also seen the unfortunate severance of Michel St. Denis, Glen Byam Shaw and George Devine from the organisation, must be the subject of a future chronicle. Suffice it to say that the Bristol Old Vic, including its dramatic school, has continued to function, and at the time of writing the London Old Vic, with three exciting successive productions of *Julius Caesar* (Hugh Hunt), *Murder in the Cathedral* (Robert Helpmann) and *King Henry VIII* (Tyrone Guthrie), is showing a new upsurge of vitality and endeavour. The leap into prominence, after what might be termed a long gestation period, of a young actor, Paul Rogers, in remarkable and diverse performances of Shylock, Cassius and Henry VIII, is an encouraging sign that the Vic still has the capacity to develop its own stars as well as to draw them (as it often must do, to attain the highest standards) from outside.

In the autumn of 1953 Michael Benthall will succeed Hugh Hunt as director of productions, and Claire Bloom, whose Juliet was deservedly one of the major successes of the 1952-3 season, will return to play Ophelia in his opening production of *Hamlet*.

London,
May, 1953.

BIBLIOGRAPHY

A. G. BRADLEY : *Shakespearean Tragedy.*

HARLEY GRANVILLE-BARKER : *Prefaces to Shakespeare* (4 vols.)

WILLIAM POEL : *Shakespeare in the Theatre.*

J. DOVER WILSON : *What Happens in Hamlet.*

„   „   *The Essential Shakespeare.*

WILLIAM HAZLITT : *Characters of Shakespeare's Plays.*

CHARLES LAMB : *Essays of Elia.*

C. E. MONTAGUE : *Dramatic Values.*

G. BERNARD SHAW : *The Quintessence of Ibsenism.*

S. T. COLERIDGE : *Lectures on Shakespeare.*

Ed. JAMES AGATE : *The English Dramatic Critics, 1660-1932.*

Ed. A. C. WARD : *Specimens of English Dramatic Criticism.*

CONSTANTIN STANISLAVSKY : *My Life In Art.*

JOHN MASON BROWN : *Seeing Things.*

INDEX